Fredric Jameson

Marxism and Culture

Series Editors:
Professor Esther Leslie, Birkbeck, University of London
Professor Michael Wayne, Brunel University

Fredric Jameson

The Project of Dialectical Criticism

Robert T. Tally Jr.

www.plutobooks.com

First published 2014 by Pluto Press
345 Archway Road, London N6 5AA

www.plutobooks.com

Distributed in the United States of America exclusively by
Palgrave Macmillan, a division of St. Martin's Press LLC,
175 Fifth Avenue, New York, NY 10010

British Library Cataloguing in Publication Data
A catalogue record for this book is available from the British Library

ISBN   978 0 7453 3211 6   Hardback
ISBN   978 0 7453 3210 9   Paperback
ISBN   978 1 7837 1159 8   PDF eBook
ISBN   978 1 7837 1161 1   Kindle eBook
ISBN   978 1 7837 1160 4   EPUB eBook

Library of Congress Cataloging in Publication Data applied for

10   9   8   7   6   5   4   3   2   1

Typeset by Stanford DTP Services, Northampton, England
Text design by Melanie Patrick
Printed and bound by CPI Group (UK) Ltd, Croydon, CR0 4YY

In memory of Rick Roderick,
who encouraged me to do better

Contents

Series Editors' Preface

It is entirely appropriate that the first book in this series to be devoted exclusively to a single figure should focus on Fredric Jameson. The longevity of Jameson's research program, along with the authority he brings to his work, means that several generations of students and scholars alike have become acquainted with Marxist cultural theory in a context (academia) which is often at best ignorant or indifferent to it, and at worst actively hostile. Jameson has pursued his interest in and defense of such key concepts for Marxism as the dialectic, totality, and utopianism with a remarkable consistency. This is especially the case when we consider how driven by fashionable trends academia can be. The scope of Jameson's interests in culture and the range of alternative theoretical paradigms he engages with (and subsumes) have often been remarked upon and may be regarded as a model for maintaining the vibrancy and relevance of academic Marxism. Yet second only to Jameson's position within academe, the contours of his work have perhaps been most shaped by the fact that, for all his cosmopolitanism, he is emphatically an American Marxist. While British Marxists might be especially concerned with the cultural power and characteristics of the most successful ruling class in the world, French Marxists with the centrality of the state, and Marxists in the global South with the legacies of colonialism and imperialism, Jameson is above all concerned with capital in one of the 'purest' capitalist economies in the world. This makes his work at once highly particular and, given the global hegemony of the United States and its increasing power to shape others in its own image, internationally resonant. Jameson's continued extraordinary productivity means that happily this book will not be the definitive exposition of his still expanding *oeuvre*.

We can only hope that this series will last as long as Jameson's project. If it proves to be even slightly as influential as his work, we will be happy indeed. We would like the series to become, for academics, activists and artists everywhere, a natural home for Marxists interested in the cultural question.

Series Editors
Mike Wayne
Esther Leslie

Acknowledgements

As is indicated in the title of my introduction and implicit throughout this study, the literary critic and cultural theorist Fredric Jameson is above all an educator. I have benefited from being his student, first in the classroom, then while a visiting scholar in the Graduate Program in Literature at Duke University, and more recently in my own career as a literature professor. As a teacher, mentor, and scholar, Jameson has contributed mightily to my own intellectual and professional formation. Many others have helped along the way, and I would especially like to thank the professors, students, and friends who contributed to my studies of dialectical criticism and who helped foster a sense of community, among them Jonathan Arac, John Beverley, Paul A. Bové, Eric Clarke, Sara Danius, Lawrence Goodwyn, Sabine Hake, Stefan Jonsson, Ronald Judy, Carol Kay, Marcia Landy, Toril Moi, Michael Morton, Michael V. Moses, Valentin Mudimbe, Dana Polan, Rick Roderick, James Rolleston, Kenneth Surin, Xiaobing Tang, Phillip Wegner, and, above all, Sandy Mills. I would also like to acknowledge my comrades in the Marxist Literary Group, an organization Jameson helped to establish, which has provided a forum for spirited discussion and fellowship.

Koonyong Kim invited me to speak on Jameson's cultural cartography of the world system as part of his seminar at the American Comparative Literature Association's annual meeting in 2013, and my presentation there turned out to be an early version of this study's Chapter 1. I am grateful to the organizers of Simon Fraser University's Dreaming Dangerously graduate conference for inviting me to present a plenary talk on utopia as literary cartography, and the insightful comments and questions from audience members there have contributed to my thoughts on Jameson's utopianism. Moreover, I am indebted to the many generous scholars of Jameson's work whose insights have informed my reading; among these, let me single out Phillip E. Wegner, who graciously shared with me the manuscript of his then forthcoming book, *Periodizing Jameson: Dialectics, the University, and the Desire for Narrative*. The Jameson people, "Fred-heads," form a rare and marvelous community.

Although I have not included any previously published material in this book, the feedback I received from editors and readers of some of my earlier writings on Jameson has certainly helped to inform the present study. These writings include "Jameson's Project of Cognitive Mapping: A Critical Engagement," in Rolland G. Paulston, ed., *Social Cartography: Mapping Ways of Seeing Social and Educational Change* (New York: Garland, 1996); my reviews of *Valences of the Dialectic* in the *Marx and Philosophy Review of Books* and of *Representing Capital* in *Historical Materialism*; parts of my *Spatiality* (London: Routledge, 2013); and much of the overall argument in my *Utopia in the Age of Globalization: Space, Representation, and the World System* (New York: Palgrave Macmillan, 2013). I am grateful to the editors, publishers, and readers whose attentiveness and support have aided me in thinking about Jameson's work. I would also like to thank David Castle of Pluto Press, copy-editor Anthony Winder, and the anonymous referees, whose sharp eyes and insightful comments have helped to make this book better than it would otherwise have been. I am especially grateful to Esther Leslie and Mike Wayne, editors of the Marxism and Culture series, for their enthusiastic and encouraging support for this project.

This book is dedicated to my late advisor and friend Rick Roderick, who first recommended *Marxism and Form* as essential reading if I wished to integrate my literary and philosophical interests and who encouraged my explorations in modern critical theory. Rick was an inspiring teacher, scholar, and activist, a comrade who thoroughly embodied a commitment to the spirit of Marx's eleventh thesis on Feuerbach.

And, as always, Reiko Graham has been there for me with love and support.

Selected Works by
Fredric Jameson

(in chronological order)

Sartre: The Origins of a Style. Second edition. New York: Columbia University Press, 1984. (First published by Yale University Press, 1961.)

"On Politics and Literature," *Salmagundi* 2.3 (Spring–Summer 1968), pp.17–26.

Marxism and Form: Twentieth-Century Dialectical Theories of Literature. Princeton, NJ: Princeton University Press, 1971.

The Prison-House of Language: A Critical Account of Structuralism and Russian Formalism. Princeton, NJ: Princeton University Press, 1972.

Fables of Aggression: Wyndham Lewis, the Modernist as Fascist. Berkeley, CA: University of California Press, 1979.

The Political Unconscious: Narrative as a Socially Symbolic Act. Ithaca, NY: Cornell University Press, 1981.

"Third-World Literature in an Era of Multinational Capitalism," *Social Text* 15 (Autumn 1986), pp.65–88.

"A Brief Response" (to Aijaz Ahmad), *Social Text* 17 (1987), pp.26–28.

The Ideologies of Theory: Essays, 1971–1986, Volume 1: Situations of Theory. Minneapolis, MN: University of Minnesota Press, 1988.

The Ideologies of Theory: Essays, 1971–1986, Volume 2: The Syntax of History. Minneapolis, MN: University of Minnesota Press, 1988.

Late Marxism: Adorno, or, the Persistence of the Dialectic. London: Verso, 1990.

Signatures of the Visible. London and New York: Routledge, 1990.

Postmodernism, or, the Cultural Logic of Late Capitalism. Durham, NC: Duke University Press, 1991.

The Geopolitical Aesthetic: Cinema and Space in the World System. Bloomington and London: Indiana University Press and the British Film Institute, 1992.

The Seeds of Time. New York: Columbia University Press, 1994.

The Cultural Turn: Selected Writings on the Postmodern, 1983–1998. London: Verso, 1998.

The Cultures of Globalization, co-edited with Masao Miyoshi. Durham, NC: Duke University Press, 1998.

Brecht and Method. London: Verso, 1998.

The Jameson Reader. Ed. Michael Hardt and Kathi Weeks. Oxford: Blackwell, 2000.

A Singular Modernity: Essay on the Ontology of the Present. London: Verso, 2001.

Archaeologies of the Future: The Desire Called Utopia and Other Science Fictions. London: Verso, 2005.

The Modernist Papers. London: Verso, 2007.

Jameson on Jameson: Conversations on Cultural Marxism. Ed. Ian Buchanan. Durham, NC: Duke University Press, 2007.

The Ideologies of Theory. London: Verso, 2008. (Expanded version of the two-volume, 1988 collection of essays, omitting one, but including 13 additional articles.)

Valences of the Dialectic. London: Verso, 2009.

The Hegel Variations: On the Phenomenology of Spirit. London: Verso, 2010.

"A New Reading of Capital." *Mediations* 25.1 (2010), pp.5–14.

Representing Capital: A Reading of Volume One. London: Verso, 2011.

The Antinomies of Realism. London: Verso, 2013.

Introduction
Jameson as Educator

I would like to begin with a memory, one that is quite personal and therefore not entirely trustworthy, but which lends color to my thinking about Fredric Jameson's diverse body of work. I first encountered Jameson in the classroom, rather than in print, when I was a student in an introductory course in comparative literature at Duke University in 1989. The course was titled—simply, fittingly, and with its recognizable echoes of Jean-Paul Sartre—"What is Literature?" In a mid-semester lecture introducing the intellectual culture of postwar France, as a means of getting into the text for that week's reading (Roland Barthes's *Mythologies*, I believe), Professor Jameson approached the blackboard, stick of chalk in hand, and fluidly narrated a stream of cultural and historical events, ideas, and personages. Near the center of the board, he wrote, in large capital letters, *SARTRE*, commenting on the supreme position occupied by the author of *Being and Nothingness* in France during the years just after World War II. Underneath, in somewhat smaller letters, Jameson wrote two names on the same line, *Lévi-Strauss* and *Lacan*, smoothly transitioning to introduce the structuralist response to existential phenomenology. Soon words like *Saussure, Barthes, Althusser,* and *Foucault* appeared underneath the others. But then Jameson started drawing lines outward, making what had looked to be a pyramidal structure into more of a rhizomatic diagram, or perhaps something along the lines of those Greimas semiotic rectangles that Jameson has become so notorious for producing in his writings. Names on the edges included Simone de Beauvoir, Merleau-Ponty, Derrida, and Deleuze, and, outside of the French tradition, Heidegger, Lukács, Adorno, and Benjamin. Eventually, now more distant but with bigger letters, the names *Nietzsche, Freud,* and *Marx* loomed over even the initial "Sartre," with various lines crisscrossing the whole, connecting various thinkers, or curiously juxtaposing one with another.

By the end of the lecture, with my notebook page a messy assemblage of proper names, book titles, dates, and interspersed arrows, I felt as if I had experienced a sort of bibliographic tornado, a whirlwind of information in which utterly new ideas interlocked with traditions I had thought I knew well, such as existentialism, but which appeared now fresh and exciting. In the bewildering array of authors and texts, some familiar and many others unknown to me, I found ample material for pursuing my existing interests and for venturing into completely new areas of research. Afterwards, as I often did after these class meetings, I made my way straight to the Lilly Library on Duke's East Campus to look up some of these exotic texts. But what I remember best from this course, and from others like it, is the way that Jameson managed to integrate such novelties into a cognizable whole, such that the strangest new ideas—the fundamental "arbitrariness of the sign," *pensée sauvage*, reification, "ideological state apparatuses," and so on—seemed to fit within a broader structure of knowledge, namely the narrative of twentieth-century intellectual history, or perhaps just History itself. In learning about a given, discrete new idea, theory, or writer, I felt that I was participating in a much vaster universe of literary, philosophical, and historical knowledge.

I think this is merely to say, uninterestingly perhaps, that Jameson that day was doing what teachers nearly everywhere, nearly every day, are also doing. But the experience is also similar to that which the reader discovers in studying Jameson's writings. In more than 20 books and in hundreds of shorter pieces, Jameson has consistently introduced often difficult and frequently novel ideas or texts, while invariably situating them in a meaningful cultural, historical, and intellectual context, and then, armed with both the new knowledge and a structure that gives shape to it, the reader, like the student, is prepared to strike out upon his or her own critical adventures or literary explorations. In his literary criticism and theory as well as in his university teaching, Jameson is above all an educator.

Jameson is arguably the leading literary and cultural critic in the world today, a status symbolically registered in his receipt of the Modern Language Association's prestigious lifetime achievement award and of the Holberg International Memorial Prize, which is something of a Nobel Prize for philosophy, criticism, law, and theology, and whose recent winners include Julia Kristeva, Jürgen Habermas, Ian Hacking, and Bruno Latour. Additionally, Jameson is probably the world's most prominent Marxist critic, one whose writings have kept alive a tradition thought by many in a post-Cold War era to be moribund or no longer relevant. Jameson's dialectical criticism has reinvigorated Marxism by connecting its lessons to the cultural sphere, broadly imagined, and to the exigencies of theory in an era of globalization. Perhaps for this reason, his worldwide influence has been especially notable in eastern Asia and Latin America, emergent powers within the postmodern world system. What is more, as I will emphasize throughout this study, Jameson has been one of the most important *literary* thinkers in a time when literature, literary criticism, and literary theory, properly speaking, are considered by many to be *passé* or irrelevant, whether in the face of new media and technology or in contrast to other apparently pragmatic or utilitarian fields of study. Terry Eagleton, long considered Jameson's chief rival amongst the leading Marxist critics in the English-speaking world, has enshrined him in a pantheon of modern critical theory. As Eagleton put it:

> There is surely no doubt that Fredric Jameson is not only an eminent critic but a great one, fit to assume his place in a roll-call of illustrious names stretching from Edmund Wilson, Kenneth Burke, F.R. Leavis and Northrop Frye to I.A. Richards, William Empson and Paul de Man. Even this is to limit the judgement to Anglophone colleagues only, whereas the true field of comparison ranges much more widely. No literary scholar today can match Jameson's versatility, encyclopaedic erudition, imaginative brio or prodigious intellectual energy. In an age when literary criticism, like so much else, has suffered something of a downturn, with forlornly few outstanding figures in the field, Jameson looms like a holdover from a grander cultural epoch altogether, a refugee from the era of Shklovsky and Auerbach, Jakobson and Barthes, who is nonetheless absolutely contemporary.[1]

Eagleton identifies a curious aspect of Jameson's *oeuvre*: its simultaneous evocation of an august past and engagement with an utterly present, even seemingly near-future condition. This most postmodern of theorists is also among the last of the great cultural critics of yore.

Jameson's varied work continues to challenge orthodoxies while retaining close ties to what some would consider rather old-fashioned philosophical discourses. In particular, Jameson has remained committed to the dialectic, or more broadly to a Hegelian Marxist dialectical criticism, which had been under attack if not wholly disregarded by both the more positivist Anglo-American philosophers and the *au courant* theorists of French poststructuralism and its advocates. Beginning with his earliest writings on Jean-Paul Sartre, Theodor W. Adorno, Walter Benjamin, and Georg Lukács, Jameson has endorsed and extended dialectical criticism throughout his career, frequently engaging opponents within and outside of the Marxist tradition, including his notorious encounters with poststructuralism and postmodernism. At the same time, Jameson has maintained a persistent defense of Marxist criticism as the most (indeed, the only) viable critical practice for making sense of the world system, broadly conceived, in the era of multinational capitalism. Jameson's most recent writings—the *tour de force* that is *Valences of the Dialectic*, along with his brief, innovative readings of Hegel's *Phenomenology of Spirit* and Marx's *Capital*—return him to the earliest studies of Sartre and of dialectical criticism in *Marxism and Form*.[2] Or rather, these works demonstrate the degree to which Jameson's lifelong critical project, though constantly modified, updated, refined, and extended into other domains, has remained dedicated to the vocation of dialectical criticism.

Along with his commitment to the dialectic, Jameson has never abandoned the project of utopia, which he has considered central to Marxist criticism and theory. Indeed, he maintains that the dialectic is itself a properly utopian mode of thought, the kind of thinking best suited for critically apprehending the societies organized under the capitalist mode of production and for projecting alternatives. Jameson demonstrates how dialectical criticism allows us to make sense of the social and cultural forms that shape our lives. Over his more than 50-year career, Jameson has extended the vocation of dialectical criticism, using the tools of literature, philosophy, and criticism to interpret the world in which we live and to imagine radical alternatives, or, famously, to analyze our apparent inability to do so. In *Fredric Jameson: The Project of Dialectical Criticism*, I consider Jameson's overall career and argue that his Marxist approach is well suited for understanding, interpreting, and perhaps even changing the world in the twenty-first century.

Jameson's ideas are not easily summarized, in large part because his dialectical criticism resists the static encapsulation that summaries so usefully provide. For example, as Ian Buchanan has argued in response to another critic's complaint that Jameson never clearly defines what he means by the term *political unconscious* in the book by that name, "*The Political Unconscious* taken as a whole, *is* the definition of this concept—a very precise definition, to be sure, encompassing a panoply of nuances and permutations, but containing nothing inessential or extraneous."[3] That is, the entire book discloses the definition in the process of its meditation on the problems of interpretation, its critical assessment of other literary theorists, and its readings of Balzac, Gissing, and Conrad, among the many other things that this extraordinary study attempts to accomplish. Summaries, while helpful up to a point, inevitably mislead the reader by effacing the very process by which Jameson is doing what he does. Jameson's thoughts rarely stay motionless long enough to be captured, mostly because his work strives to map an ever-changing, ever more complex totality that itself cannot be reduced to a static, stable image. So, for instance, one cannot help but note in Jameson's writing a tentative, aspirational, and above all projective sense, at both the conceptual level of his philosophy and the formal level of his sentences and paragraphs. In Jameson, it seems, we are always moving toward something just beyond our grasp, even as we are simultaneously looking back on the historical circumstances that make such an attempt even conceivable, while also persistently taking note of our current, all-too-real situation in the here and now. Jameson's overall body of work constitutes an exploration of consciousness, representation, narrative, interpretation, history, utopia, and the world system. Reading Jameson's writings involves a similarly exploratory project. Although my study aims to highlight and make clear many aspects of Jameson's project of dialectical criticism, it is unlikely to produce any easily maintained *précis* of his key ideas, assuming such a thing is even possible. Rather, I hope this work functions as an adventurer's guide for those who, through reading his books, wish to accompany Jameson in the adventures of the dialectic.

Perversely, perhaps, I have chosen to approach this body of work by examining in chronological order each of Jameson's books, from *Sartre: The Origin of a Style* to *Representing Capital: A Reading of Volume One*.[4] This is not a very Jamesonian methodology, to be sure, but a study of Jameson's career as it unfolds over the course of 20 or more books across some 50-plus years reveals the paradoxically consistent and innovative project of his dialectical criticism. In some respects, elements of his earliest forays into literary and cultural criticism remain powerful parts of his most recent work, while the development of certain themes over time underscores the historical pressures helping to shape his project. In his *Periodizing Jameson*, Phillip E. Wegner argues that Jameson's critical project between the early 1960s and mid-1990s develops along the lines of his own periodization of literary forms or modes of production at various stages of capital. That is, to oversimplify the argument for the moment, Jameson's early studies of Sartre and *Marxism and Form* constitute investigations of the problems of narrative realism, while his writings of the 1970s up through *The Political Unconscious* examine modernism and its concomitant crisis of representation, before Jameson launches his full-scale critical intervention into the notoriously slippery problems of postmodernity in the 1980s, particularly in his magnum opus on the subject, *Postmodernism, or, the Cultural Logic of Late Capitalism*. It happens that the *Postmodernism* book emerges as the fourth volume (but the first published) of Jameson's announced six-volume *Poetics of Social Forms* project, of which *A Singular Modernity* and *Archaeologies of the Future* represent Volumes 5 and 6, respectively. Jameson's explorations of the relationship between globalization and culture have occupied his thinking for much of the past two decades, but at the same time he has never stopped delving into the past, for example, by returning to nineteenth-century realism, medieval allegory, and ancient myth (to mention the reverse-chronological trajectory of the "first" three volumes of the *Poetics of Social Forms* series), nor has he ceased to take aim at the phenomena of a quite contemporary moment (see, for example, his analysis of Walmart's business model in *Valences of the Dialectic*), while always keeping an eye out for an anticipated but not-yet-discernible future, as with the omnipresent utopian impulse in his writings. By reading along with Jameson, in this admittedly artificial chronological order, I hope to preserve the developmental narrative of his project, at the same time highlighting its remarkable consistency and flexibility.

As I discuss in Chapter 1, Jameson's work poses a difficulty above and beyond that which attaches to many other "difficult" literary theorists. As Jameson puts it, "the dialectic requires you to say everything simultaneously, whether you think you can or not," so any scholarly analysis of this most dialectical literary critic must come to terms with an impossibility from the outset. Jameson's own theory and criticism has developed over the decades, and he has throughout his career addressed the most novel, apparently *avant-garde* cultural phenomena in real time, as it were, while never losing sight of what might be considered a more traditional discourse, Marxism itself, and the dialectic more generally. The paradoxical result is that the most contemporary cultural theorist in the United States is also among the most old-fashioned: someone who is as likely to quote Balzac as Baudrillard (in the French, no less), someone equally at ease discussing Dante's view of allegory and Andy Warhol's pop art, or someone who would have no trouble analyzing the gritty television drama *The Wire* by looking at Henry James's theory of the novel. But aside from this mixture of high and low, old and new, sophisticated and vulgar, which after all help to make Jameson's cultural criticism so pleasurable for readers, his overall project remains consistent even as it unfolds, gains complexity, extends into ever new territories, and then doubles back, revisiting sites with new theoretical equipment, seeing familiar landscapes with fresh eyes, and so on. The trajectory is both daunting and exhilarating.

In retrospect, Jameson's early books read like a Who's Who of twentieth-century European critical theorists. Jameson has said that being among the first critics in the United States to write about Adorno, Bloch, perhaps Benjamin, and Sartre's critique, is a "service" of which he is still rather proud.[5] In Chapter 2, I examine his first three books, *Sartre: The Origins of a Style* (1961), *Marxism and Form: Twentieth-Century Dialectical Theories of Literature* (1971), and *The Prison-House of Language: A Critical Account of Structuralism and Russian Formalism* (1972). There I suggest Jameson begins to elaborate his own project in part by assuming "the task of the translator" and ushering these thinkers into the critical conversation. These studies introduced many in the English-speaking world to little-known and previously untranslated works of critical theory, and they exhibit Jameson's acute attention to formal and stylistic elements while also bringing an array of social and cultural phenomena to bear on what had seemed a merely literary critical argument. In these early texts, Jameson astutely considered the significance of style in contemporary France's most famous intellectual, Sartre, and he argued for the importance of a number of less well known theorists, such as Adorno, Benjamin, and Lukács, prior to the appearance in English of much, or any, of their writings. Also, in an extremely timely intervention, Jameson offered a Marxian critique of the linguistic turn in philosophy and literary studies at a moment when what came to be known simply as "theory" was beginning to transform the study of literature in the United States and elsewhere. Jameson's study of Sartre's style drew upon such apparently traditional critical practices as the philology of Erich Auerbach or Leo Spitzer, and, less visibly, it benefited from the theoretical writings of Adorno and Barthes. In *Marxism and Form*, Jameson "translated" a tradition of European Marxist criticism and made the case for a dialectical criticism, a case he has continued to make throughout his career, and *The Prison-House of Language* presented a critical translation of Russian Formalism and French Structuralism. Translation, of course, does not mean simply moving from one language to another, but suggests from its Latin root a "carrying across." In these early books, Jameson carried Marxist theory across the ocean, introducing American readers to lesser-known texts while expanding the range of his

own project. As Benjamin had pointed out, the translation is the afterlife
of a work of art, and the translator breathes new life into the work,
while seeing that it retains an aspect of its foreignness. Jameson's early
writings display his gift for "translation," which remains a key aspect of
his later work.

As a leading scholar of modern French literature, particularly of
"French theory" *avant la lettre*, Jameson was well positioned to respond
to the tidal wave of contemporary European thought, doing business as
structuralism, semiotics, poststructuralism, or *deconstruction,* that swept over
many British and American literature programs and journals in the 1970s
and 1980s. Jameson's writings during this period took the temperature of
these theoretical practices and their contributions to literary studies while
also criticizing their weaknesses, and always incorporating them into a
broader framework of Marxism. Given that much of this theory presented
itself in opposition to Marxism and to the dialectical tradition, Jameson
might have been put on the defensive. His responses, though measured,
were often polemical and, as with the postmodernism debates he was
about to enter and reconceptualize, Jameson frequently countered his
opponents by attempting to overcome and assimilate their arguments,
thus demonstrating the superiority of dialectical criticism by taking
advantage of its immense flexibility. Borrowing an expression from Sartre,
Jameson averred that Marxism was the "untranscendable horizon" of
contemporary thought, subsuming and extending beyond other critical
practices. It is during this period that Jameson established himself as the
leading Marxist critic in the United States, and his tactical maneuvers
in the theory wars of the 1970s only served to make clear his unique
project of dialectical criticism. In particular, he used these occasions to
elaborate a properly Marxist hermeneutic, by which one could glimpse
both the meaning of a given text and the social totality that functions as
the absent cause of that meaning. It is perhaps noteworthy that Jameson
published just two monographs, plus a collection of essays, between
1972 and 1990.[6] In *Fables of Aggression: Wyndham Lewis, the Modernist as
Fascist* (1979), *The Political Unconscious: Narrative as a Socially Symbolic
Act* (1981), and *The Ideologies of Theory: Essays, 1971–1986*, a collection of
previously published articles, thematically arranged into two volumes,
Situations of Theory and *The Syntax of History* (1988), Jameson argued for
a distinctively Marxist hermeneutic practice, one that superseded and
incorporated such varied competitors as psychoanalysis, semiotics, myth
criticism, and phenomenology. In Chapter 3, I examine these works in

their historical context, while focusing on several of Jameson's innovative and influential concepts, including metacommentary, national allegory, and the political unconscious.

Dipping his toes into the turbulent waters of the debate over postmodernism in the early 1980s, Jameson risked diluting his properly Marxian critique and losing allies who found postmodernism to be antithetical and anathema to Marxism.[7] But, as Perry Anderson makes clear in *The Origins of Postmodernity*, Jameson's intervention immediately altered the terms of the debate, as Jameson "captured" postmodernism on behalf of Marxism. Jameson's signature achievement was to redefine postmodernism, not as a style or a period, but as a *cultural dominant*, a conception that simultaneously limited the exuberantly inflated rhetoric of postmodernism as a new social order itself and expanded the meaning of the term to allow for "the presence and coexistence of a range of different, yet subordinate, features."[8] At the same time, Jameson definitively grounds postmodernism in a materialist historical dimension, the mode of production itself, and invokes critical traditions well suited to contribute to the critique of this elusive phenomenon. In particular, he enlists the critical theory of Adorno, who, as Jameson asserts in *Late Marxism: Adorno, or, the Persistence of the Dialectic* (1990) is perhaps more useful in the postmodern condition than he had been in an earlier epoch, to aid in laying the foundation for his own broader engagement with postmodernity. Meanwhile, Jameson's ongoing exploration of the vicissitudes of narrative representation increasingly leads him to examine other media, notably film, and *Signatures of the Visible* (1990) gathers several of his most important essays on cinema, as well as offering a lengthy new chapter on the problem of realism in the postmodern moment. In Chapter 4, I discuss these books along with the monumental *Postmodernism, or, The Cultural Logic of Late Capitalism* (1991), paying particular attention to the development of Jameson's critique of the postmodern and his conception of cognitive mapping as the most suitable response to the representational and political crisis of postmodernity.

In his analysis of the postmodern condition, Jameson comes to see as fundamental the crisis of representation occasioned by multinational capitalism, a system in which capitalism has expanded to such an extent that, as Marx had anticipated, its relations become global; in the early 1990s, this tendency increasingly becomes cognizable under the auspices of a new concept, *globalization*. Employing a cartographic metaphor (but only somewhat metaphorically), Jameson calls for an aesthetic of cognitive mapping that could provide, if only provisionally, a practical means of representing the global social and spatial totality. Following up on this somewhat prospective or tentative notion in the *Postmodernism* book, Jameson in *The Geopolitical Aesthetic: Cinema and Space in the World System* (1992) analyzes the ways in which films and other narratives perform what I call *literary cartography* in order to make sense of the perplexing and ominous social forces affecting our lives. Hence, the importance of the "conspiracy film" genre for Jameson, for conspiracies offer a formal means of constructing some kind of totalizing vision. Such literary maps call for a critical approach—geocriticism, perhaps—that responds to the peculiarly spatial aspects of this crisis, while also paying attention to the dialectic of form and content that makes these narratives or works of art so compelling, from both an aesthetic and political vantage. Such is the project of Jameson's utopian critique of globalization in this book, but also in his vastly underrated *Seeds of Time* (1994) and in another collection of essays, *The Cultural Turn: Selected Writings on the Postmodern, 1983–1998* (1998), which restates but also amplifies Jameson's positions on postmodernism as it delves into the material, political–economic bases of globalization. In Chapter 5, I examine these texts and show how Jameson's call for a "cognitive mapping on a global scale" is answered, at least in part, by his own critical mapping project.

Jameson's ambiguous relationship with modernism has been the subject of some debate, but he has throughout his career frequently returned to the problems of modernism and modernity. In his reflections on Adorno, Benjamin, and Brecht, especially with respect to the so-called "Brecht–Lukács" debate, Jameson wrestles with the apparent contradictions between formal innovation and social content in modernist literature and art. Chapter 6 examines his passionate defense of dialectical criticism in *Brecht and Method* (1998), in which he considers an exemplary, but problematic, modernist theorist and artist. This study is Jameson's fourth book devoted to a single author—after *Sartre*, *Fables of Aggression* (on Lewis), and *Late Marxism* (on Adorno)—and it is probably no coincidence that all of these writers have a complex relationship with modernism, each being fundamentally modernist in some respects, while also maintaining a critical distance from it. The more extended argument in *A Singular Modernity: Essay on the Ontology of the Present* (2002), along with its "source-book" *The Modernist Papers* (2007), offer the most complete vision yet of Jameson's thinking about the modern, even as they point to an ultimate dead-end—and, hence, to a limit to be surpassed.[9]

Drawing also upon Jameson's reflections on Lukács's theory of reification, I discuss the "thing" that leads the analysis of modernism into so much difficulty, which explains in part why Jameson concludes that "[r]adical alternatives, systematic transformations, cannot be theorized or even imagined within the conceptual field governed by the word 'modern.' […] Ontologies of the present demand archaeologies of the future, not forecasts of the past."[10]

With *Archaeologies of the Future: The Desire Called Utopia and Other Science Fictions* (2005), Jameson fulfilled the wishes of many of his students and "fans" who had awaited his definitive statements on both utopia and science fiction. Of course, Jameson's meditations on utopia can be found throughout his writings, and the concept is discussed at some length in *Marxism and Form*, *The Political Unconscious*, *Postmodernism*, and *The Seeds of Time*, not to mention in dozens of essays. In Chapter 7, looking especially at Part I of *Archaeologies*, "The Desire Called Utopia," I discuss in more depth Jameson's commitment to utopia, in theory and in practice, focusing on his sense that utopian thought is a necessary critical activity, supplying not only a means of negating the actual but also the wherewithal to imagine the possible, which is itself a function of literary art. This chapter also examines the revised and expanded edition of *The Ideologies of Theory* (2008), considering the many new essays included while also revisiting some of the earlier pieces in a twenty-first-century context. Finally, I discuss Jameson's *Valences of the Dialectic* (2009), which collects essays written over the previous two decades or so, but which also presents over 250 pages of new material, including a book-length study of "The Valences of History," in which Jameson patiently intertwines a Marxist analysis with the narrative theory of Paul Ricoeur, among others. Jameson's return to the dialectic in this book is, of course, no return at all, as he never left it. Rather, I see *Valences* as something like Jameson's *Summa Dialectica*, a forceful and no-holds-barred defense of dialectical criticism combined with a cool-headed review of his own work in this area. What is more, Jameson's theory of the dialectic as presented in *Valences* enables us to recognize the power of the dialectical reversal or the Aristotelian figure of *peripeteia*, by which we see that what goes around sometimes comes around, as the unity of opposites may open up new vistas for thought. The rousing, open-ended ending to *Valences of the Dialectic* discloses once more that utopian vision in which we may dimly perceive that "other systems, other spaces, are still possible."[11]

To employ another image from Benjamin, one can get to know a critic by unpacking his or her library. Given the breadth of his interests and the omnivorous tastes in literature, the encounter with Jameson's writings often seems like a trip through a well-stocked, perhaps utopian library of modern thought. Jameson's readings also give shape to the project of dialectical criticism, whereby one may approach virtually anything—Kantian philosophy, French psychoanalysis, urban geography, popular music, the Homeric epic, pulp science fiction, and horror movies, to name but a few—in order to find a germ of the social totality in which we work and live. In the Conclusion, I examine Jameson's most recent "readings," *The Hegel Variations* (2010) and *Representing Capital* (2011), in which he returns to two ur-texts of the dialectic, *The Phenomenology of Spirit* and *Capital*. The critical discussion of the Hegel and Marx opuses was conspicuously absent from *Valences of the Dialectic*, and the brevity of Jameson's studies suggests that they might function as appendices to that larger tome. However, these two little books might also be representative of a kind of Jamesonian project, whereby a close reading of difficult, old texts may disclose not only insights into the texts themselves and their own times but also a newly discovered significance to our own time and place. The deceptively simple act of reading, the vocation of dialectical criticism, becomes another way to unpack our own libraries, to return to work, and, with a bit of luck, to make possible new thoughts and actions. To a certain extent, this is also what I imagine as literary cartography, and the role of the critic, whose exemplar here is Jameson himself, is to map this literary terrain. In Jameson, the project of dialectical criticism, the cultural cartography of the world system, is another way of envisioning the functions of literature and of criticism itself.

In a fairly straightforward sense, Jameson's fundamental vocation is that of a literature professor, and all of his writings may be considered pedagogical in a certain sense. By this I do not refer primarily to his various discussions of the role of a Marxist pedagogy or the importance of the academic study of literature or some such thing, although these are also important matters.[12] I mean to indicate the degree to which Jameson's work provides an education in dialectical criticism and inspires those aspects of the utopian impulse in such a way that pedagogy, broadly conceived, pervades his entire critical theory. Like any good literature professor, Jameson introduces us, his students or readers, to texts and contexts; he teaches us how to read them, and he aids us in handling and sharpening our own critical tools for future, independent learning. I confess that part of my reading is here influenced by my own, largely precritical experience as an undergraduate scholar, experiencing such teaching for the first time in the university classroom. Hence, my decision to call this introduction to a study of Jameson's critical *oeuvre* "Jameson as Educator." The reference to Nietzsche's great essay on Schopenhauer is apt, I believe, inasmuch as Nietzsche there shows how a thinker becomes truly original and creative through an engagement with teachers or philosophical forebears.[13] This is doubly true for Jameson, whose own highly original thought draws from so many predecessors—Hegel and Marx, especially, but then Sartre, Adorno, Lukács, Barthes, Brecht, Marcuse, Althusser, Deleuze, and so on—and, like the translator in Benjamin's famous essay, Jameson's critical engagement with the work of these others makes new thought possible.

Casting my mind back 25 years to my own experience as an undergraduate student of Professor Jameson, I find that various bits of lectures, responses to my own questions or observations, or still-remembered marginal comments on my papers, all continue to inform my own reading, teaching, and thinking today. My own library, partially stocked with books purchased on the cheap from used bookstores in Durham, North Carolina, still reflects Jameson's immeasurable influence. (How else does one explain the ease with which I could find so many $2.00 and $3.00 paperback editions of Georg Lukács in a mid-sized city of the American South?) Above all, it is the heady mixture of close reading or detailed textual analysis with the grand philosophical ideas and broad historical sweep on display in Jameson's classes, as well as his writings, that I cherish now as a teacher and critic. Back then, as a philosophy major interested in nineteenth- and twentieth-century social thought, I was somewhat familiar with and interested in Marxism before I enrolled in the university, and I was already participating in Duke University's "Marxism and Society" certificate program when I encountered Jameson the educator.[14] But apart from the credential, my education in literature, criticism, and theory, as well as in film and film history, social theory, historiography, politics, philosophy, anthropology, not to mention Marx's own writings and those of many other Marxists, was established, to a greater or lesser degree, in my student–teacher interactions with Professor Jameson. Only after all of this did I begin to read Jameson's own writings, and to explore on my own the literary, cultural, and philosophical texts that his work so productively engages. There is no substitute for the university classroom, obviously, but reading Jameson's books is like a graduate-level education in comparative literature, literary criticism, and cultural theory. As educator, Jameson invites us to explore this world system of which we are a part, and his project of dialectical criticism may enable us to situate ourselves historically, to understand the present system, and to imagine potential alternatives.

1

"… the dialectic requires you to say everything simultaneously …"

On January 7, 2012, a standing-room-only crowd gathered in the large ballroom of a Seattle hotel to honor Fredric Jameson as he received the Modern Language Association's lifetime achievement award. In his brief remarks,[1] Jameson graciously but pointedly accepted his award as a ratification of the idea that formal analysis of literary texts is in no way incompatible with social and political approaches to literature, which was itself a slight dig at his erstwhile enemies and a recollection of past battles. He then offered a spirited defense of the project of the literary humanities and of the vocation of humanists (whom he preferred to call "culture-workers"), which were, and are, under attack both within and outside of the academy. Jameson asserted the radical difference between the work of literary critics and that of philosophers or other types of intellectuals, and he noted in particular the specific functions of narrative as distinct from those of epistemology. That is, Jameson suggested, our principal task as critics is not to determine what we can or cannot *know*, in the philosophers' sense, but to figure out what it is we think we can *tell*. In Jameson's view, the project of the literary critic is inextricably intertwined with the aesthetic and social forms of narrative.

As I listened to this brief speech, I thought that I detected echoes of a well-remembered passage from an earlier work, in which Jameson had referred to "a continuous and lifelong meditation on narrative, on its basic structures, its relationship to the reality it expresses, and its epistemological value when compared with other, more abstract and philosophical modes of understanding."[2] But this was Jameson speaking of Georg Lukács's career, 41 years earlier, in *Marxism and Form*. To those familiar with Jameson's criticism, which has remained remarkably consistent even as he ventured into always novel areas of cultural theory and practice over more than six decades, this echo from the past will not be surprising. Jameson's arguments somehow manage to be fresh and engaging with each new article and book, while at the same time appearing to reiterate, restate, or simply emphasize conceptions that he has articulated throughout his career. Ironically, perhaps, the passage just quoted appears in connection with Jameson's defense of treating Lukács's long career as a coherent critical project, as against those who would embrace the early Lukács but dismiss the later one, or vice versa. Given his practice of revisiting and expanding upon his earlier ideas, incorporating new elements into his theoretical practice while maintaining his own, some would say idiosyncratic, form of Marxism, it is unlikely that many readers would be able to definitively locate an "early" Jameson distinct from the "later" one. With each new cultural or theoretical phenomenon encountered—existentialism, structuralism, semiotics, poststructuralist theory, deconstruction, cinema, postmodern architecture, postcolonialism, globalization, and so on—Jameson's dialectical criticism has at times eviscerated, at others embraced them, while consistently advancing and building upon itself. In his own version of the Hegelian *Aufhebung*, Jameson's writings simultaneously cancel, preserve, and elevate the objects of cultural criticism.

Jameson is the most significant literary theorist and cultural critic of the past 50 years, and he remains the most important Marxist literary critic in the world today. From his first book on Jean-Paul Sartre, published in 1961, to his most recent writings on Hegel's *Phenomenology of Spirit* and Marx's *Capital*, not to mention his forthcoming books on realism, allegory, and myth, among other things,[3] Jameson has often operated at the cutting edge of cultural theory, while always retaining close ties to what many would consider a rather old-fashioned philosophical tradition. That is, even where he has taken as his ostensible subjects *avant-garde* theories and movements, from structuralism or poststructuralism to postmodernism and globalization, Jameson has ever grounded his discussion of these phenomena in an intelligible universe of a versatile, Marxist body of thought. Notably, Jameson has maintained a commitment to Hegel and the dialectic in the face of an onslaught of ostensibly anti-dialectical theory, whether in the staid, upright form of Anglo-American empiricism and positivism or in the alluring conceptual phantasmagoria of French poststructuralism's *différance*, *délire*, or *jouissance*. (However, as Jameson has argued throughout his career, as in his *Valences of the Dialectic*, many of these apparently anti-dialectical positions turn out to be, in a sort of ruse of history or dialectical reversal, dialectical after all.) Moreover, despite his sometimes eccentric usage, Jameson has gleefully embraced an almost "vulgar Marxism," insofar as he has always asserted that the economic base or mode of production conditions the superstructural products of the arts and sciences. Finally, and in contrast to the views of both his anti-Marxist opponents and many of his political fellow travelers, Jameson has resolutely defended the prospects of utopia, utopianism, and the utopian impulse. Operating simultaneously within these three seemingly *passé* traditions—that is, dialectical criticism, Marxism, and utopia—Jameson has deftly weighed in on, and sometimes then dominated, contemporary debates in literary theory, cultural studies, film and media criticism, architectural movements, and political philosophy, among other discourses. As Colin MacCabe famously observed, "it can truly be said that nothing cultural is alien to him."[4] In these interventions, Jameson has suggestively introduced such concepts as metacommentary, national allegory, the political unconscious, postmodernism as the cultural logic of late capitalism, cognitive mapping, ontologies of the present, and archaeologies of the future, to name but a few of the more memorable ones. Taken piecemeal, each intervention represents a significant contribution to a relevant cultural situation, phenomenon, text, or event, and the reader frequently comes away from a given Jameson article or book with a radically different perspective on the subject at hand, one that partakes of a powerful sense of novelty and alterity while, at the same time, finding its place in an established interpretative or epistemic structure. The effect is both strikingly new and eerily familiar. Jameson's rigorously formal analysis, Marxist critical theory, and utopian discourse come together in his distinctive project of dialectical criticism, and taken in its entirety, Jameson's work constitutes a cultural cartography of the world system.

My use of the mapping metaphor is more than a personal preference, something the author of geocritical or spatial literary studies might understandably favor. I take seriously Jameson's sense that the postmodern condition is somehow typified by a "new spatiality"[5] and that part of our job as critics is to make sense of these social and spatial forms that go a long way toward shaping the content of our lived experience in the era of globalization. Moreover, as a way of apprehending Jameson's own critical theory, the figure of the map can be imagined as helpfully combining the formal features of a visual register, the interpretive possibilities of the text, and a profoundly political content. The flexibility of the map might be said to replicate the immense versatility of Jameson's project. As Gilles Deleuze and Félix Guattari put it, "The map is open and connectable in all of its dimensions; it is detachable, reversible, susceptible to constant modification. It can be torn, reversed, adapted to any kind of mounting, reworked by an individual, group, or social formation. It can be drawn on a wall, conceived of as a work of art, constructed as a political action or a meditation."[6] Jameson's own concept of cognitive mapping, which I discuss at greater length in the chapters that follow, offers one form by which to envision his overall project of dialectical criticism.

I have argued elsewhere that *cognitive mapping* could be an apt label for Jameson's lifelong project.[7] In this chapter, I would like to examine an aspect of this spatiality in Jameson that is not, strictly speaking, cartographic, but that requires one to think spatially or to project a map of Jameson's own career. I refer to the "spatial form" of Jameson's project over a nearly 60-year career, using that phrase in the sense that Joseph Frank made famous in his 1945 essay, "Spatial Form in Modern Literature."[8] What I mean is that all who wish to discuss Jameson's career in its totality must face a curious, spatiotemporal dilemma: that is, the problem of trying to say everything at once. As Jameson has acknowledged, this is one of the impossible imperatives of the dialectic itself. So, at the start, I want to offer a brief survey of Jameson's career while noting along the way the paradoxical co-presence of a temporal development over one critic's *longue durée* and an apparently static position or a perpetual repetition of the same concepts. In Jameson's astonishingly wide-ranging and yet meticulously detailed body of work, the itinerary is the map which is also the territory, simultaneously.

Timely Meditations

As I suggested above, Jameson's career may be characterized by a curious *détente* between the undoubtedly *avant-garde* and the seemingly old-fashioned tendencies in literary criticism and theory. That is, on the one hand Jameson's work has always operated at the cutting edge of contemporary intellectual culture. But, on the other, Jameson has never appeared to follow fashion or waver in his own positions, and he has consistently held that Marxism is not just the best, but the only theoretical and critical practice capable of adequately comprehending the narratives by which we make sense of, or give form to, the world. In sum, Jameson's project of dialectical criticism analyzes and evaluates the cultural landscape with an almost up-to-the-minute calibration, while always situating these interventions in a consistent yet flexible and complex system through which may be glimpsed that totality that ultimately gives meaning to each discrete element within it. In this way, Jameson seems to be a hip, ultra-contemporary postmodern theorist and a traditional, almost nineteenth-century thinker, all at the same time.

Jameson's earliest writings on Jean-Paul Sartre in the 1950s critically assessed France's leading intellectual at the very moment when Sartrean existentialism would become a dominant force in American literature and philosophy. During the Sixties, and culminating in his monumental 1971 opus, *Marxism and Form*, Jameson was among the first in the United States to write about such European thinkers as Theodor W. Adorno, Walter Benjamin, Ernst Bloch, and Georg Lukács, and this before many of their works had been translated into English. As a scholar of French and German culture so attuned to Sartre and twentieth-century European thought, Jameson was ideally positioned to recognize and respond to the explosion of criticism and philosophy—what came to be known simply as *theory*— in the late 1960s. Such books as *The Prison-House of Language*, *Fables of Aggression*, and *The Political Unconscious* deftly articulated the linguistic turn in literature and philosophy, the concepts of desire and national allegory, and the problems of interpretation and transcoding in a decade when continental theory was beginning to transform literary studies in the English-speaking world. Jameson's essays of the 1970s and early 1980s, including many assembled in *The Ideologies of Theory* (published in 1988, with a revised and expanded edition appearing in 2008), gave insight into the ostensibly strange, new ideas associated with structuralism, post-structuralism, psychoanalysis, semiotics, and critical theory. Fearlessly and unexpectedly wading into the troubled waters of the postmodernism debates in the early-to-mid-1980s, Jameson immediately became the central theorist of this famously decentered cultural phenomenon, and his books and essays of this era addressed the postmodern in art, architecture, cinema, literature, philosophy, politics, social theory, and urban studies, to name just a few of the areas. His *Postmodernism, or, the Cultural Logic of Late Capitalism* helped to reorient the postmodernism debates, and he demonstrated the power of Marxist theoretical practice to make sense of the system underlying the discrete phenomena. By the early 1990s, Jameson had become an unavoidable theorist and critic for anyone engaged in contemporary literary and cultural studies, broadly conceived. Grounding the seemingly groundless postmodernism in the material condition of a postcolonial and post-Cold War epoch of globalization, as well as the economics of postindustrial capital and financialization, Jameson's work helped to redefine the millennial moment, the ramped-up war on terror, and the pervasive uncertainty attendant to the present historical conjuncture. This twenty-first-century moment has called for new ways of imagining both the past and the future, as Jameson nicely indicates in the title of his extended analysis of the utopian impulse, *Archaeologies of the Future*, while it has also opened up a space for renewed attention to such putatively superannuated subjects as modernism, the dialectic itself, Hegel and Marx, and perhaps realism, allegory, and myth, to follow the chronologically complicated trajectory of Jameson's recent and forthcoming books. Throughout all of this, Jameson's dialectical mapping project has emphasized the need for a sense of totality, which in turn has made possible new ways of understanding and engaging with the world system in the era of late capitalism.

As this ridiculously condensed *précis* of his career already demonstrates, Jameson has consistently found himself near the center of the most current cultural and critical controversies of the day, moving with remarkable agility through the theoretical thickets of existentialism, structuralism, poststructuralism, postmodernism, and globalization. Yet, throughout all of these post-contemporary interventions (to use the evocative, if somewhat eccentric phrase made famous as the name of the Duke University Press series co-edited by Jameson and Stanley Fish), Jameson has been among the more resolutely traditional Marxist theorists and critics. For instance, when faced with a rising tide of virulent anti-Hegelianism from both the left and the right, Jameson has consistently embraced both Hegel and the dialectic, going so far as to reinterpret contemporary theories and critical practices as merely so many instances of the dialectical unity of opposites, thereby absorbing any errant positions in his overall system. To put it less charitably, as I once heard one friendly critic assert, Jameson embraces all things—but like a python, squeezing the life out of them. At the time of this writing, Jameson's two most recent books are studies of Hegel's *Phenomenology of Spirit* and Marx's *Capital*, and although several other important theorists have returned to these texts of late,[9] it is hardly likely that the *Phenomenology* (1807) and *Capital* (1867) are considered *avant-garde* works of cultural theory in the twenty-first century. And Jameson's insistence on "the persistence of the dialectic," to borrow the subtitle of his study of Adorno,[10] establishes his position as a bulwark against the putatively anti-dialectical, poststructuralist and postmodern theories that have come to dominate critical discourse in the humanities and social sciences in recent decades.

Moreover, to speak more generally, Jameson's commitment to a properly literary critical project, even when he ventures into other disciplinary fields, might also be deemed old fashioned. In a somewhat post-literary age, with media theory and cultural studies usurping the roles previously played by literary criticism and literary history, Jameson's criticism and theory, especially in their attention to narrative, form, genre, and tropes, appear to represent an almost perversely Luddite perspective. Even when he has ventured into architecture, film, visual arts, or media criticism, Jameson has always done so as a literary critic, paying closest attention to the forms and functions normally associated with narrative fiction. Despite his remarkable breadth of cultural inquiry, Jameson in some respects remains the student of Erich Auerbach, his teacher in graduate school at Yale University in the 1950s, and of the great philological tradition of the early twentieth century. From his earliest writings to his most recent, Jameson has been concerned above all with the ways in which individual expressions—sentences, in fact—relate to forms, which in turn derive their force and significance from the totality of social, political, and economic relations at work in a given mode of production. For Jameson, the critical perspective peculiar to literary criticism enables a properly Marxist critique of the world system.

This literariness, in fact, comports with Jameson's Marxism and his overall project of dialectical criticism. Jameson understands that the existential condition of personal and social life in societies organized under the capitalist mode of production (and, perhaps, under other modes as well) necessarily requires a form of interpretative or allegorical activity, which ultimately means that the task of making sense of one's world falls into the traditional bailiwick of literary criticism. Literary texts come to the reader as already constructed objects, situated in a complex literary and social history, and therefore cannot necessarily be read literally even if that is the preferred approach, since even a "literal" reading will involve some forms of interpretation. Just so, our interpretation of the social text—that is, the world in which we live—will also require a kind of metacommentary, to invoke a famous Jamesonian concept. As Jameson explains in *The Political Unconscious*, no society has ever been quite so mystified in quite so many ways as our own, saturated as it is with messages and information, the very vehicles of mystification (language, as Talleyrand put it, having been given us in order to conceal our thoughts). If everything were transparent, then no ideology would be possible, and no domination either: evidently that is not our case. But above and beyond the sheer fact of mystification, we must point to the supplementary problem involved in the study of cultural or literary texts, or in other words, essentially, narratives: for even if discursive language were to be taken literally, there is always, and constitutively, a problem about the "meaning" of narrative as such; and the problem about the assessment and subsequent formulation of the "meaning" of this or that narrative is the hermeneutic question.[11]

Because narratives are themselves what Lukács called "form-giving forms" by which individual and collective subjects make sense of the world,[12] the project of the literary critic coincides with that of other sense-making systems, such as religion, philosophy, and science. Yet, as Jameson's own dialectical criticism makes clear, the literary critic is professionally attuned to the presumption of mystification or, to put it differently, to the need for interpretation, in advance. As Jameson had expressed this position in his brief acceptance speech in Seattle, for "culture-workers" in the literary humanities the question is less a matter of determining what we can know and more pertinently a matter of what we think we can tell.

In Jameson's own career, this project of dialectical criticism is both the point of departure for his system of thought and itself a discursive practice unfolding over the course of some 20-odd books published in a span of more than 50 years. The problem for students of this remarkable body of work, then, becomes all too visible. How can one deal with Jameson's timely interventions in the moment while also drawing upon this supreme reservoir and untranscendable horizon of history? At each point along the way, the entire journey must be in constant view, for each moment is meaningful only in reference to the overarching project that makes possible our very recognition of a moment as "momentous", and hence recognizable, in the first place. Or, to recast it in a more geographical register, how can we determine what is a "place" if we do not also and already comprehend the space of which it is a discernible part? How does one talk about Jameson's individual works while also keeping in mind his lifelong project, a project that does seem to transcend the individual works, even as it comprises and is constituted by them? Tracing the trajectory of Jameson's career will thus require a spatiotemporal approach, one that follows the chronological unfolding of his work over six decades and, at the same time, synoptically maps the theoretical territory upon which this work unfolds and which also conditions the work. In order to discuss Jameson's project in the present study, I find myself in the awkward position of trying to say everything simultaneously, even if I do not think I can.

As we have already seen, this last sentence echoes a line from Jameson in which he explains the potential for repetition, contradiction, and overall heterogeneity in a selection of his own writings. In *The Modernist Papers*, Jameson writes that, "for good or ill, the dialectic requires you to say everything simultaneously whether you think you can or not."[13] If the dialectic requires us to say everything at once, that is, to attempt a retrospective survey of the long historical march that led to this particular spot while extrapolating the imaginary itineraries of future journeys and also maintaining at all times a clear sense of the totality of the here-and-now, then the project of dialectic criticism would appear to be an almost impossible task—impossible, perhaps, but no less worthy of the effort. There is something vaguely Proustian about the whole thing: at the moment when you discover that the writer—having detailed his ambitions, his frustrations, his false starts, and his determination to become a writer who will detail his ambitions, his frustrations, his false starts, and so on—is about to begin his novel, you realize that you have just finished it. Alexander Nehamas aptly likened this process to Nietzsche's *eternal recurrence*, a decidedly undialectical (or, at least, non-Hegelian) theory which nevertheless offers one figure for imagining how to say everything simultaneously after all.[14] As a way of introducing what comes next and of surveying what has come before, this Janus-faced approach discloses the challenges, as well as the delights, of Jameson's multifaceted body of work.

Making Things Difficult

The imperatives of dialectical criticism partially explains an almost universally acknowledged, although not necessarily true, characteristic of Jameson's prose: its purported difficulty. I suppose it would be churlish to deny that Jameson's writing is "difficult," even if I do believe that the notorious difficulty is overstated, and I suspect that sometimes this assessment is deliberately overstated by those who wish to discredit him, Marxist criticism, or literary theory more generally. Other, more generous readers, might mistake the complexity and indeterminacy of the topics Jameson's writings explore for a personal, stylistic choice to write in a way that seems overly complicated, if not downright obfuscatory. Still others may merely wish that Jameson would write more simply, in so doing possibly confusing the simple with the clear—something that Jameson himself has found surprising. For example, he has pointed out that even those who have found his sentences "hard to read" have discovered that the same lines "turned out to be very lucid" when spoken.[15] In fact, I find his writing to be rather consistent with his lecture style, and perhaps the cadences of his voice are not always so easily registered by punctuation in print. Many of these apparently complicated, tortuous, and above all long sentences—with parenthetical asides and subordinate clauses, not to mention the frequent use of temporal language that adverts the reader's attention to coming attractions or reminds the reader of territories previously traversed—have a salutary pedagogical function. In my own experience as an undergraduate student, Jameson's lectures and his approach to leading discussions in a seminar setting are fairly well replicated in his prose. It might be that I read him this way because I first encountered this "style" in a classroom, but I do think that Jameson's prose, despite the frequent references to its difficulty, when read carefully or listened to attentively, is actually quite clear, even if the concepts and practices he is discussing can be surpassingly complicated and nuanced.

This writing is also, at times, quite beautiful. Detractors of theory might snicker to hear it, but Terry Eagleton's assessment of Jameson as a writer one reads "for pleasure," as one would read a Baudelaire or a Faulkner, resonates strongly with me, and I believe that Jameson's style, the ultimate merger of content and form in his prose, is essential to his critical project in general. Eagleton writes that, for him, it is "unimaginable that anyone could read Jameson's [...] magisterial, busily metaphorical sentences without profound pleasure, and indeed I must acknowledge that I take a book of his from the shelf as often in place of poetry or fiction as literary theory."[16] Referring elsewhere to *The Political Unconscious*, Eagleton sums up "Jameson's now familiar strengths," before again evoking the pleasures of his elegantly crafted sentences and paragraphs: "his global range of literary and theoretical allusion, his combination of an insistently 'structural' habit of mind with a rich responsiveness to textual detail, his prestidigitatory ability to produce striking, original insights of his own out of received notions. Jameson composes rather than writes his texts, and his prose, here as in previous works, carries an intense libidinal charge, a burnished elegance and unruffled poise, which allows him to sustain a rhetorical lucidity through the most tortuous, intractable materials."[17] Nonetheless, while Jameson's work has remained both popular and influential among students of critical theory for decades, there remains a pervasive view of Jameson's writing as thoroughly, and perhaps unnecessarily difficult.

Jameson has rightly complained of a double-standard when it comes to the terminology or language of cultural theory when compared to other areas of inquiry. The injunction to write in a non-specialized vernacular that somehow seems natural to the uninitiated reader is almost never applied to intellectuals working in the natural sciences, for example. As Jameson has put it,

> it is always surprising how many people in other disciplines still take a relatively belles-lettristic view of the problems of culture and make the assumption—which they would never make in the area of nuclear physics, linguistics, symbolic logic, or urbanism—that such problems can be laid out with all the leisurely elegance of a coffee-table magazine (which is not to be taken as a slur on good cultural journalism, of which we have little enough as it is). But the problems of cultural theory— which address the relationship between, let's say, consciousness and representation, the unconscious, narrative, the social matrix, symbolic syntax and symbolic capital—why should there be any reason to feel that these problems are less complex than those of biochemistry?[18]

The idea that cultural criticism does not require, or is artificially aggrandized by, a vocabulary suited to its own field of study implies a certain chauvinism, as well as a type of mystification. To assert that molecular biologists or astrophysicists need to speak in a specialized professional language in order to do their jobs, while maintaining that literary and cultural critics must at all times limit themselves to a vocabulary and syntax already familiar to lay readers, is to devalue, perhaps intentionally, the work produced in the humanities. But, beyond this elitism masquerading as populism, this looking-down upon the very thing that such people would claim ought to belong to everyone, the advocates for less jargon-laden or "plain language" cultural criticism also, in fact, pose a false problem. As Eagleton noted in *After Theory*, the word "signifier" is not more abstract and specialized than the word "symbol," the definition of which is actually a good deal more difficult to pin down, even by experts, and "[a] lot of so-called ordinary language is just jargon which we have forgotten is jargon."[19] In effect, Jameson's notorious "difficulty" has been used against him as a grounds for dismissing his work, whether as elitist, out of touch, or simply irrelevant to real world concerns. Sometimes such criticisms have been leveled at literary theory as a genre, if not at the entire field of academic writing in the humanities, *tout court*.

There is, of course, a political dimension to such a view. As Jameson has pointed out, the insistence upon ordinary language in the Anglo-American philosophical tradition may ultimately have less to do with conceptual clarity than with an unintended ideological purpose, "to speed the reader across a sentence in such a way that he can salute a readymade idea effortlessly in passing, without suspecting that real thought demands a descent into the materiality of language and a consent to time itself in the form of the sentence."[20] As Northrop Frye observed even in the early 1960s, the study of literature itself was the only antidote to becoming overwhelmed by "the speech of the mob," whose representatives were "advertisers" and "politicians at election time"; such degraded language "stands for cliché, ready-made idea and automatic babble, and it leads us inevitably from illusion to hysteria."[21] Similarly, the calls for plain language and simple writing often mask a potentially undesirable program of making works of literature and of the intellect easily consumed commodities. Under such circumstances, one might argue that producing deliberately "difficult" writing could be viewed as an act of resistance. The difficulty of the dialectical sentences of a writer like Adorno (or Jameson) may manifest itself in the need for readers to pause, to take a moment for reflection, and to think through the difficult matters that such an apparently difficult style is used to represent. Prose that facilitates understanding may in fact be facile, and the ease with which a reader consumes it may belie the consumerist quality of its project.

Before moving on, I would like to make a couple of other, rather banal points about this perception of Jameson as a "difficult" writer, whether or not that assessment is a fair one. First, it really ought to go without saying that difficulty is in no way incompatible with pleasure. There is something obnoxious about the idea that a work of literature or of literary criticism could only be enjoyed if it were "easy to read" (whatever that phrase might mean, given the diversity of audiences, literacies, tastes, and so on). Undoubtedly, part of the joy that comes with experiencing great literature is the challenge of its language or its ideas; grappling with a difficult text, working through its perplexing forms or thoughts, coming to an understanding about it or learning something new from the experience— presumably, these activities do much to constitute the pleasure of the text, to use Roland Barthes's felicitous phrase. In fact, I could just as well make a similar case for the desirable difficulty of other kinds of human activity. The unbridled joy that comes with successfully working out a frustrating mathematical problem, achieving a breakthrough in some confounding scientific experiment, or solving a particularly irksome matter of home repair is also surely the result of our engagement with the given task's perceived difficulty. At the risk of sounding like an overly enthusiastic football coach, no pain, no gain. Therefore, even if we concede that Jameson's writings are difficult, that should not daunt us in the least. If anything, it should whet our appetites for the fare.

Second, in the matter of Jameson's style, I think that the influence of literary modernism on his own writing has been underestimated, perhaps understandably, since Jameson is a theorist and critic rather than a poet or novelist. But Jameson has acknowledged the effect that such writers as Ezra Pound or William Faulkner had upon him, and Jameson has listed as early influences the philological writings of an Auerbach or Spitzer and perhaps especially Sartre's essays on Faulkner.[22] Perhaps Jameson's "long sentences" owe as much to those of Faulkner as they do to the dialectical tradition? In his *Sartre: The Origins of a Style*, Jameson asserts that "[t]he writers with the most striking, most nakedly accessible sense of time are those who use long sentences: the exaggeration of the rhythms of normal breathing yields a kind of time whose texture is gross and easily perceived."[23] As an author and critic whose own work has been specifically attuned to valences of history and of temporality, Jameson's formulation of lines comparable to the Faulknerian "long sentence," with its "breathless gerundives," might itself be said to represent a sort of unity of form and content in his project of dialectical criticism.[24]

In this way, it becomes apparent that what is sometimes taken to be the difficulty or density of Jameson's prose is part and parcel of his project of dialectical criticism itself. As he has observed in response to a question about the supposedly difficult style of the so-called "Jamesonian sentence," it is really about "making connections," which is what dialectical criticism is all about. "It is not a question of making statements, it is to make connections of all kinds of pieces of the problem, or the situation or the contradiction, that those sentences try to represent."[25] Considering the degree to which what might have seemed to be Jameson's idiosyncratic style is actually an essential element of his overall critical project, I must agree with Ian Buchanan that the attention to Jameson's purported difficulty is unhelpful and ultimately perplexing.[26] If Jameson's prose is somehow too complex, reflexive, tortuous, or dense, it is likely because the problems that it attempts to represent and bring into intelligible form, much like the multinational world system in its totality, are equally complicated and stubbornly resist simplistic descriptions or interpretations. I therefore conclude this digression on difficulty by invoking once more the impossible task of saying everything simultaneously, whether we think we can or not. Far from being obscurantist or needlessly difficult, Jameson's work quite clearly and straightforwardly registers the difficulties imposed upon us as readers and writers in our attempts to make sense of the world.

Meanwhile

In attempting my impossible task of saying everything about Jameson's dialectical criticism and theory simultaneously, I have had recourse to various tactics or strategies that seem to fly in the face of that goal. Unexpectedly, I have chosen to approach Jameson's books in more-or-less chronological order, starting with *Sartre: The Origins of a Style* (1961) and working my way up to *Representing Capital: A Reading of Volume One* (2011). For a number of reasons, I do not always cleave fastidiously to the timeline, but chronology provides an Ariadne's thread to guide students of Jameson's immense and dynamic *oeuvre* through this labyrinth. As the line about "saying everything simultaneously" suggests, Jameson himself acknowledges his own polychronic writing, whether he is actually compiling documents that originated in disparate eras (as with 2009's *Valences of the Dialectic*, which includes some materials first presented in the 1980s) or revisiting themes first sounded with other instruments (such as the permutations of the concept of "cognitive mapping" over several decades). Partly for this reason I have also focused my attention primarily on Jameson's books, as distinct from his many influential journal articles. Jameson often returns to his own essays, frequently developing them further in later studies—as with "Metacommentary," whose central argument is explored in greater theoretical detail in the long, first chapter of *The Political Unconscious* ("On Interpretation")—if not incorporating them directly into his books. Jameson has published collections of previously published essays, such as *The Ideologies of Theory* and *The Cultural Turn*, and he has also reprinted earlier essays in connection with his own new interventions. Thus, Part II of *The Archaeologies of the Future* collects many of Jameson's influential articles on science fiction from the 1970s through the early 2000s, while Part I (itself a book-length essay titled "The Desire Called Utopia") contains almost entirely new material. Jameson's practice of revisiting and reworking his earlier essays in later book projects may itself have something to do with that dialectical imperative to say everything simultaneously, but a careful reading of his 20-odd books in roughly the order in which they were produced offers a useful survey of his entire career, while highlighting the key moments or themes which appear along the way.[27]

Chronological order thus offers a provisional means of organizing the explorations of Jameson's thought, but it is not a fixed or unilinear path. Given the profound influences of such figures as Hegel, Marx, and Nietzsche (and, more silently, Faulkner) on Jameson's corpus, perhaps I should add that this chronological approach is not meant to suggest either a teleology or a genealogy. In other words, I am not trying to show how the exposure to existentialism and "style studies" in the 1950s inexorably led to Jameson's provocative vision of Walmart as a potentially representative form of utopia in *Valences of the Dialectic*; nor do I mean to examine Jameson's most recent thought and delve for its origins in this or that precursor text. It makes sense that Jameson's thought has developed over time, *and* it makes sense that his overall project has remained rather consistent throughout, but neither of these sensible observations requires us to adopt a strictly synchronic or diachronic perspective. Jameson's position might be summed up in a marvelous little piece of advice supplied by one of Neil Gaiman's helpful ghosts in *The Graveyard Book*: "You're always you, and that don't change, and you're always changing, and there's nothing you can do about it."[28] I hope that my study of Jameson and the project of dialectical criticism will sufficiently register the degrees to which Jameson's cultural cartography of the world system both transforms and maintains itself over time.

I might add, in passing but also by way of a conclusion, a comment about my titles, that is, the title of this chapter and of the book as a whole. The ellipses used to bracket Jameson's phrase ("the dialectic requires you to say everything simultaneously") are intended to indicate, not just my scrupulosity in noting that the words are taken from a sentence that begins earlier and ends later than the quotation, but my sense that "the dialectic" requires us to see how we are always and already in the midst of things, *in mediis rebus*, and that we necessarily begin our projects *in medias res*. This is the Sartrean lesson of the *situation*, one that Jameson took to heart and developed throughout his own career. Kurt Vonnegut once stated that all stories about people should end with the three-letter phrase "ETC.," which partially explained why Vonnegut chooses to "begin so many sentences with 'And' and 'So,' and end so many paragraphs with '… and so on.'"[29] Of course, narrative is itself a primary means by which subjects who find themselves "in the middest" project a sensible, if provisional map or plan of the world. Jameson's project of dialectical criticism simultaneously explores the narratives we use to make sense of this world from our limited spatial and historical situations and provides its own map by which we can guide ourselves through that world.

The subtitle of this book thus provides a label for Jameson's career and names a larger project of which all of Jameson's critical interventions are a part. The project of dialectical criticism in Jameson's *oeuvre* is nothing less than the cultural cartography of the world system, itself broadly conceived so as to include not only the geopolitical or economic relations in the present international configuration à la Immanuel Wallerstein's world systems theory, but also the spatiotemporal constellation in which we find ourselves and by which we imagine our world, its past, present, and future: in a word, History. Jameson's multivalent Marxism requires that we try to understand or to map the totality in order to make sense of our apparently local or timely situations. This requires "saying everything simultaneously," an impossible task, but no less worthy of the attempt for being merely impossible. The model for such a project, of course, is provided by Jameson himself, who is both a stylist and teacher, even down to the level of his meticulous diction and his carefully crafted sentences. Benjamin Kunkel has pointed out, for instance, that Jameson's prose frequently employs the word *meanwhile*, "a favourite Jamesonian transition, as if everything was present in his mind at once, and it was only the unfortunately sequential nature of language that forced him to spell out sentence by sentence and essay by essay an apprehension of the contemporary world that was simultaneous and total."[30] Similarly, in any given text Jameson almost constantly alludes to what is to come (with phrases like "as we shall see" or "as I discuss below") and what has come before ("as we have seen," "thus," "we can now return to …"), making his very sentences enact that spatiotemporal condition that the dialectic is uniquely suited to assess and comprehend, in theory as in practice. Not surprisingly, Jameson's content merges with his form, dramatizing the unity of opposites and, therefore, persistently advancing his sustained vision of Marxist critical theory. Merely reading Jameson, then, is already an education in the project of dialectical criticism.

2

The Task of the Translator

It probably ought to go without saying—but, as Michel Foucault liked to point out, perhaps it goes better *with* saying—that Jameson is not a professor of English. Although he has certainly contributed a great deal to studies of English literature and culture, and he has often written on Anglophone texts, Jameson's disciplinary formation lies in continental European literature. Having majored in French at Haverford College, then studying in France and in Germany, and receiving his Ph.D. in French at Yale University, Jameson has largely spent his career in French, Romance Studies, and Comparative Literature departments. Since 1985 he has served as the William A. Lane Professor of Comparative Literature and Romance Studies at Duke University.

I feel the need to emphasize this uncontroversial fact for two reasons. First, because I continue to see frequent, casual, and erroneous references to Jameson as an English professor, and I believe that the mistake leads to another: that of viewing Jameson's literary theory as a response to British or American critical traditions, such as Leavisite humanism, the New Criticism, or even the Marxist criticism exemplified by Raymond Williams and later Terry Eagleton. As his early writings clearly demonstrate, Jameson's work draws upon a rather different intellectual heritage. Second, more importantly, because Jameson himself emphasizes the difference between his intellectual formation and that of many who were trained in English. By studying French in the early 1950s, Jameson was exposed to contemporary fiction, criticism, and philosophy (in a word, "theory," *avant la lettre*), without being restricted to earlier, canonical, and mainly poetic texts of British and American literature. Additionally, his approach to literature was informed by Romance philology or "style studies" in the vein of such giants as Erich Auerbach, Leo Spitzer, or Ernest Robert Curtius, and hence Jameson largely avoided the powerful influence of the New Criticism, then dominant in English programs in the United States.[1] Thus, even as a graduate student just beginning his career in literary criticism and theory, Jameson was well positioned to take up, after his own fashion, the task of the translator.

Jameson's early works were self-conscious attempts to bring various traditions of what would become known as Western Marxism into the critical discussions taking place in the United States and elsewhere. Beginning with his first book, a seemingly apolitical investigation of Sartre's style, Jameson explored a Marxist tradition of cultural criticism largely unknown to American readers. In his second and third books, Jameson explicitly attempted to introduce German and French critical theory to an audience that not only had little to no native, operable, Marxian intellectual culture, but whose popular view of Marxism was at best simplistic and at worst a grotesque misrepresentation. "The whole ambition of *Marxism and Form* [was] to make available in English some of those traditions, and to make it more difficult for people to entertain these clichés and caricatural ideas of what Marxism was on the cultural level."[2] *Marxism and Form* included lengthy chapters on Theodor Adorno, Georg Lukács, and Sartre's *Critique of Dialectical Reason*, with slightly briefer discussions of Walter Benjamin, Herbert Marcuse, and Ernst Bloch, and concluded with a long, programmatic essay on the prospects and character of a truly dialectical criticism. In *The Prison-House of Language*, published one year later and originally conceived as part of the overall project of *Marxism and Form*,[3] Jameson addresses Russian formalism and French structuralism, examining from a Marxist perspective the "linguistic turn" in critical theory made possible by Ferdinand de Saussure's influential *Course in General Linguistics*. In the three early books, then, Jameson established himself as one of the leading critics of continental criticism and theory, largely through his engagement with other writers. Although he was not literally translating works from French or German into English, Jameson here fulfilled the task of the translator by bringing these foreign ideas across the linguistic, philosophical, and historical divide and making them available for use on new shores.

Jameson's early work appears to be a sort of commentary on other theorists rather than an unfolding of his own critical and theoretical practices, but I believe this is misleading. Like Gilles Deleuze, who wrote several books "on" various philosophers before producing work written "in his own voice," Jameson in reality develops his own distinctive critical theory through his engagement with these other writers.[4] So, just as Deleuze's *Nietzsche and Philosophy* is both a study of Nietzsche's work and a powerful example of what is now recognizable as Deleuzian thought, so too are Jameson's readings of, say, Sartre or Adorno not only helpful in introducing those influential, sometimes difficult theorists to new readers, but also useful for understanding Jameson's own dialectical criticism. Jameson faithfully translates this work, while also demonstrating the degree to which these various theories shape his Marxist literary criticism and theory.

My use of Walter Benjamin's phrase in this chapter is thus metaphorical, but only partially so. In "The Task of the Translator," Benjamin explains how translation as a mode differs from literary writing, inasmuch as the latter operates at the level of its specific linguistic situation while the former must direct its efforts toward language itself, in its totality. As Benjamin put it, "The task of the translator consists in finding that intended effect [*Intention*] upon the language into which he is translating which produces in it the echo of the original. [...] Unlike a work of literature, translation does not find itself in the center of the language forest but on the outside facing a wooded ridge; it calls into it without entering, aiming at that single spot where the echo is able to give, in its own language, the reverberation of the work in the alien one."[5] Moving from the literal languages to the more figurative "language" of critical theory, we might see how Jameson's project of dialectical criticism draws upon the individual works of these foreign authors in order to produce a novel effect in the "language" of Anglo-American criticism. In the process, Jameson remains faithful to the meanings of Sartre, Adorno, Lukács, Lévi-Strauss, Althusser, and so on, while also maintaining the integrity of his theoretical practice. The result, in these three early books, is a stunningly executed expository maneuver in which the theories of the European critics become legible within, and constitutive of, Jameson's own critical project.

Sartre

Throughout his career Jameson has remained somewhat loathe to engage in intellectual autobiography, but he has consistently acknowledged the profound effects of his literary and philosophical formation in the writings of Jean-Paul Sartre. In a 2012 interview, for instance, Jameson remarked that "in lots of ways I am always surprised to find to what degree I am still a Sartrean."[6] Jameson's first book was a study of Sartre's style. In retrospect, the choice of Sartre as the writer and of style as the topic seem significant, for the influence of Sartre and the close attention paid to formal matters of style are characteristic of Jameson's lifelong project. Even his most recent statements on realism have revisited Sartre's essays and examined, as he has throughout his career, the sentence-level details of literary works with as much care as that with which he has explicated grand philosophical systems. Hence, Jameson's early study of Sartre is not merely a preliminary exercise or precursor to his critical project, but an important part of it.

Nevertheless, *Sartre: The Origins of a Style* has been either ignored entirely or given short shrift in studies of Jameson's career. For example, the book is not mentioned by name at all by Adam Roberts, who allows only that Jameson wrote "his PhD thesis on Sartre (which was later published as a book)"; indeed, Sartre's name appears just three times in Roberts's study.[7] Sean Homer's *Fredric Jameson* pointedly begins with *Marxism and Form*, relegating the discussion of *Sartre* to an oddly out-of-place portion of his introduction, as if to suggest that Jameson's Sartre study is prefatory to, but not directly part of, his overall project.[8] Clint Burnham acknowledges Sartre's influence, but pays no attention to Jameson's study of Sartre's style.[9] In contrast to these others, Ian Buchanan takes such critics to task in his *Fredric Jameson: Live Theory*, as Buchanan identifies Sartre as one of four principal figures—the others are Adorno, Brecht, and Barthes—whose work permeates the entire Jamesonian critical endeavor.[10] Buchanan's list could no doubt be extended, but Sartre is unquestionably a significant presence in Jameson's work.

A reason some critics have felt confident in skipping over Jameson's first book is the mistaken belief that Jameson himself turned to Marxism only after *Sartre*, and that anyone interested in Jameson's Marxist criticism can therefore safely ignore it. For instance, Vincent B. Leitch has written that "Jameson began his career in the sixties as a philological and phe-nomenological critic. Sometime early in the decade he evidently became a Marxist."[11] It is true that *Sartre: The Origins of a Style* lacks the most visible signs of Marxist theory, including Karl Marx's name (although Sartre's Marxism is mentioned), but this owes more to the material facts of its production and circulation than to any change of heart on the part of its author. As is well known, *Sartre* emerged from Jameson's Ph.D. dissertation in the French department at Yale University in 1959, where he studied under the legendary critics Henri Peyre and Erich Auerbach, and the aims as well as the requirements of an academic thesis are not the same as those of other books. Even so, it is worth mentioning that McCarthyism and the Cold War moment—after the Rosenbergs, Hungary, Sputnik, and the Cuban Revolution, not to mention Khrushchev's "We will bury you" and the purported missile gap between the USA and the Soviet Union—undoubtedly placed the discourse of Marxism in the United States under a certain erasure, to use a Derridean formulation, but as in Derrida, this would not have made it less significant for criticism. In response to the suggestion that his ideas changed during the 1960s, Jameson has said, "No, I don't think so at all. I always thought in these ways. But the framework of the Sartre study, which was a dissertation and focused on style, was designed to explore formal aspects in Sartre's work that people hadn't noticed."[12] Jameson also pointed out that even before beginning his dissertation he had embraced a Marxist critical perspective: "I always felt even at an early age that Marx was right, and even though my first experience of Marxism as a creative movement came from the spirit of France in the 1950s, and in particular from the example of Sartre. [...] But I did read a good deal of Lukács when I studied in Berlin in the mid-1950s (and also a good deal of Brecht); and as for the Frankfurt School, they were always on the horizon too, as superb practitioners of the dialectic."[13]

Curiously, Jameson himself criticizes a similar misapprehension concerning Sartre's career. In *Marxism and Form*, Jameson notes that, while most critics think that Sartre was first an existentialist who only during or after World War II turned to Marxism, in reality the two philosophies, so-called, were concurrent and "coexisted [...] throughout Sartre's career." Indeed, "Sartre studied *Das Kapital* in 1925, two years before the publication of *Sein und Zeit*," and he later demonstrated the basic complementarity of the two "philosophies," since "Marxism is a way of understanding the objective dimension of history from the outside; existentialism a way of understanding subjective, individual experience."[14]

However, even in a work of "style studies," Jameson offered a clue to his more pervasive and widespread critical argument in his foreword, in which he acknowledges the "heavy debt" owed to the writings of Theodor W. Adorno and Roland Barthes. (It should be remembered that the Barthes of *Writing Degree Zero* and *Mythologies* was himself a Marxist critic in these days, if not always thereafter, and Jameson himself, in *Late Marxism*, has made the case that Adorno, "one of the greatest of twentieth-century Marxist philosophers,"[15] is perhaps the pre-eminent Marxist theorist for the postmodern condition.) In his afterword to the 1984 reissue of this book, Jameson elaborates the degree to which these writers, as well as Benjamin, contributed to his thinking, and he there situates *Sartre* among his more overtly Marxist critical theory of the intervening decades. Jameson's philological and even phenomenological early work was nevertheless written under the sign of Marxist theory, and the germinal element of the peculiarly expansive and intricately nuanced Marxism that characterizes his later work is at work in his first book on Sartre's style.

In *Sartre*, Jameson already demonstrates the remarkable fluidity with which he is able to analyze different cultural forms. By the 1980s, he would be nearly as well known for his writings on art, architecture, film, and philosophy, as for those on literature or literary theory proper. Of course, as he himself would be quickest to point out, all of these analyses are subsumed under the critical practice of Marxism, which simultaneously grants to each cultural form its own limited place and transcends them by projecting the broader social totality of which they are necessarily a part. With what will become characteristic dexterity, Jameson deftly moves among Sartre's diverse types of writing, from plays to novels to philosophical texts and back again, without ever losing sight of the fundamentally literary or stylistic critical project in which he is engaged.

Jameson begins by asserting that "a modern style is somehow in itself intelligible, above and beyond the limited meaning of the book written in it, and beyond even those precise meanings with the individual sentences that make it up are designed to convey." He undertakes to identify and analyze Sartre's unique style. In the main, Jameson's examination will turn on the opposition between consciousness and things, thus nominally evoking the existential phenomenology of Sartre's philosophical work. But Jameson proceeds by focusing on what he calls "the Event," which is not understood as "any particular type of happening" but as that which "directs our attention toward those moments when something essential *is* happening, whether in an old-fashioned kind of scene climax, or the description of a face, a suddenly electric gesture of a different quality from the gestures with which the scene is filled, or the nervousness with which certain sentences differentiate themselves from the more indifferent prose in which they take place."[16] As Jameson works his way through Sartre's writings, his chapters are organized around distinctive "events," and in a sense Jameson's *Sartre* operates a bit like Auerbach's *Mimesis*, in which a key scene or fragment—often presented through a single, more or less lengthy quotation of the original text—is singled out for meticulous, close reading. Jameson's *Sartre* is thus also a performance of a type of literary analysis, as well as a more objective explication of something belonging to Sartre himself.

Jameson starts with the "problem of acts," in which he explores Sartre's most famous play, *No Exit*, which is ostensibly a drama without action. The characters remain in an utterly static place, a hell or a limbo, and their torments are rooted in a consciousness of their inability to act or, perhaps, to have acted differently in the past. *No Exit* is thus a dramatization of the existentialist conception of *Angst*. But Jameson also demonstrates how such anxiety is dramatized even at the formal level, by observing that the play consists of "language in a void, of sentences that can never cross the distance that separates them from the acts they attempt to describe, of thinking turning around and around in a sealed past without the oxygen of a real present or future." This rupture between language and the world it is supposed to represent typifies a certain modernist vision of life within societies in which all that is solid melts into air, but in Sartre's play this seems to lack the modernist's complementary aspect of a sense of the new and of a transformative future. Already Jameson notes that the world of *No Exit* "reflects the condition of a society without a visible future, a society dazzled by the massive permanence of its own institutions in which no change seems possible and the idea of progress is dead."[17] The lack of historicity, in turn, reflects the problem of narrative itself.

In his 1984 afterword, Jameson reveals that "the basic propositions of this study turned around the question of narrative," particularly "the relationship of narrative to narrative closure, the possibility of storytelling, and the kinds of experience—social and existential—structurally available in a given social formation." For Jameson, the crisis of historicity necessarily evokes a crisis in narrative. Citing a lengthy exposition in *Nausea* of how lived experience cannot be told, Jameson remarks that "it is characteristic of Sartre's way of dealing with such literary problems that he should tell an anecdote to demonstrate the impossibility of anecdotes, that he should possess the means to make this lived time spring drearily from the page at the same time that he is demonstrating how irreducible it is to language."[18] In *Sartre*, Jameson explores this dilemma by examining the fundamental unit of narrative prose, the sentence itself; Jameson demonstrates that a sentence forms a complete "event," while somehow placing in brackets the larger matter of temporality. The discontinuity imposed by such punctuation as periods or colons establishes the "rhythm of time" for the reader.[19] As Jameson also makes clear, the distinction between the content and the form of a literary or philosophical work—and Sartre remains an exemplary model of the hybrid form of creative writer and philosopher— is ultimately false: "the search for the proper expression is the same as the search for the wholly adequate notion."[20] The matter of style, for Sartre as for others, is thus inextricably tied to the ability to represent experience.

In order to attempt to do so, new formal techniques, themselves tied to a social and historical moment in which the writer and text are situated, are required.

Already, then, Jameson has established in this perceived "crisis of narratable experience"[21] in Sartre's writings a theme that he revisits throughout his career, what Buchanan has called his "twin concerns" as cultural critic, "namely that historical memory is deteriorating and our sense of the future shrivelling."[22] In Sartre's style, Jameson discovers a formal mechanism for simultaneously restoring a kind of historicity while holding open a possibility for a future that is quite different from the present, or what might also be called the utopian impulse. As he notes, Sartre faced the same aesthetic problems—"the collapse of a single literary language, a period style, the expression of a relatively homogeneous class, into a host of private styles and isolated points in a fragmented society," for instance— that earlier modernists had countenanced; but Sartre's "literature of consciousness" resists both the naturalism and the psychologism of early or high modernism in favor of an intensely artificial and willful authorial style. Sartre's works are not "natural," writes Jameson, for "behind them we sense a motive-power of great violence bringing them into being, the mere feeling of uniqueness of a personal world pushed and extended until it becomes work, until it generates out of itself the narratives through which it can come to expression."[23]

Even this, however, might be viewed as a failed endeavor, as the task of crystallizing both experience and the objective world in a narrative form appears impossible. Jameson acknowledges this in his conclusion, but also demonstrates why this effort in Sartre's multidisciplinary writings remains so worthwhile. As he puts it, inimitably snatching a victory from the jaws of hopeless defeat,

> the vision of the world from which all more progressive content springs, the split between being and consciousness, seems to render language powerless. Language, one of the most fundamental syntheses of things and consciousness, falls useless between them when they are too radically separated. Yet a language is forced up into existence in the very silence which ought to take its place, and the imperfection of language does not inspire an attempt to correct it, or become the grounds for an utter failure, an abandonment of any speech and a silence, but is made the very instrument for speaking: the inhumanity

of things is revealed through the humanized language, and the purity of consciousness unveiled at the very moment when consciousness is intolerably being treated as a thing. Thus action, both in the subject matter of the works, and in the work itself of elaborating it, is resolutely undertaken in a situation which seemed to make it impossible: and the very imperfections of the works are merely another face, the negative dimension, of their vastness; for when all forms are impossible, no single one is any more impossible than any other, and suddenly they all come into being, all possible, criticism and plays, philosophy, novels, and political and historical and biographical analyses, bringing us face to face with the image of a consciousness for which everything can be understood, and of an unintimidated language for which there is nothing that cannot be said.[24]

One does not really need to read too minutely between the lines to find in this dialectical reversal a Marxist, and somewhat utopian, vision of Sartrean style, where style itself becomes a kind of class struggle against the baleful effects of a system characterized primarily by alienation.

As noted above, in an afterword to the 1984 reissue of *Sartre: The Origins of a Style* Jameson takes the opportunity to revisit his study and Sartre more generally by assessing both in a more recognizably Marxist idiom. However, it would be a mistake to see this as a revisionist intervention into his own work, even if Jameson himself seems to signal that he is "retelling" the story. In fact, he attempts to show how the "style studies" approach is remarkably consistent with the more elaborate French theory and Marxist criticism (here, represented mainly by Benjamin and, in particular, his essay on the work of art in the age of mechanical reproducibility) that had come to prominence in the intervening years. Jameson also takes the opportunity to discuss some of Sartre's work published after 1961, including his monumental and unfinished biography of Gustave Flaubert, *L'Idiot de la famille*. Jameson invokes the Sartrean conception of the *situation*, which enables him to consider Sartre's narratives outside of some facile opposition between individual will and a deterministic *Zeitgeist*. Drawing on this concept, Jameson shows how Sartre's apparently static narratives nevertheless "deconceal" the historical situation underlying, and necessary for the production of, any utopian impulse.[25] Through the formal study of Sartre's sentences and narratives, then, Jameson uncovers the dialectic of ideology and utopia that is fundamental to his Marxist criticism.

Marxism and Form

If Jameson's first book seemed to submerge any Marxist critique beneath the more philological, formal analysis of individual sentences or events, his second book, *Marxism and Form: Twentieth-Century Dialectical Theories of Literature* (1971) would place Marxism and the project of dialectical criticism at the center of discussion. As noted above, however, this does not mean that Jameson's Marxism was not present throughout his early writings, only that the express explication of a Marxist criticism would emerge through Jameson's effort to introduce, translate, and above all work through the vast intellectual productions of a number of key figures in what became known, after Perry Anderson's use of the term, as Western Marxism. By looking at, while also thinking *with*, the writings of "T.W. Adorno, Walter Benjamin, Herbert Marcuse, Ernst Bloch, Georg Lukács, [and] Jean-Paul Sartre" (to cite the list on the book's cover), Jameson establishes a properly Marxist criticism suited to the social and historical moment of what he still referred to as "the new modernism," but which would later become better known as postmodernism. The ten-year gap between *Sartre* and *Marxism and Form*, then, does not represent a major shift in Jameson's own project, so much as a continued unfolding of it. "And then," as Jameson has also pointed out, "it's not just people who change, it's also history itself that changed from 1959, when I finished *Sartre*, and 1969, when I was finishing *Marxism and Form*."[26] Or, to quote a character from Gillo Pontecorvo's majestic 1969 film, *Burn!* (one of Jameson's favorite movies, incidentally), "very often between one historical period and another, ten years suddenly might be enough to reveal the contradictions of a whole century."[27]

Jameson's task in *Marxism and Form* is formidable. "The crucial fact about the United States then and now is the utter absence of anything like what we would come to call western Marxism later on; my own contribution was (in books like *Marxism and Form*) to make that tradition known."[28] There are at least two problems for Jameson to overcome at the outset. First, he had to introduce this alien, almost exclusively German and French, tradition to an audience that was constitutionally resistant to it on both political and philosophical grounds. A powerful anti-Marxist and anti-dialectical strain runs through the intellectual discourse of a country with almost no operative socialist political culture; equally powerful, perhaps, is the fact that such theoretical traditions are anathema to the empirical and positivistic methods of most Anglo-American philosophy.

Hence, Jameson felt the need to introduce and to make available as viable critical practices Marxism and the dialectic to an audience likely uninterested in these concepts, if not openly hostile to them. Second, Jameson also had to contend with the residual Marxist traditions in the United States, specifically those of the dimly remembered struggles of the 1930s, in which the Marxist criticism tended to propound a sociology of literature and offer what might be viewed as simplistic readings of class in relation to a novel's content, such as determining which characters represent the corrupt *bourgeoisie*, for instance.[29] Not only did that older criticism pay little attention to form, but, in the debates of that era, any attention to the formal or even aesthetic qualities of a literary work might be viewed with suspicion. In some instances, form itself was considered a bourgeois concern, and, in any event, formal considerations might be seen as distractions from the underlying content. Additionally, the perceived cultural elitism of aesthetics could be viewed by a certain sort of leftist as ideologically undermining the working-class reader, who was presumed to take greater interest in the stories themselves and their allegorical import to the class struggle. Thus, in the very title of *Marxism and Form*, Jameson stakes out a somewhat polemical position.

So significant is that older vision of Marxism that Jameson felt the need to counter it in the book's very first paragraph:

> When the American reader thinks of Marxist literary criticism, I imagine that it is still the atmosphere of the 1930's which comes to mind. The burning issues of those days—anti-Nazism, the Popular Front, the relationship between literature and the labor movement, the struggle between Stalin and Trotsky, between Marxism and anarchism—generated polemics which no longer correspond to the conditions of the world today. The criticism practiced then was of a relatively untheoretical, essentially didactic nature, destined more for use in the night school than in the graduate seminar, if I may put it that way; and has been relegated to the status of an intellectual and historical curiosity, as which, in the form of an occasional stray reprint of an essay by Plekhanov or a passing reference to Christopher Caudwell, it is presently maintained.[30]

The reference to "night school" is suggestive of the purported elitism attributed to Jameson and the Marxist Literary Group by the more "practical" proponents of reform among the Modern Language

Association's Radical Caucus.[31] But, as Jameson maintains, in the United States and other "overdeveloped countries" in the postindustrial era, in which the material relations between personal experience and a larger social system seem invisible if not unimaginable, "there is no tactical or political question which is not first and foremost theoretical."[32] In such circumstances, Marxist literary criticism provides a vantage from which to glimpse the problem and to give it form.

Although the chapters of *Marxism and Form* deal with each thinker separately, Jameson's discussion of Adorno, Benjamin, Marcuse, Bloch, Lukács, and Sartre constitutes a continuous argument, building up to the long concluding chapter in which he sketches the outlines of a dialectical criticism suited to the exigencies of the present world system. As Phillip E. Wegner has argued recently, *Marxism and Form* reads like a realist novel, whose characters appear on the stage only when needed, and whose plot is "rich and exhilarating."[33]

Jameson begins by examining the work of Adorno, whom he takes as the exemplary figure of the dialectical critic. Noting the irony implicit in presenting to the public the work of a writer notorious for his pessimism with respect to the possibilities of the public sphere, Jameson uses the wide-ranging and difficult work of Adorno to establish the basic ground for Marxist literary criticism: that is, the relationship between superstructure and infrastructure, which are constantly in the mind of the dialectical critic, who "recognizes an obligation to transcend the limits of specialized analysis at the same time as [such criticism] respects the object's integrity as an independent entity." Thus, for Jameson, following Adorno, "the sociology of culture is […] a *form*." That is to say, the relationship between a work of culture and its underlying historical background becomes, for the truly dialectical critic, the crucial question. The critic attempts "to link together in a single figure two incommensurable realities, two independent codes or systems of signs, two heterogeneous and asymmetrical terms: spirit and matter, the data of individual experience and the vaster forms of institutional society, the language of existence and that of history."[34] Jameson's discussion of this criticism in Adorno will depend on what he calls "historical tropes," which are the formal attempts to think this impossible representational linkage.

In elaborating this historical vision, Jameson focuses on Adorno's *Philosophy of Modern Music*, in which Adorno famously assesses the twelve-tone system of Arnold Schoenberg as emblematic, or an expression, of the contemporary, rationalized European society. In Jameson's reading of Adorno, who is in turn "reading" Schoenberg's music, "the twelve-tone system serves as a kind of unified field theory for music, in which the data of harmony and that of counterpoint can now be translated back and forth into each other. [...] Thus there is carried into completion in the musical realm that basic tendency of all modern art in general toward a kind of absolute *overdetermination* of all of its elements." The effect is a sort of rational control over the contingent elements of art or of the lived experience to which works of art give shape. As Jameson summarizes, "the total organizational principle of Schoenberg's system reflects a new systemization of the world itself, of which the so-called totalitarian political regimes are themselves only a symptom. For in the later stages of monopoly and post-industrial capitalism not only the multiplicity of small business units, but also distribution, and ultimately the last free-floating elements of the older commercial and cultural universe, now are assimilated into a single all-absorbing mechanism."[35] In this case, the form of modern music serves to illuminate the abject condition of humanity in modern (or postmodern) society.

The historical narrative which can disclose such a present condition relies, inevitably it seems, upon some notion of an earlier, more Edenic past, from which the deteriorating processes descended. In Adorno, the musical predecessor is Beethoven, who represents a moment when form and content, experience and structure, are still unified. "Beethoven's reconciliation between the subjective and the objective faithfully registers the enlarged horizons of the revolutionary transition period itself, when the positive and universalistic thinking of the middle class during its struggle for power has not yet given way to the *esprit de sérieux* of money, business, and *Realpolitik*." Notably, this is also the spatiotemporal moment of Hegel and the dialectic, by which "Hegel is able to overcome the separation between subject and object."[36] Hegel is the philosophical *analogon* to Beethoven, in this view, and our inability to replicate a system such as Hegel's in the twentieth century is, for Adorno and Jameson, a sign of the historical limitation upon our thought in the present situation. Ultimately, in identifying this moment when, if only briefly and imperfectly, the unity of subjective experience and an objective world in music or philosophy is possible, Adorno seems to reveal the ironclad hopelessness of the present system. Although Jameson does not mention it here, Adorno is, after all, the dour scholar famed for remarking on the impossibility of poetry after Auschwitz, and Adorno's well-earned pessimism is perhaps justified considering the epoch in which he developed his theories. However, as Jameson recognizes in *Marxism and Form* as elsewhere, Adorno's "failure" to represent the totality or to imagine a way out of the modern "administered world" or "institutionalized society" nevertheless reveals the success of his attempts to come to terms with a historical situation all too familiar to most of his readers.

Building upon the form of Adorno's dialectical criticism, Jameson turns to three rather different thinkers in exploring "versions of a Marxist hermeneutic." In a way, Jameson's inquiry into Benjamin's sense of nostalgia, Marcuse's revival of the utopian vocation of the aesthetic sphere, and Bloch's forward-looking principle of hope supplements and responds to the apparently stagnant condition of postwar, postindustrial societies in Adorno's vision. Each of these other writers offers a means of interpreting the present that holds open the possibility for an alternative to the status quo. And, in Jameson's narration, this chapter invokes these Marxist critics as figurations of past, present, and future, each a partial fulfillment of the promise of the historical trope, and, in the aggregate, a compelling vision of a totality toward which Marxist hermeneutics must strive.

In Benjamin's varied work, memory and nostalgia predominate, either in such personal reflections as *Berlin Childhood* or in his historical researches into the German Baroque (in his *Trauerspiel* study) and nineteenth-century Paris ("On Some Motifs in Baudelaire," for instance). In Jameson's view, Benjamin seeks these exemplary moments when a kind of "psychic wholeness or unity of experience" can be recovered. Jameson argues that Benjamin's thought is best understood as allegorical, "as a set of parallel, discontinuous levels of meditation" that could be adequately compared to the great Dantean formula, as laid out in Dante's famous letter to Can Grande della Scala, for reading his own *Commedia*. Dante identified four dimensions of meaning (literal, moral, allegorical, and anagogical), which Jameson translates here—and again later, perhaps more famously, in *The Political Unconscious*—as psychological, moral, aesthetic, and political. So, for Benjamin, the psychological drive toward unity takes the form of "an obsession with the past or memory," which is then mediated by the Freudian "distinction between unconscious memory and the conscious act of recollection." This, in turn, leads to a moral judgement, "a vision of the reconciliation of the past and present which is somehow an ethical one," but *moral* in a special sense of personal development or *Bildung*. In Jameson's thinking *with* Benjamin, this moves into the aesthetic realm in Benjamin's great study of allegory, *The Origins of German Tragic Drama*, in which the baroque world of seventeenth-century German culture registers its radical alterity from the present; it is a world whose unity can be grasped allegorically. In moving from the baroque to the modern society of Baudelaire's Paris (or even of Benjamin's Paris of the 1930s), Benjamin shifts from primarily aesthetic concerns to historical and political ones, focusing on such matters as "The Work of Art in the Age of Mechanical Reproduction" and "Paris, Capital of the Nineteenth-Century," as well as his late "Theses on the Philosophy of History." Jameson discovers in Benjamin's notion of the "aura," apprehensible in modern art, a "Utopian component" that is ultimately available to the thinker "only in a simpler cultural past."[37] In this manner, Benjamin recovers for a Marxist criticism the value of nostalgia from its more familiar, reactionary uses, since "a nostalgia conscious of itself, a lucid and remorseless dissatisfaction with the present on the grounds of some remembered plenitude," could easily "furnish as adequate a revolutionary stimulus as any other." As Jameson concludes this section on Benjamin, fittingly with the Benjaminian image of the *Angelus Novus*, Benjamin's experience of time is "a present of language on the threshold of the future, honoring it by averted eyes in meditation on the past."[38]

In the following section, Jameson juxtaposes the thought of his senior colleague Herbert Marcuse with that found in Friedrich Schiller's *Letters on the Aesthetic Education of Mankind*, mediating the two with a related discussion of surrealism. These are some strange bedfellows gathered for an argument in which hermeneutics, the traditionally religious textual practice, is shown to be a thoroughly political discipline, whereby freedom may be glimpsed amid the "sudden perception of an intolerable present."[39] Jameson shows how Schiller constructs "a hermeneutic machine which permitted the critic to identify the concrete experience of the work of art with the broader problems of freedom," on both personal and political levels. Drawing upon André Breton and the surrealists, Jameson argues that the commodified culture of the 1920s, with its artificial stimuli and artificial longings, creates a similar problem for the artist, and as the industrial civilization begins to yield to a postindustrial capitalism, the works of art themselves no longer seem to bear much relation to the psychological or personal investments in them.[40] At this point, Jameson pivots to the work of Marcuse, the preeminent cultural critic of the postindustrial moment, in whose writings the promise of a critical utopianism is revived. For Marcuse, "it is the Utopian concept—'the attempt to draft a theoretical construct of culture beyond the performance principle'—which henceforth, absorbing and replacing the function of art for Schiller and for the Surrealists, embodies the newest version of a hermeneutics of freedom."[41]

In the third and final "version of a Marxist hermeneutic," Jameson considers the eccentric and sometimes neglected work of Ernst Bloch, who is seen as less of a Marxist philosopher than a "theologian of the revolution." Jameson considers the formal comparison of Marxism to religion (frequently made as an insult by anti-communists but, as Jameson notes, ironically so, since they must thereby admit that religion is itself ideological), and observes that Marxism does indeed have much, albeit superficially, in common with Christian thought in their historical situation and their claims to universality. Thus, for Jameson, the allegorical model supplied by medieval religious thought may be usefully translated for a properly Marxist criticism. Bloch's principle of hope, with its Messianic orientation toward the future, extends the utopian impulse in Marcuse and makes it available in the consideration of those traces or seeds of utopian futurity to be discovered in past and present works. In Bloch's hermeneutic, as Jameson describes it, "little by little, wherever we look everything in the world becomes a version of some primal figure, a manifestation of that primordial movement toward the future and toward ultimate identity with a transfigured world which is Utopia, and whose vital presence, behind whatever distortions, beneath whatever layers of repression, may always be detected, no matter how faintly, by the instruments and apparatus of hope." For Bloch, the unconscious attraction is less that tending toward a past plenitude or unity and more "an ontological pull of the future, of a tidal influence exerted upon us by that which lies out of sight below the horizon, an unconscious of what is yet to come."[42]

In Jameson's analysis, all three of these dialectical thinkers, Benjamin, Marcuse, and Bloch, make possible a Marxist hermeneutic that discloses the political dimensions of the varied texts produced in modern industrial (and postindustrial) societies. Whether principally oriented toward the past, present, or future, each discovers in the texts they examine certain "figures—whether of psychic wholeness, of freedom, or of the drive toward Utopian transfiguration—of the irrepressible revolutionary wish."[43] The apparently pessimistic thought of Adorno is thus countered, in a sense, by these versions of a hermeneutic, but the ultimate ground upon which such revolutionary critiques and desires unfold is history itself, which becomes the subject of *Marxism and Form*'s next chapters.

In naming his chapter on this preeminent Marxist philosopher and critic "The Case for Georg Lukács," Jameson implies both an apologia and a polemic. Given the vicissitudes of the Hungarian thinker's career and reputation, it is perhaps not surprising that Jameson feels the need not only to explicate, but to advocate for, Lukács's own form of dialectical criticism. The influence of Lukács, perhaps behind only that of Sartre and Adorno, is visible in nearly all of Jameson's writing, but here Jameson endeavors to demonstrate the coherence and actuality of Lukács's Marxist criticism. And, as I mentioned in the Introduction, Jameson disputes the facile division of Lukács's career into various self-contained segments or phases (such as early Hegelianism, followed by a middle-period of Bolshevik philosophy, then a later socialist realism, etc.). Instead, he views Lukács's project as "a continuous and lifelong meditation on narrative, on its basic structures, its relationship to the reality it expresses, and its epistemological value when compared with other, more abstract and philosophical modes of understanding."[44]

Jameson begins by noting that inherent in the Hegelian distinction between abstract and concrete is the Marxist concept of alienation. That is, alienation is implied by abstraction, and the movement from the concrete to the abstract can be viewed as part of the process of increasing alienation. In considering Lukács's *Theory of the Novel*, a supposedly pre-Marxist or merely Hegelian work, Jameson observes that Lukács already projects a historical and political world system in which the era of the novel, typified by a "world abandoned by God," signals the profound alienation of soul and forms (to invoke the title of Lukács's first book).[45] In such a world, narrative itself offers the concrete means for imagining utopia, "a world in which meaning and life are once more indivisible, in which man and the world are one." But Lukács's apparent nostalgia for a lost plenum or *Lebenstotalität* of the age of the epic is quickly projected into a future, and thus already situates itself within the Marxist theory of history. In order to achieve his aims in *The Theory of the Novel*, then, Lukács will require the complete theory of totality that he is able to formulate only in *History and Class Consciousness*. In a typically Jamesonian dialectical reversal, Jameson contends that Lukács did not abandon his Hegelianism when he became a communist, thus disavowing his earlier theory, but that "the problems of narration raised in the *Theory of the Novel* required a Marxist framework to be thought through to their logical conclusion."[46] Jameson goes on to demonstrate how the seemingly non-literary *History and Class Consciousness* in fact resolves its own epistemological problematic of "the antinomies of bourgeois thought" by demonstrating the degree to which the nineteenth-century novel, not nineteenth-century philosophy, is capable of reflecting the truth of the world under industrial capitalism. As such, Lukács's turn toward the forms of the historical novel and realism are perfectly in line with his political and philosophical endeavor, and his ultimate accomplishment will be his insistence on the relationship between narrative and totality.[47]

In his elegant retracing of Lukács's critical trajectory, Jameson emphasizes the way in which Lukács's meditation on the relationship between narrative and the social totality forms the basis of Marxist, dialectical thought. A quasi-scientific ordering of the world into seemingly static categories cannot really hope to give shape to the shifting realities of social experience in modern, capitalist societies, whereas the realist novel and narrative more generally might provide an adequate representation. Narrative thus assumes the role that philosophy had previously occupied in establishing a meaningful ontology of the present. What is lacking still is a sense of agency, which Jameson will recover through his reading of Sartre's *Critique of Dialectical Reason* in the next chapter of *Marxism and Form*.

Sartre's *Critique*, which was ultimately unfinished but whose first, influential volume appeared in 1960, was published after those works Jameson considered in the earlier study, so the chapter on "Sartre and History" may be of interest to students of Jameson's thought as a supplement to *Sartre: The Origins of a Style*. However, this chapter also completes the "realist narrative" that Wegner has identified in *Marxism and Form* by providing the unification of the subjective and objective in Sartre's conception of totalization or, rather, in history itself. As noted above, Jameson disputes the idea that Sartre's career can be meaningfully split between an early, existentialist Sartre of *Being and Nothingness* and a later, Marxist Sartre of the *Critique*, but he convincingly demonstrates the relationship between the two forms or modes. "Marxism is a way of understanding the objective dimension of history from the outside; existentialism a way of understanding subjective, individual experience. The 'search for a method' therefore does not take the form of a reconciliation of contraries, but rather of a kind of unified field theory in which two wholly different ontological phenomena can share a common set of equations and be expressed in a single linguistic or terminological system." In practice, Jameson finds Sartre's conception of totalization to be an updated and expanded version of what Sartre had earlier termed a *project*, but with totalization such a project necessarily takes on a collective, historical dimension.[48] Overcoming the merely subjective experience of the individual and the seemingly detached, objective condition of society, Marxism considers both subjectivity (in the form of class struggle) and objectivity (in the form of the mode of production) in order to disclose the workings of history itself, which is necessarily both subjective and objective, material and ideal, diachronic and synchronic, and so on. As a method and a mode of thinking, then, Sartre's Marxism attempts to overcome the splintering and fragmentation of knowledge into discrete, necessarily incomplete, and hence false fields. In considering the concrete historical situation, Marxism thus includes the social, political, economic, and other spheres while demonstrating their inextricable connections to each other in what may be glimpsed as a totality. As Jameson concludes, citing James Joyce's famous line, if history is a nightmare from which we cannot awake, then "one cannot awake until one has first measured the extent and the intensity of the nightmare."[49]

At the risk of appearing insufficiently historicist myself, I might point out that Jameson's reading of Sartre here already anticipates his conceptions of national allegory, the political unconscious, and cognitive mapping, insofar as the coordination of individual lived experience and a projection of a larger, social totality is very much the point of Sartre's totalization. There is also that utopian element, never very distant from Jameson's critical theory, in Sartre's vision. To name another theorist admired by Jameson, this is something like Gilles Deleuze's assessment of Sartre in 1964, at a moment when the founder of existentialism was starting to be considered rather *passé* by the younger generation of French intellectuals: "Sartre allows us to await some vague future moment, a return, when thought will form again and make its totalities anew, like a power that is at once collective and private. That is why Sartre remains my teacher."[50]

The narrative trajectory of *Marxism and Form* would seem to conclude at this point, since Jameson is no longer "translating" twentieth-century European theorists, but he appends a long final chapter titled "Toward a Dialectical Criticism," in which, arguably, he adds his own name to the roster that included Adorno, Benjamin, Marcuse, Bloch, Lukács, and Sartre. This chapter is not exactly a survey of Jameson's personal theories, but demonstrates his own remarkable synthesis of these and other theorists' ideas as he sketches the project of dialectical criticism. In a sense, the 300 or so pages before this might be viewed as a prolegomena to this section.

"The peculiar difficulty in dialectical writing," Jameson asserts, "lies indeed in its holistic, 'totalizing' character: as though you could not say any one thing until you had first said everything else." This totalizing aspect of dialectical criticism accounts not only for its difficulty, but also for its apparent unwillingness to make simple propositions or draw definitive conclusions. Jameson famously refers to dialectical thinking as "thought to the second power: an intensification of the normal thought processes," and he argues that "dialectical thought tries not so much to complete and perfect the application of such procedures [i.e., those of the "nonreflective thinking mind"] as to widen its own attention to include them in its awareness." Such thought aims "not so much at solving the particular dilemmas in question, as at converting those problems into their own solutions on a higher level, and making the fact and the existence of the problem itself the starting point for new research."[51] Those familiar with Jameson's notoriously tortuous prose style and the expansiveness of his terrains of critical inquiry will recognize this principle at work in nearly all of his writings.

A fundamental element of dialectical criticism is its attention to what Aristotle called *peripeteia*, the reversal of the situation, which makes possible that later recognition (*anagnorisis*), which in turn is necessary for true understanding. As Jameson explains:

> The basic story which the dialectic has to tell is no doubt that of the dialectical *reversal*, that paradoxical turning around of a phenomenon into its opposite of which the transformation of quantity into quality is only one of the better known manifestations. It can be described as a kind of leap-frogging affair in time, in which the drawbacks of a given historical situation turn out in reality to be its secret advantages, in which what looked like built-in superiorities suddenly prove to set the most ironclad limits on its future development. It is a matter, indeed, of the reversal of limits, of the transformation from negative to positive and from positive to negative.[52]

Jameson's then timely example of such a dialectical reversal involved the Cold War arms race. He notes that the technological superiority of the United States in producing atomic weapons led the Soviet Union to experiment with missiles that could carry their much more cumbersome nuclear bombs, which resulted in a benefit to their space program; but the consequent Soviet superiority in rocket technology led the Americans to develop smaller, more efficient transistorized instruments, and so on. An apparent disadvantage turns out to have been a clear advantage when judged from a certain point of view, but this situation is itself reversed when perceived from a different spatiotemporal vantage. As Jameson concludes, this example neglects the various events and reversals which came before but which constituted the conditions for the possibility of the technological arms race or space race: "a complete picture of this particular set of dialectical reversals would ultimately have involved a reimmersion in the very element of concrete history itself."[53]

More recently, in *Valences of the Dialectic*, Jameson uses the example of India and the phenomenon of "outsourcing." Jameson observes how the seemingly negative (at least, from the point of view of American capitalism), Soviet-style policies of Jawaharlal Nehru in the 1960s led to the formation of technical institutes, thus creating a generation of well-educated workers perfectly suited to constitute the productive labor force for the (positive) outsourcing booms of the 1990s. But the dot-com bust (negative) facilitated the cheaper employment of outsourced, Indian workers (positive). Such dialectical reversals remain part of the geopolitical and world economic history of the present.[54]

What seems *ironic* to the limited, empiricist perspective is an example of the "dialectical union of opposites" in Jameson's view. Any dialectical criticism must necessarily be attuned to these reversals, which is one of the many reasons why Jameson is so impatient with social criticism that he deems "moralizing." What seems "good" in one historical situation may be a great "evil," or (to follow Jameson's own more Nietzschean conception) merely "bad," when considered from a different spatiotemporal position.[55] The dialectic requires taking the good with the bad, Jameson insists, which sometimes means recognizing the seeds of utopia in the most baleful and repressive circumstances.

Jameson has pointed out that the dialectic is committed to the "logic of the situation," as opposed to logics of individual consciousness or abstract notions like "society." As he puts it, "The emphasis on the logic of the situation, the constant changeability of the situation, its primacy and the way in which it allows certain things to be possible and others not: that would lead to a kind of thinking that I would call dialectical."[56] From this position, Jameson's exploratory elaboration of a dialectical criticism at the end of *Marxism and Form* is intimately related to his later work, and demonstrates once more its essentially Sartrean heritage. And, although the word itself is not yet in his mind, Jameson's reflections on the "new modernism" of the 1960s, distinct from its *fin-de-siècle* predecessor, suggest the degree to which *postmodernism* was already insinuating itself into Jameson's criticism.[57] In such a postmodern situation, the project of dialectical criticism is all the more needed, since only that project heroically attempts to square the circle of, and give form to, both lived experience and the social totality, which is impossible from the limited perspective of various specialized disciplines. "The works of culture come to us as signs of an all-but-forgotten code, as symptoms of diseases no longer even recognized as such, as fragments of a totality we have long since lost the organs to see." Today, Jameson asserts, everything "cries out for commentary, for interpretation, for decipherment, for diagnosis," in other words, for the traditional duties of literary criticism.[58] Marxist criticism, not only because it does a better job than those other, more specialized or local varieties, but also because it always and already contains their concerns within its own, is uniquely suited to this situation.

The Prison-House of Language

If part of Jameson's aim in *Marxism and Form*, among his other works of the 1970s, is to make a case for the actuality of Marxism and the dialectic in literary studies, the linguistic turn in literature and philosophy, heralded especially by the influence of structuralism in France and its initial gains in the English-speaking world, presented a special challenge. Just as Jameson was introducing important work by continental Marxist theorists to an Anglophone audience, an apparently anti-dialectical, sometimes anti-Marxist model was gaining momentum. As a scholar of European and particularly French critical theory, Jameson was well positioned to assess fascinating ideas emerging under the sign of structuralism, and *The Prison-House of Language* (1972) was among the first critical studies to do so.[59]

While Jameson has said that the materials covered in *The Prison-House of Language* were originally conceived as part of *Marxism and Form*, which may explain the latter's imbalance with respect to the German and French writers, it is clear that *The Prison-House of Language* has a rather different focus and produces different effects. For one thing, Jameson's subtitle, *A Critical Approach to Structuralism and Russian Formalism*, establishes in advance a somewhat more polemical stance. Whereas *Marxism and Form* had purported to present *Twentieth-Century Dialectical Theories of Literature* (its subtitle), which suggests, perhaps misleadingly, a more dispassionate presentation of the literary critics and theorists discussed, Jameson expressly labels his discussion of the linguistic approaches "critical." And, indeed, Jameson's tone throughout is far more critical, as that term is used in everyday parlance, than the earlier study's had been. By introducing and "translating" the theories of Adorno, Bloch, Benjamin, Lukács, and the later Sartre, Jameson also defends and even champions their work. This is not to say that his presentation of their work is uncritical. Far from it. It is just that Jameson seeks to demonstrate how these lesser-known (in the United States, at least) theorists deserve our attention, and he demonstrates that by revealing how powerful and interesting their work really is. The approach in *The Prison-House of Language* is similar, but the results are slightly different. Jameson duly and fairly presents the linguistic theory of Ferdinand de Saussure, its influence on Roman Jakobson and Claude Lévi-Strauss, and so on, but he does so in such a way as to show the limitations of those models when considered from a properly Marxist perspective.

Such a stance is not surprising when one considers that the linguistic model and structuralism in particular effectively displaced Sartrean existentialism and phenomenology at the summit of French intellectual culture. As a leading Sartrean, Jameson could not help but feel somewhat defensive about a theory that presented itself, in part, as anti-Sartrean, not to mention anti-Hegelian and, at times, anti-Marxist. Michel Foucault, for instance, established his work in opposition to Sartre's, and he seemed to delight in taking jabs at the left, as when he mischievously wrote in *The Order of Things* that the controversies of Marxism in the field of economics were but "storms in a children's paddling pool."[60] Even though many of the leading French structuralists and Russian formalists were themselves Marxists, the theoretical attention to synchrony rather than diachrony and to structures rather than processes seemed rather antithetical to Marxism. Yet, as usual, Jameson cautions against dismissing theories or concepts on strictly ideological grounds, and he seems to easily incorporate even an enemy's arguments into his own, dialectical criticism. As if in response to those who wonder why a Hegelian Marxist critic would even bother with structuralism, Jameson writes: "my own feeling is that a genuine critique of Structuralism commits us to working our way completely through it so as to emerge, on the other side, into some wholly different and theoretically more satisfying philosophical perspective."[61]

Jameson begins by observing that "[t]he history of thought is a history of its models," thus signaling that his consideration of "the linguistic model" (the first chapter of *The Prison-House of Language*) places the study in the field of intellectual history.[62] This is itself a distancing maneuver, although Jameson's sense of history readily incorporates the more limited field into its broader totality. Yet, by invoking other "models" that have emerged, had their day, and then evanesced after a period of stale dogmatism, Jameson is already gently provoking the proponents of structuralism, supposedly the most *au courant* theory going, by suggesting that theirs is one of any number of ultimately failed theories. Before laying out the principles of Saussure's field-changing work in the first chapter, Jameson notes how even Saussure's linguistics responded to the Romantic philology and the Neo-Grammarians of the nineteenth-century. But, for all that, Jameson also acknowledges that Saussure's reaction to these older models constituted a release of great intellectual energies.[63]

In Jameson's view, the most significant contribution of Saussure is the separation of the synchronic from the diachronic in linguistics. Whereas historical philology had focused upon discrete changes in a word or phrase over time, the synchronic approach enables a scientific apprehensive of the system of language itself. "Saussure's originality was to have insisted on the fact that language as a total system is complete at every moment, no matter what happens to have been altered in it a moment before. This is to say that the temporal model proposed by Saussure is that of a series of complete systems succeeding each other in time; that language is for him a perpetual present, with all the possibilities of meaning implicit in its every moment."[64] Although Jameson finds that the opposition between the synchronic and diachronic seems anti-dialectical, an antinomial opposition that cannot be resolved, *within* Saussure's synchronic system, the dialectic of *langue* and *parole* plays out. *Langue*, or language, is the system or structure as a whole, whereas *parole*, speech or utterance, is the individual instance within the system. The dialectical relation of a part to the whole, the mutual dependence upon one another, distinguishes this Saussurean opposition from the empirical attention to discrete statements or words.[65] The individual speech act is thus distinguished from the structure within which it may take on meaning. The *langue/ parole* distinction, along with its larger counterpart in synchrony versus diachrony, forms the basis of Jameson's discussion of the effect of Saussure on literary criticism and theory in the subsequent chapters.

Jameson's consideration of "the formalist projection" and "the structuralist projection" is simultaneously an exposition and extrapolation of this Saussurean model. As Jameson sees it, the Russian formalists seized upon the *parole*, particularly in the discrete and discernibly literary act, whereas the French structuralists focused upon the *langue*, the system of signs itself. In that sense, the two complementary theories essentially followed divergent paths through the territory surveyed by Saussurean linguistics.

Jameson notes that the Russian formalists were stubbornly committed to the literary fact, to *literaturnost* (literariness), from which their investigations proceeded. Famously, Viktor Shklovsky defined literary art, or art in general, as defamiliarization or estrangement (*ostranenie*), which is richly developed in a more overtly political and Marxian way in Bertolt Brecht's idea of the *Verfremdungseffekt* (or "estrangement effect," *Verfremdung* being roughly the German equivalent of *ostranenie*).[66] In Shklovsky's approach, the goal of criticism was to "bare the device" by which a work of art defamiliarized the commonplace objects of everyday life. However, as Jameson explains, the historical situation of the work of art and of its public determines the degree to which the familiar may be apprehended as strange, and thus "what gave itself as universal law proves with the turning over of the calendar to have been nothing more than the ideology of the day in disguise."[67]

Under the influence of Lévi-Strauss, French structuralism went in the direction of the *langue*, the system or structure of language. Partly for this reason, the individual literary act (*parole*) became less significant, and a structuralist theorist like the Barthes of *Mythologies* could interpret the "language" of wrestling, fashion magazines, and the like. Clearly the specifically literary language of the formalists ceased to have much import when nearly all texts could be apprehended as part of an overarching sign system. Jameson suggests that the structuralist project is "a study of super-structures, or, in a more limited way, of ideology,"[68] thus introducing a Marxist terminology at the outset of his analysis. In their intense focus on the signifier, on relations among signifiers even more than on the relation between signifier and signified, the structuralist projection becomes a mediation on the synchronic, to the extent that even the diachronic comes to be an inaccessible concept, subordinated to the synchronic system. According to A.J. Greimas (and also Louis Althusser), "understanding is essentially a synchronic process, even when it takes diachronic events as its object. It follows that insofar as we can 'apprehend' history at all conceptually, such apprehension must have taken the form of a translation of genuine diachrony into synchronic terms. Real diachrony, therefore, real history, falls outside the mind as a kind of *Ding-an-sich*, unattainable directly: time becomes unknowable."[69] This is suggestive of the dialectical opposition between form and content, not to mention description and narrative (as in Lukács's distinction between naturalism and realism),[70] and it will have lasting effects on Jameson's discussion of cognitive mapping or other means of attempting to apprehend history or the totality. The encounter with structuralism allows Jameson to think synchrony without entirely abandoning the diachronic field that was to have formed the basis of any Marxist theory of history. Jameson concludes *The Prison-House of Language* by revisiting the philosophical overcoming of Kant's static categories through Hegel's historical dialectic, thus recasting structuralism as a kind of neo-Kantianism, and Jameson's own position as that of a properly poststructuralist dialectical criticism.

It is not surprising to find that Marxism itself is capable of reconciling the antinomial conflict between synchrony and diachrony, as Marxist criticism effects that characteristically Hegelian *Aufhebung*, canceling, preserving, and elevating the problem by demonstrating the ultimate unity of instance and system. For the synchronic snapshot of a mode of production, like Saussure's ever present and always complete *langue*, discloses the system as we attempt to know it, while the diachronic class struggle, like each *parole* of Saussure, is revealed as the motor of history itself. In Jameson's view, the partial readings made possible by this or that limited perspective, while valuable in their own way, must yield before the untranscendable horizon of Marxism, the only philosophy constitutionally capable of apprehending the totality of which all of these discrete instances are parts and by which they attain their significance. "Truth as transcoding, as translation from one code to another," Jameson concludes *The Prison-House of Language*, makes possible a genuine hermeneutic practice "by disclosing the presence of preexisting codes and models and by reemphasizing the place of the analyst himself," which would in turn "reopen text and analytic process alike to all the winds of history."[71] Ultimately, then, the task of the translator is to bring these diverse discourses back into relation with the one language through which all of these things may be intelligible and narratable—Marxism itself.

3

The Untranscendable Horizon

Marxism and Form, along with *The Prison-House of Language*, established Jameson as both a leading Marxist intellectual and one of the most prominent literary critics in the United States. At a moment when "theory," as it would come to be called, was beginning to infiltrate major academic literary journals and university curricula, Jameson's critical interventions were both timely and transformational. In his writings, Jameson coolly assessed the shifting territories and terminologies associated with continental theory, as well as its influence on more traditional forms of literary criticism, while he energetically lobbied for the priority of a Marxist approach. In a seminal essay, "Metacommentary" (1971), Jameson attempted to outflank in advance many of the emerging methodologies by observing that the literary text, by virtue of its inherently social production and existence in language, comes to us as an always and already interpreted thing. As such, any particular interpretative method—New Critical, psychoanalytic, semiotic, deconstructive, etc.—limits itself to a particular kind of hermeneutic model that cannot but ignore a more basic question of why we need to interpret in the first place.[1] Any commentary upon a given literary text must involve metacommentary, which for Jameson stands as another code word for the project of dialectical criticism itself. "Metacommentary" won the Modern Language Association's prestigious William Riley Parker Prize, awarded to the year's most outstanding article published in *PMLA* (the organization's principal organ), and thus the essay further established Jameson's place among the leading critics of the day.[2] Ian Buchanan has suggested that metacommentary is cornerstone of the entire Jamesonian enterprise,[3] and, although Jameson refrains from emphasizing the specifically Marxian content of his argument there, in this early and quite public intervention Jameson serves notice that the only theoretical practice capable of making sense of literature, which itself represents various attempts to make sense of one's experience in an unrepresentable social totality, is Marxism.

Borrowing a well-known expression from Sartre, Jameson nominates Marxism as the "untranscendable horizon" of critical thinking in the contemporary world. Elsewhere, he also asserts that history (or, in his frequently Hegelian or perhaps just Germanic usage, History) itself is this "untranscendable horizon"; but it amounts to the same thing, as Marxism is the preeminent discourse by which History with a capital "H" might be disclosed. Sartre had stated this himself in his *Search for a Method*: "I consider Marxism the one philosophy of our time which we cannot go beyond."[4] In his 1979 essay "Marxism and Historicism," Jameson invokes this conception as the basis for his eclectic or holistic embrace of other literary theories and methods within his own Marxist framework. Noting that various schools of interpretation focus upon certain themes— for example, language or communication for structuralism, desire for Freudianism, temporality for phenomenological approaches, archetypes for myth criticism, and so on—Jameson explains that

> no intelligent contemporary Marxism will wish to exclude or repudiate any of the themes listed above, which all in their various ways designate objective zones in the fragmentation of contemporary life. Marxism's "transcendence" of these other methods therefore does not spell the abolition or dissolution of their privileged objects of study, but rather the demystification of the various frameworks or strategies of containment by means of which each could lay claim to being a total and self-sufficient interpretive system. To affirm the priority of Marxist analysis as that of some ultimate and untranscendable semantic horizon—namely the horizon of the *social*—thus implies that all other interpretive systems conceal a *seam* which strategically seals them off from the social totality of which they are a part and constitutes their object of study as an apparently closed phenomenon.[5]

Whereas linguistic, psychological, ethical, or political methodologies and theories are valuable inasmuch as they provide a handle by which to grasp these extremely important elements of social experience, only Marxism, properly understood, aims at apprehending the social totality that both conditions individual experience and evades individual perception.

A similar theory is outlined in the opening pages of *The Political Unconscious*, in which Jameson conceives of Marxism as "that 'untranscendable horizon' that subsumes such apparently antagonistic or incommensurable critical operations, assigning them an undoubted sectoral validity with itself, and thus at once canceling and preserving them."[6] In establishing Marxism as the untranscendable horizon of contemporary thought, Jameson's writings of the 1970s and 1980s engaged directly with the diverse panoply of theoretical practices which were then dominating critical discussions. But his dialectical criticism remained paradoxically rigid and flexible, as he doggedly maintained a sort of Hegelian Marxism that even among Marxist critics seemed terribly old-fashioned, while at the same time also demonstrating a veritably gymnastic conceptual dexterity in grappling with, parrying, and ultimately subduing each novel interpretive system as it entered the arena.[7] That is, rather than hastily dismissing psychoanalysis, poststructuralism, reader response theory, the new historicism, and other decentralized "schools" of thought as irrelevant or wrongheaded, as so much fashionable nonsense, Jameson becomes a prominent interlocutor in these debates. As in his earlier role as a "translator" of mostly German and French theory into an American critical idiom, he patiently and generously analyzes the texts under consideration, but inevitably demonstrates how they may be subsumed within a dialectical, Marxist criticism.

As we have seen, between 1972 and 1990, Jameson published only two new books, *Fables of Aggression* and *The Political Unconscious*, plus an important two-volume collection of essays, *The Ideologies of Theory: Essays, 1971–1986*. This apparent slow-down in his literary productivity is misleading, however, particularly when one considers that he published no fewer than 130 journal articles and book chapters between 1971 and 1989.[8] Moreover, as with many of the materials related to the postmodernism debates, which I will discuss in Chapters 4 and 5, Jameson's labors during this period bore a great deal of fruit in the 1990s and beyond. At a personal level, Jameson's career proved more tumultuous and peripatetic in these years, as he moved from the University of California, San Diego, to Yale University in 1976; from 1983 to 1985, he taught at the University of California at Santa Cruz, before establishing himself at Duke University, where he founded the Graduate Program in Literature (now the Program in Literature), transforming the comparative literature curriculum and founding the Institute for Critical Theory, among other significant accomplishments as an administrator and teacher. During this period, in books, essays, public lectures, and undoubtedly in the classroom as well, Jameson endeavored to prove that Marxist criticism was not only capable of interpreting literary and cultural artifacts more effectively than other forms of criticism, but that those other methods ultimately generated only partial or incomplete versions of the interpretations produced by a properly dialectical criticism.

Fables of Aggression

Jameson's methodology is on full display in *Fables of Aggression: Wyndham Lewis, the Modernist as Fascist* (1979), in which he lists "ideology, psychoanalysis, and narrative analysis" as the "coordinates" within which to construct an interpretive model for reading Lewis's work.[9] Lewis is probably among the least known figures in the British modernist canon, and his loathsome politics and misogyny would have further relegated the author of *Tarr* to obscurity. Thus, it is astonishing that Jameson not only pays critical attention to such a figure, but also in several ways rehabilitates his work for Marxist criticism. The eccentricity of this choice probably accounts for another odd fact; as Phillip E. Wegner has pointed out, *Fables of Aggression* is the only one of Jameson's books to have gone out of print for any significant period of time.[10] Yet, by producing a careful analysis and even "sympathetic" reading of the *oeuvre* of an ideological enemy, Jameson demonstrates all the more clearly the flexibility and interpretive power of dialectical criticism.

Although Jameson's theory will be given fuller exposition in *The Political Unconscious*, the Lewis study presents the most thoroughgoing example to date of Jameson's heady mixture of Marxist and Freudian theory, with it of course understood that the psychoanalytic materials are ineluctably subsumed within the Marxist conceptual framework. In his 1977 essay "Imaginary and Symbolic in Lacan," Jameson had observed that the "attempt to coordinate a Marxist and Freudian criticism" has to confront the problem of the subject, or more specifically, "mediations between social phenomena and what must be called private, rather than merely individual."[11] As with Herbert Marcuse's *Eros and Civilization*, Jameson's own Marxist criticism is likely strengthened by its encounter with psychoanalytic theory, for the latter, through its characterization of the unconscious, enables him to give shape to the complex relationships between private desires and the social totality. This problem then becomes a key aspect of his conception of the political unconscious and the utopian impulse.

In *Fables of Aggression*, Jameson borrows from Jean-François Lyotard the idea of the *libidinal apparatus*, partly as a way of moving past unsatisfying or reductively simplistic conceptual divisions between the psychological and the social. "The theory of the libidinal apparatus marks an advance over psychologizing approaches in the way in which it endows a private fantasy-structure with a quasi-material inertness." From this perspective, then, the libidinal apparatus becomes "an independent structure of which one can write a history: and this history—the story of the logical permutations of a given fantasy-structure, as well as of its approaches to its own closure and internal limits—is a very different one from that projected by the conventional literary psychoanalysis or psycho-biography."[12] Thus Jameson overcomes the specious division between the enclosed, semiautonomous psychological subject of bourgeois biographical criticism and the reductive determinism of some cruder Marxist view. In this way, too, Jameson bypasses the sometimes tedious critical distinction between form and content, or between a formalist analysis and a historicist approach, since the structure of language itself, of language as used by the writer and interpreted by the reader, is itself a mediation of the social sphere.

Consistent with Jameson's early professional formation in "style studies" and with his characteristically formalist approach to even the most political of writings, Jameson analyzes Lewis's sentence-level prose with as much care as that used in examining the ideological import of the work, although, as we have seen, these two registers are never mutually exclusive in Jameson's work. He begins *Fables of Aggression* by observing the unique style of Lewis's writing. "To face the sentences of Wyndham Lewis is to find oneself confronted with a principle of immense mechanical energy. Flaubert, *Ulysses*, are composed; the voices of a James or a Faulkner develop their resources through some patient blind groping exploration of their personal idiosyncrasies from work to work. The style of Lewis, however, equally unmistakable, blasts through the tissues of his novels like a steam whistle, breaking them to its will."[13] Faced with a powerful crisis of representation, at a social and historical moment in which the previous era's techniques seemed insufficient if not utterly useless, the modernist artist attempts to craft an aesthetically plausible solution. "Since there exists no adequate language for 'rendering' the object, all that is left to the writer is to tell us how he would have rendered it had he had such a language in the first place. There thus comes into being a language beyond language, shot through with the jerry-built shoddiness of modern industrial civilization, brittle and impermanent, yet full of a mechanic's enthusiasm."[14]

In Jameson's view, Lewis develops a style suited to his engagement with the modern, capitalist system of his era, in which the "traditional faith in the transparency of language and an unselfconscious practice of mimetic representation" are increasingly called into question. The older realism is no longer seen as an adequate mode, and the modernist writer seeks other means by which to give form to the fragmentary and disconnected elements of everyday life. As Jameson writes, "The modernist gesture is thus ideological and Utopian all at once: perpetuating the increasing subjectivization of individual experience and the atomization and disintegration of the older social communities, expressing the anxiety and revulsion of intellectuals before the reification of social life and the ever intensifying class conflicts of industrial society, it also embodies a will to overcome the commodification of the late nineteenth-century capitalism, and to substitute for the mouldering and overstuffed bazaar of late Victorian life the mystique and promise of some intense and heightened, more authentic existence."[15]

Fables of Aggression introduces another well-known Jamesonian concept, that of *national allegory*, a term that would gain notoriety and stir up more than a little controversy after Jameson's discussion of it in his 1986 essay "Third-World Literature in an Era of Multinational Capitalism." National allegory, according to Jameson, "must be read as an instable and provisory solution to an aesthetic dilemma which is itself the manifestation of a social and historical contradiction," a provisional definition that announces its affiliation with Louis Althusser's striking reconception of ideology. Much like what Jameson will later call cognitive mapping, national allegory is understood as "a formal attempt to bridge the increasing gap between the existential data of everyday life within a given nation-state and the structural tendency of monopoly capital to develop on a worldwide, essentially transnational scale."[16] This model reaches its apotheosis, for Jameson and with respect to Lewis's *Tarr*, with World War I, in which the system of nation-states breaks down amid the rise of new superstates and broader ideological movements, namely Communism and Fascism. To return to the Freudian idiom, this becomes an appeal to the death drive, and more broadly to the "energy model" of Eros and Thanatos, and the modernist response to the postwar cultural constellation becomes visible in Lewis as acts of aggression.[17]

In *Fables of Aggression*, Jameson discloses and analyzes the "political unconscious" of Lewis's works, demonstrating through a combination of narrative theory, psychoanalysis, and good old-fashioned *Ideologiekritik* how the modernist-as-fascist was able to produce a body of work somehow representative of the modernity it partially opposed, while also undermining its own critical force in the face of structural limitations, as its formal artistry is necessarily bound to those very cultural artifacts that the author disdains. Moreover, in another dialectical reversal, Jameson reveals how even the anti-progressive, fascist, oppositional intellectual is twisted into a kind of apologist for, or at least a tacit endorser of, a Marxian vision of history. "The figural value of fascism as a reaction is determined by the more central position of Communism, against which the anticapitalist posture of protofascism (of which Lewis approved) must always be understood." For Lewis understood Communism to be "a historical inevitability, and thus, in a sense, the final and most irrevocable form of the *Zeitgeist*, that against which the oppositional mind must somehow always take a stand."[18] Here is a powerful demonstration of a political unconscious at work, then: a consciously anticommunist artist manages to evoke the historical necessity of communism itself. *Fables of Aggression*, which certainly stands up well on its own as an exemplary reading in the mode of Jameson's dialectical criticism, is also a useful prolegomenon to his much more celebrated study, *The Political Unconscious*. There Jameson's literary methodology and hermeneutics are most clearly elaborated in relation to the broader Marxist program.

The Political Unconscious

The Political Unconscious: Narrative as a Socially Symbolic Act (1981) probably remains Jameson's most influential and well-known book, even if his *Postmodernism* and other later works may have produced more spectacular shockwaves throughout cultural studies, broadly conceived. There are many reasons why this might be the case, but I believe that the primary one may be that *The Political Unconscious*, more than any other study, is inherently methodological, focusing as it does on interpretation itself, and offering rich examples of how Jameson's own dialectical criticism operates with respect both to individual authors or texts and to larger themes, genres, theories, and historical periods. Hence, for those wishing to understand Marxist *literary* criticism—and particularly Jameson's dialectical version of it—*The Political Unconscious* remains the touchstone.

In the famous opening words of its preface ("Always historicize!"), *The Political Unconscious* announces a crucial aspect of its project, but the thoroughgoing historicism of Jameson's dialectical criticism is not easily reducible to the interpretive methods sometimes associated with the term *historicism.* For one thing, Jameson seldom allows one to rest easy in the assumption that placing a given author or text in its historical context will, by itself, yield the desired results. He is also extremely wary of the various historicist methods, including the so-called "New Historicism" then gaining currency in the United States, which he feels are insufficiently dialectical or Marxist. Above all, Jameson finds the historical investigation of a particular cultural artifact without regard to its inevitable situation within a supra-individual frame of reference, a larger social structure or system such as the mode of production, to be at best rather limited and incomplete, and at worst misleadingly false or ideologically suspect. So, while "always historicize" is the "one absolute and we may even say 'transhistorical' imperative of all dialectical thought," and while it "will unsurprisingly turn out to be the moral of *The Political Unconscious*," Jameson's more pressing argument in this study will involve the categories by which such a historicist project is possible or even conceivable. Not unexpectedly, Marxism will offer the key to solving the theoretical and methodological problem facing the committed historicist. "Only Marxism can give us an adequate account of the essential *mystery* of the cultural past, which, like Tiresias drinking the blood, is momentarily returned to life and warmth and allowed once more to speak, and to deliver its long-forgotten message in surroundings utterly alien to it."[19] In this way, the Marxist hermeneutic outlined in this book will not only counter other interpretive models and oppose the putatively anti-interpretive theories associated with poststructuralism or deconstruction, but it will also propose a model by which texts can be read in their comprehensive historical and cultural contexts, as well as in our own. Thus, the very possibility of interpretation, as well as the interpretive act itself, is the real focus of *The Political Unconscious*.

Interpretation, therefore, cannot be simply "read off" the text in question, as if the phenomenological *Ding-an-sich* could be perceived by the astute observer. For texts are themselves historical and cultural objects that contain within them, as it were, the perceptions and interpretations of them throughout their history. Following his earlier argument in "Metacommentary," Jameson explains that "we never fully confront a text immediately, in all its freshness as a thing-in-itself. Rather, texts come before us as the always-already-read; we apprehend them through sedimented layers of previous interpretations, or—if a text is brand-new— through the sedimented reading habits and categories developed by those inherited interpretive traditions."[20] Interpretation is thus never an isolated act performed by a reader upon a text, "but takes place on a Homeric battlefield, on which a host of interpretive options are either openly or implicitly in conflict."[21] One does not so much interpret a text as translate it into an interpretive code, in order to reveal or construct a meaning that is itself situated within a semantic battleground of different, sometimes opposed, meanings. Hence, in Jameson's view, interpretation is a fundamentally allegorical act, by which one must translate from one code into another, along different registers and according to a particular master code. Such "master codes" may ultimately refer to the various methods or "schools" of criticism. Marxist criticism, which for Jameson is marked by its dialectical and totalizing vision, can reveal the limitations of these partial or local methods, identifying the "strategies of containment" by which texts and interpretations foster the illusion of completeness while suppressing the historical (and, therefore, also social and political) content. In this sense, Jameson's theory of interpretation may be viewed as a properly literary version of the older practice of ideology critique, in which the false consciousness of a given class is exposed and the "scientific" analysis of the total system discloses the social relations hidden beneath the visible surfaces of things, much like Marx's own revelatory investigation into the fetishism of the commodity in *Capital*. However, Jameson does not maintain that Marxist interpretation stands free of ideology, since all thought is necessarily ideological. Rather, he views Marxism as the practice that can reflexively recognize its own ideological position and, in wrestling with itself in this way, open up the possibility of transcending ideology.

Thus, the essentially polemical argument in *The Political Unconscious* is directed against those who would segregate the "political" from other areas of human experience and, in so doing, deny or occlude the historical as well. Obviously, this includes non-Marxist approaches to literature, but Jameson's argument ultimately confronts something like false consciousness in societies organized under the capitalist mode of production as a whole. The theory of a "political unconscious," then, is formulated as a means of apprehending and making visible the repressed narrative of history, which, following Marx, Jameson understands as the history of class struggle and, therefore, as political. Those critics or thinkers who would distinguish cultural texts that are social and political from those that are not are, in Jameson's view, not merely in error, but are (perhaps unintentionally) apologists for and reinforcers of "the reification and privatization of contemporary life." As Jameson continues,

To imagine that, sheltered from the omnipresence of history and the implacable influence of the social, there already exists a realm of freedom—whether it be that of the microscopic experience of words in a text or the ecstasies and intensities of the various private religions—is only to strengthen the grip of Necessity over all such blind zones in which the individual subject seeks refuge, in pursuit of a purely individual, merely psychological, project of salvation. The only effective liberation from such constraint begins with the recognition that there is nothing that is not social and historical—indeed, that everything is "in the last analysis" political.[22]

In this manner, we may see that Jameson is not advocating for a political interpretation, as distinct from psychoanalytic, religious, linguistic, or other hermeneutic methods, but rather is arguing for a Marxist and dialectical criticism capable of making visible the unseen but all-too-real social totality of which all texts are ultimately a part.[23]

As far as methodology goes, Jameson insists that the insights of Marxist criticism offer "an ultimate *semantic* precondition for the intelligibility of literary and cultural texts," and that the "semantic enrichment and enlargement of the inert givens and materials of a particular text" takes place within three overlapping or "concentric" frames of reference. That is, the text would be situated first in its own time or political history (in a narrow sense of the event placed in its own chronological sequence), then in its society as a whole (a somewhat more synchronic system), and finally in history itself, "now conceived in its vastest sense of the sequence of modes of production and the succession or destiny of the various human social formations, from prehistoric life to whatever far future history has in store for us."[24] In practice, these phases of reading will mainly move in an ever-widening gyre from the individual text itself to the social order of which it is a part, and thence to a broader view of the text in history. But Jameson makes clear that these are all understood in Marxist terms, so that even the first, more discretely textual analysis, which might appear similar to the traditional form of an *explication de texte*, will necessarily understand the work as a "socially symbolic act." At the social level, Jameson's analysis would extend deeper into or beyond the text to examine the *ideologeme* or "the smallest intelligible unit of the essentially antagonistic collective discourses of social classes." And at the horizon of history, the text and its ideologemes may be seen in terms of what Jameson calls "the ideology of form," in which the mode of production may be somehow discerned in the organization of the forms themselves.[25] In *The Political Unconscious*, the central chapters, nominally on Honoré de Balzac, George Gissing, and Joseph Conrad, respectively, explore these three horizons of interpretation.

Lingering on this last "horizon" for a moment, Jameson indicates that at this point the *form* itself is recognized as *content*, thus marking a dialectical reversal in which a formal analysis can reveal the heterogeneous processes of a given cultural text and ascertain a social "content of the form." That is, it has become possible "to grasp such formal processes as sedimented content in their own right, distinct from the manifest content of the works." Jameson endeavors to demonstrate this by examining genre, a primarily formal category that he shows to contain sociopolitical content in its own right. His lengthy chapter on "the dialectical use of genre criticism," which engages productively with a compelling non-Marxist literary theory (i.e., that of Northrop Frye's *Anatomy of Criticism*), draws out social implications of that theory while demonstrating Jameson's provocative notion of the ideology of form. Jameson's idea of "generic discontinuities"—that is, the presence of multiple genres within a given literary text (even, or especially, a text already placed in a recognizable genre, such as a romance)—stages at a level of literary history the sort of textual heteroglossia that Mikhail Bakhtin has considered so fundamental to the form of the novel. Using "a kind of x-ray technique," the reader may reveal "the layered and marbled structure of the text," thereby showing that the novel is "not so much an organic unity as a symbolic act that must reunite or harmonize heterogeneous narrative paradigms which have their own specific and contradictory ideological meaning," such as the social versus the psychological, for example.[26] In this sense even the seemingly apolitical and ahistorical characteristics of a given generic form are revealed to be imbued with social content.

The aim of this theory of a political unconscious is ultimately to disclose the unseen or repressed historical dimension of both lived experience and the representations of reality in literary and cultural texts. But, as Jameson makes clear, history cannot be experienced and understood in itself, as a thing or even as a story, but may only be uncovered through the processes of narrative, which, famously, Jameson takes to be "the central function or *instance* of the human mind."[27] Drawing upon Althusser's conception, itself derived from Spinoza, of the "absent cause," Jameson proposes that "history is *not* a text, not a narrative, master or otherwise, but that, as an absent cause, it is inaccessible to us except in textual form, and that our approach to it and to the Real itself necessarily passes through its prior textualization, its narrativization in the political unconscious."[28] Working through the aforementioned phases or horizons of textual interpretation, from the timely symbolic act to broader social system and on to the vast spatiotemporal territory of human history, the hermeneutic process of *The Political Unconscious* arrives at "a space in which History itself becomes the ultimate ground as well as the untranscendable limit of our understanding in general and our textual interpretations in particular."[29] But for Marxists history must be understood as "the experience of Necessity," no longer in terms of its content (as in an older discourse of "needs," such as food and shelter) but as "the inexorable *form* of events. [...] History is what hurts, it is what refuses desire and sets inexorable limits to individual as well as collective praxis, which its 'ruses' turn into grisly and ironic reversals of their overt intentions."[30] Understood in this way, then, the methodological and hermeneutic program of *The Political Unconscious* to uncover the historical dimension that had been obscured or repressed in cultural texts themselves, as in other interpretive practices, may be seen as a critique of ideology or false consciousness, however much Jameson, perhaps rightly, wishes to avoid the implications of these older slogans in other respects. In disclosing the narrative of history, as Jameson will make clear in the study's conclusion, the critic may also orient his or her vision toward a utopian alternative.

In that conclusion, revealingly titled "The Dialectic of Utopia and Ideology," Jameson discusses how his innovative conception of a political unconscious is also very much a part of the "classical" Marxian *Ideologiekritik* and points toward a comprehensive sense of class consciousness. But Jameson's position expands and refines this project. He proposes that "*all* class consciousness," including that of the ruling class, is fundamentally utopian, insofar as it expresses "the unity of a collectivity" in an allegorical or figurative manner.[31] It becomes clear that even the reactionary or conservative political positions of a class (and, of course, of the narratives produced by members of that class) maintain a utopian kernel that cannot be ignored by a properly dialectical criticism. Almost tacitly criticizing the moralism that he finds objectionable in many radical philosophies and methods, Jameson avers that "any Marxist analysis of culture [...] can no longer be content with its demystifying vocation to unmask and to demonstrate the ways in which a cultural artifact fulfills a specific ideological mission," but must seek "to project" a cultural object's "simultaneously Utopian power."[32] Hence, he implies a "bad faith" on the part of Marxists or other critics who neglect that ultimate lesson of the dialectic, that is, the dialectical reversal, in which the negative and the positive may be combined in the unity of opposites. (Arguably, Jameson's retreat here from the simplistic conception of "false consciousness" is itself an affirmation of a more complex, robust version of the same, since he is suggesting a kind of false consciousness on behalf of critics unable or unwilling to see the utopian elements of ideological forms.) In apprehending the coexistence of both positive and negative, utopian and ideological, one also concedes that the work, as well as the interpreter, is situated within the nightmare of history. Jameson's political unconscious may be seen as another means by which we orient ourselves within and attempt to map this totality.

The Ideologies of Theory: Situations of Theory and *The Syntax of History*

The publication of a collection of previously published essays signals at once both the importance of those essays in their own original contexts and their lasting significance for criticism. Transferring an article from its time and place in an issue of a scholarly journal or multi-author collection to a chapter in a single-author book not only changes its audience and its context, but it arguably alters its function as a whole. The essays included in the two-volume 1988 collection, *The Ideologies of Theory: Essays, 1971–1986*, are thus historical artifacts, representing moments along the way during the previous 16 years not only of Jameson's career, but also of debates in literary theory and criticism. But, as essays presented to be read anew or reread in 1988, now formed into a coherent book project for the University of Minnesota Press's influential *Theory and History of Literature* series, they take on the qualities of book chapters, revealing themselves as parts of a more sustained argument in Jameson's project. The discrete essays become segments in a larger critical structure comprising *Situations of Theory* (Volume 1) and *The Syntax of History* (Volume 2), themselves halves of Jameson's project in organizing this collection. So, while it is not to be forgotten that an essay like "Metacommentary" belongs to the situation in which it was originally published in 1971, the essay is also an important text in its new and different situation as the first chapter of *The Ideologies of Theory*.

It may be worth considering the aims of a collection such as this. Consistent with standard academic publishing practices, Jameson had regularly published various journal articles, book chapters, and other occasional pieces, some of which went on to be incorporated into his book-length studies. Thus, his earlier essays on Adorno and Lukács became chapters in *Marxism and Form*, and early versions of several chapters of *The Political Unconscious* had appeared as articles in *New Literary History*, *SubStance*, and so on. In those cases, the original circumstances of publication seem to be quickly forgotten, for the overall argument of a monograph absorbs them, while all but erasing their previously autonomous being. In a "collection of essays," the chapters are expressly given their own semi-autonomy, and the reader is asked to view each essay as a discrete intervention made at a particular time in the past and at another place, while simultaneously agreeing to see it as an integral part of the present project. Apart from its intrinsic value as a convenient, efficient, and worthwhile service to the reader (that is, by simply gathering disparate articles together in one place), the collection of essays *as form* delivers a satisfying experience of the historical survey that is also a contemporary event. *The Ideologies of Theory* brings together important and influential essays that represent Jameson's contributions to literary critical debates over the period in question, but it also reinforces Jameson's present position as author of *this* book and, hence, as an expert on the ideologies of theory.[33]

Jameson himself addresses this ambiguity in his introduction, where he declines the opportunity to "reconstruct the polemic contexts in which, over a number of years, the following essays were composed."[34] He also proposes, but then dismisses, certain strategies that might have been used to frame the essays in such a way as to "confer some semblance of unity" upon the collection. Instead, Jameson refers to the problem that animates all of his writing, and that certainly animates the essays included in *The Ideologies of Theory*, namely "the gap or tension between literary criticism (and its practice and theory) and the simultaneous vocation to explain and to popularize the Marxist intellectual tradition." Attempting always to do both at the same time, Jameson reflects that his career up to that point had involved trying to effect "two types of changes" to "the North American intellectual and cultural climate": first, "to enlarge the conception of the literary text itself, so that its political, psychoanalytic, ideological, philosophical, and social resonances might become audible (and describable) *within* that experience of literary language and aesthetic form"; second, "to stage the attractiveness of a worldview—the only one, I think—for which those multiple dimensions and temporalities we sometimes crudely call the political, the history of forms, the dynamics of desire, the class texture of the social, the originality of the act, and geological rhythms of human history, all unimaginably coexist."[35] *The Ideologies of Theory*, as a whole, attempts to render visible both "impulses" of Jameson's project of dialectical criticism.

In choosing to divide the collection into discretely named volumes, Jameson invites us to consider the significance of *Situations of Theory* and *The Syntax of History*. The former, with its clear Sartrean overtones, allows the reader to conceive of the essays in that volume as part of a literary history, which Jameson notes is always "a history of the *situation* of the texts, and not some 'history' of the texts themselves."[36] Although not limited to readings of individual texts, the theoretical essays in Volume 1, starting with the programmatic "Metacommentary," each offer some careful consideration of how individual texts may (or may not) be interpreted. In Volume 2, as Jameson explains in an introductory note, emphasis shifts from problems of textual interpretation to broader issues of cultural and historical analysis. He describes the "transmigration" of the earlier concept of metacommentary from the "reflexive operation proposed for staging the struggle within an individual literary or cultural text of various interpretations" to a sort of "transcoding" by which the conflict of whole theoretical models or methods is rendered visible. As he puts it, it is "less a question of finding a single system of truth to convert to, than [...] of speaking the various theoretical codes experimentally." That is, Jameson's methodological conception of a metacommentary by which one seeks not to find a singular or stable "meaning" in a given text, but rather to determine the degrees to which some meanings are possible and others are not, is here transferred or elevated to a level upon which entire sense-making systems are placed under consideration. In other words, rather than looking for a single interpretive framework or discursive practice that can provide solutions to any and every hermeneutic quandary, one must learn to speak different languages that may offer provisional or tactical advantages for grappling with a particular problem. Even Marxism, which in its unity of theory and practice is able to incorporate all other philosophies within itself, benefits from examining the other "codes" that position themselves as rivals. In looking back upon his essays from this period, Jameson asserts with a bit of irony, "What has sometimes in my own work been thought to be either eclectic or, still worse, synthesizing and 'Hegelian,' will generally be found to involve transcoding of this type, rather than random, but all-inclusionary system building."[37]

The individual essays contained in these volumes are, in varying degrees, emblematic of Jameson's dialectical criticism, both at the time of their original publication and in an almost timeless (it seems heretical to say it) Jamesonian project in which the same basic propositions appear to be reiterated over and over. Jameson's basic methodological proposition of a metacommentary remains crucial to understanding his most recent work, and his timely engagements with critical traditions at odds with Marxism—as in "The Ideology of the Text," which takes on French poststructuralism and, particularly, Roland Barthes's elaborately "post-Marxist" *S/Z* (as opposed to his clearly Marxian earlier works, such as *Mythologies*)—nevertheless continue to be important to our understanding of the project of literary theory today. Many of the essays included in *The Ideologies of Theory* volumes operate as early instances of concepts later worked out more thoroughly. For example, in "Of Islands and Trenches," Jameson's theory of utopia elaborated in *The Seeds of Time* and *Archaeologies of the Future*, among other places, is explored through a review of Louis Marin's fascinating narratological study of Thomas More, *Utopiques: Jeux d'espaces*. If anything, what the reader of Jameson's entire *oeuvre* discovers in rereading these punctual interventions into the cultural theory and critical debates from the early 1970s to the mid-1980s is how philosophically consistent and yet flexible his dialectical criticism has been.

Conspicuously absent from this collection is the aforementioned "Third-World Literature in an Era of Multinational Capitalism," which provoked widespread (and, I believe, rather overheated) controversy when it appeared in *Social Text* in 1986. Its absence from *The Ideologies of Theory* may be based on any of number of things, including mere untimeliness, as most of the essays were likely selected for this edition before it was published. What is more, one could point out that it was not, strictly speaking, a "theoretical" essay and that its argument did not neatly fit within the provisional rubrics of "situations of theory" or "syntax of history," so it did not really belong in the collection. (Given that it was primarily concerned with a peculiarly postmodern and "first-world" cultural phenomenon,[38] one might have expected it to reappear somewhere in *Postmodernism, or, the Cultural Logic of Late Capitalism*.) Without access to the principles of selection used by Jameson and his publisher, one might endlessly speculate about why a given essay was included and why another was excluded. But the "Third-World" essay gives pause in part because it was so controversial, and yet, to date—quite unlike many of his other famous essays of this period—it has not been republished in any of Jameson's other books.[39]

In "Third-World Literature in an Era of Multinational Capitalism," Jameson revives the conception of national allegory to argue that "Third-World texts, even those which are seemingly private and invested with a properly libidinal dynamic—necessarily project a political dimension in the form of national allegory: *the story of the private individual destiny is always an allegory of the embattled situation of the public third-world culture and society.*"[40] This remarkably bold thesis understandably elicited criticism, particularly from representatives of so-called "Third-World" cultures. Perhaps the most influential response to Jameson's essay came from Aijaz Ahmad, who in "Jameson's Rhetoric of Otherness and the 'National Allegory'" objected to Jameson's argument on two principal grounds.[41] First, Ahmad disputes the universalism of Jameson's assertion, noting that any hypothesis which claims to encompass *all* "Third-World texts" necessarily overlooks the specificity of, for instance, an Indian-born poet writing in Urdu, whose work must be quite different from other writers in other languages and cultures. Second, Ahmad criticizes the essentialism of Jameson's understanding of "Third-World," and, by extension, the essentialism of a cognizable "First-World" as well. Since the idea of the "third world" is "a polemical one, with no theoretical status whatsoever," Ahmad asserts, "there is no such thing as a 'Third World Literature' which can be constructed as an internally coherent object of theoretical knowledge."[42] Such universalism and essentialism becomes a sort of renewed Orientalism. For Ahmad, as for others who took up his critique, Jameson's analysis is thus fundamentally flawed.[43]

Leaving aside the outrage among many postcolonial or other critics at the perceived presumptuousness of a "First-World" Marxist intellectual pronouncing such a "sweeping hypothesis" (in Jameson's words) about cultural texts from elsewhere,[44] we may detect in Jameson's argument a continuing concern with the schism between subject and object, individual and social, private and public, lived experience and an inaccessible structural totality. In his discussion of national allegory in Third-World literature, Jameson invokes also an aesthetic practice that, by 1986, had been given another label.

As noted above, both the conception of national allegory and the earlier consideration of narrative as a means by which individual experience and a broader social totality may be somehow represented and reconciled, if only through a kind of figuration, prefigure Jameson's well-known conception of *cognitive mapping*. Cognitive mapping accrues its illustrious reputation only after being named as the political vocation of postmodern art in Jameson's 1984 essay "Postmodernism, or, the Cultural Logic of Late Capitalism," but it may surprise some readers to learn that the phrase appears, after a fashion, in *The Political Unconscious*, where it is directly associated with realism, albeit only parenthetically. Jameson writes that realism has been "traditionally in one form or another the central model of Marxist aesthetics as a narrative discourse which unites the experience of daily life with a properly cognitive, mapping, or well-nigh 'scientific' perspective."[45] Aware of Jameson's close attention to such sentence-level stylistic details as punctuation, we may take the comma between "cognitive" and "mapping" as a clear sign that "cognitive mapping," the latter concept, is not here called into being, but we could still surmise that Jameson's consideration of narrative realism and the crisis of representation anticipates his analysis in his writings on postmodernism of that spatial anxiety endemic to the postmodern condition. Here, in fact, the "cognitive, mapping, or well-nigh scientific" aspects of realism are productively contrasted with the more mythic or metaphysical cartographies associated with the genre, or generic mode, of romance. If Marxism itself unfolds as a sort of romantic philosophical discourse, that does not mean that it sheds its more properly realistic mapping project. Rather, it indicates the degree to which any apparently "realistic" mapping project must partake of the figural projections normally associated with romance, such as that of the imaginary plenum of a distinct, perhaps inaccessible past (for instance, Lukács's *Lebenstotalität* in the age of the epic) or that of an anticipatory illumination of some alternative space (for example, giving form to the utopian impulse). Whereas high realism seems to reproduce the iron cage of modern capitalism in a narrative form, the apparently outmoded form of romance offers a potentially utopian vision. "It is in the context of the gradual reification of realism in late capitalism that romance once again comes to be felt as the place of narrative heterogeneity and of freedom from that reality principle to which a now oppressive realistic representation is a hostage."[46] Later, the stylistic experiments and free play of modernist and postmodernist art may be found to exhibit a similarly utopian impulse, while also necessarily maintaining their own ideological functions.

Looking ahead to the discussion of cognitive mapping in the following chapters, we can begin to see the relationship between these two, well-known Jamesonian concepts. The *political unconscious* and *cognitive mapping* represent two distinct sides of the coin, which is perhaps most clearly understood when considering that the one refers mostly to reading or to the critic's activity, whereas the other refers to a program engaged in by the writer or producer of the aesthetic work itself. As Jameson has conceded, both ideas are epistemological in a sense: "The political unconscious implies that certain kinds of knowledge about society are encoded in literary texts and in their forms. The analysis I propose is designed to make it possible to recover some of that knowledge. The notion of cognitive mapping insists much more strongly on the way in which art itself functions as a mode of knowledge, a mode of knowledge of the totality."[47] But, as Jameson points out, the conception of "totality" itself takes on new, more concrete meaning in an era of globalization.

4

The Cultural Logic of Late Capitalism

In retrospect, it is hard to imagine the debates over postmodernism in the 1980s without Jameson's immense, influential contribution to them. But before he waded into those troubled waters, many cultural critics, Marxists in particular, had little desire to engage seriously with postmodernism, only grudgingly acknowledging it as something worth discussing at all. At the time, it was not really clear what postmodernism actually was, whether considered strictly in terms of the aesthetic sphere (especially with respect to a real or imagined break from modernist forms of art, architecture, cinema, and literature) or in connection with a philosophical tradition (notably following a Nietzschean line of anti-foundationalism represented by Martin Heidegger, Jacques Derrida, and Richard Rorty, among others). In any case, however, postmodern art or thought implied a renunciation of whole swaths of modern theory and practice, and Marxism—as one of what Jean-François Lyotard in *The Postmodern Condition* called the *grand récits* or "master narratives" of modernity—was one of the significant critical discourses apparently under siege by the postmodernists. Some of those associated with postmodernism, rightly or wrongly, were openly anti-Marxist, so it is not surprising that Marxists or leftists of other varieties would resist. Additionally, in the aftermath of the disappointments of the late Sixties—the Prague Spring and *les événements de Mai* in 1968, for instance—postmodern social or political theory appeared to be rooted in a retrenchment against or a general turning away from Marxist thought.[1] Jürgen Habermas, in "Modernity: An Unfinished Project," a 1980 lecture whose main ideas were later expanded into *The Philosophical Discourse of Modernity*,[2] launched a broadside against the postmodernist turn in philosophy; in that essay, the eminent German thinker positioned himself as a representative of the Marxian traditions of both European socialist politics and the Frankfurt School legacy of critical theory in denouncing the ideologically suspect character and apparent irrationalism of postmodernist thought.[3] With a few notable exceptions, postmodernism was generally viewed with disdain by Marxist intellectuals at the time.

Hence, the unexpectedness of Jameson's entry into the arena, first in an influential 1982 talk, "Postmodernism and Consumer Society," then in the monumental 1984 essay "Postmodernism, or, the Cultural Logic of Late Capitalism," which would become the first chapter of the award-winning book of that name.[4] Reflecting on the moment, Douglas Kellner writes,

> Fredric Jameson's intervention into the postmodernism debates was at first—to some of us—surprising. A professor of French and comparative literature at the University of California, San Diego (1967–1976), who moved to the Yale University French department from 1976–1983, Jameson's book *The Political Unconscious* (1981) had established him as one of the foremost Marxist literary critics of our era. Much of his work had focused on literary studies and contemporary theory, particularly Marxian theory which he applied to cultural analysis and used to criticize and contextualize other forms of criticism. Why, then, was a good Marxist like Jameson getting involved with the polemics and passions of the postmodern? What was really at stake in these debates? [...] Jameson's writings on postmodernism constitute both a defense of Marxism and an attempt to show that a reconstructed Marxian theory can provide the most comprehensive and penetrating theory of postmodernism itself.[5]

As Kellner astutely points out, Jameson's contribution to the discussion immediately changed it, such that in the aftermath of these essays it was difficult to speak of postmodernism or postmodernity in the arts and in cultural studies without at least some attention being paid to Jameson's Marxist representation and analysis of the phenomena.

During this time, Jameson not only offered a nuanced and rather generous reading of postmodernism, which in contrast to Habermas's intervention did not ultimately reject the *nouveau* theory in favor of a retrofitted Enlightenment sensibility, but which, in his words, attempted to "outflank" it, to force postmodernism to come to terms with its historical situation and, thus, to incorporate it into a properly Marxist, dialectical system of thought. Unlike some of postmodernism's critics on the left, such as Terry Eagleton or Alex Callinicos (to name two of the best), Jameson did not reject postmodernism or the claims of postmodernity; on the contrary, at times he might have been justly accused of celebrating postmodernism. Such simple evaluations, as we have seen, do not really have a place in Jameson's project of dialectical criticism, since the dialectic so frequently teaches that what we had thought of as good or bad will turn out to be its opposite whether we like it or not. With respect to postmodernism, then, Jameson is less interested in whether postmodern art or theory is a positive or negative development and more interested in what it represents to our ongoing investigations of the social totality or world system. Postmodernism also clearly indicates something historical, and for Jameson the concept has value as a way of periodizing our present situation, of making it available to us as a meaningful conception of our own place in a broader history, which is one of the crucial ideas he had suggested in his essay "Periodizing the 60s."[6] In the evocative title to what is probably his most famous essay, Jameson supplies his answer: postmodernism is the cultural logic of late capitalism.

Pursuing his investigation of this elusive ensemble of cultural phenomena, Jameson published three books within a span of one year in 1990 and 1991. At first blush, these texts would appear to be unrelated: a study of a somewhat "old-fashioned" mid-century German philosopher and critic, a collection of essays about film, and a grand synthesizing or, rather, "constellating" study of postmodernism. Yet, as quickly becomes clear, *Late Marxism: Adorno, or, the Persistence of the Dialectic* (1990), *Signatures of the Visible* (1990), and *Postmodernism, or, the Cultural Logic of Late Capitalism* (1991) can be viewed as part of the same overall project: that is, the attempt to map the cultural terrain of multinational capitalism at the present historical conjuncture. In this context, the first two books might be examined as theoretical and critical prologues to the larger *Postmodernism*. Taken together, these three books elaborate in some detail Jameson's curious position on the postmodern, demonstrating how his Marxist and dialectical criticism simultaneously incorporates, negates, and transcends the postmodern by situating it within a historical and materialist framework, which is to say, the world system itself.

Late Marxism

Late Marxism: Adorno, or, the Persistence of the Dialectic is not merely an updated and expanded version of Jameson's chapter on Adorno from *Marxism and Form*. In fact, as Jameson explains in his introduction, this study of Adorno is entirely different—necessarily so, given the social and cultural transformations during the intervening years. For one thing, that earlier essay drew most heavily upon Adorno's *Philosophy of Modern Music*, a text that Jameson does not address at any length in *Late Marxism*, which instead devotes the most space to *Negative Dialectics*, *Dialectic of Enlightenment* (co-authored with Max Horkheimer), and the posthumously published *Aesthetic Theory*. But the differences are not based on textual selection alone. Jameson's rehearsal of the shifting circumstances in which Adorno might be read is uncharacteristically personal or autobiographical, as Jameson reveals the extent to which even he may have shied away from Adorno's work at times during the past two decades. But he also discloses that this has less to do with the substance of Adorno's writings than with the dramatically different *situation*—the Sartrean concept is never very far from Jameson's thinking—in which one finds oneself engaging with Adorno's work. "It is not, indeed, people who change, but rather situations. This can also account for the alterations in my own views of Adorno, whose work has itself varied in significance for me according to the historical decade." He explains that Adorno had been "a crucial methodological discovery" for him during the late 1950s, when he was attempting to formulate a dialectical criticism for which the "class and ideological background" was "*intrinsic* to the business of formal analysis." But Adorno's hostility to much of what seemed liberatory in the Sixties (famously, his opposition to jazz and his skepticism with respect to the Third World), compounded by his dour, Auschwitz-oriented *Weltanschauung*, made him less appealing during that decade, while "the seventies—the age, in this country [i.e., the United States] at least, of Theory and theoretical discourse, of *jouissances* that ranged from structuralism to poststructuralism, from Maoism to narrative analysis, and from libidinal investments to Ideological State Apparatuses—were essentially French." Remarkably, with the rise in the 1980s of conservative political and economic philosophies, Thatcherism and Reaganism, Soviet *perestroika* and the collapse of the Eastern bloc, and an increasingly American-styled business management ethos, along with post-Bretton Woods monetary and trade policies, the total system that Adorno's critical theory envisioned—a system or structure that Jameson is not yet quite ready to consistently name *globalization*—had at last come into being. Unexpectedly and perhaps perversely, then, Jameson writes, "Adorno's Marxism, which was no great help to us in the previous periods, may turn out to be just what we need today."[7]

It is on this provocative basis that Jameson holds forth a preeminently old-fashioned philosopher and sociologist, a mid-century Hegelian whose words still evoke an era of air-raid warnings and bomb shelters, as *the* theorist best suited to our own postmodern condition in an era of multinational capitalism. At a historical moment of *post-Marxism* (to invoke Ernesto Laclau and Chantal Mouffe's term from their *Hegemony and Socialist Strategy*), if not simply *non*-Marxism (as the ideologues of a triumphant, liberal capitalism would have it, since *anti*-Marxism itself might be deemed irrelevant after the fall of the Berlin Wall), Jameson discovers in Adorno's thought a *late Marxism* appropriate to the contemporary stage of "late capitalism," as the phrase is understood in Ernest Mandel's sense, referring to the most recent phase of capitalist development.[8] Undoubtedly, also, Jameson intends an ironic play on words, since the declarations of Marxism's death (hence, in another sense, its "lateness") have surely been premature, and the return of Adorno's modernist dialectical criticism in the postmodern epoch is thus a kind of dramatic exposition of the persistence of the dialectic in a period from which it had supposedly evanesced. Jameson notes that the titular phrase is not of his coinage, but is merely a literal translation of a common enough German term (*der Spätmarxismus*, that is, *late* or *recent Marxism*), hence referring to a Marxism fitted to the present "late" capitalist situation in advanced, postindustrial societies, if not elsewhere. Jameson cannot help but joke, however, "better late than never!"[9]

In Jameson's assessment, the value of Adorno's work lies fundamentally in the conception of *totality*, a concept much under attack during the era of poststructuralist theory and postmodernism. From a properly Marxist perspective, this idea of totality means understanding the degree to which the mode of production or overall system conditions the particular products, including without question the intellectual and artistic products, generated within it. As may be seen, for instance, Adorno and Horkheimer's critique of the culture industry in *Dialectic of Enlightenment*, the "unique emphasis on the presence of late capitalism as a totality within the very forms of our concepts or of the works of art themselves," represents for Jameson a breakthrough in Marxist theory, distinguishing Adorno from other critical theorists of his era. As Jameson puts it, "No other Marxist theoretician has ever staged this relationship between the universal and the particular, the system and the detail, with this kind of single-minded yet wide-ranging attention."[10]

Let us stay for a moment with this notorious conception, and analysis, of the culture industry in *Dialectic of Enlightenment*. As Jameson observes, the historical condition of the emergence of Adorno and Horkheimer's critique—namely, their position as Old World intellectuals living in exile in the United States while fleeing Nazi oppression—might place the work in an older literary genre, "namely, that travel literature produced by Europeans as a result of their often horrified contact with the new North American democracy," of which Alexis de Tocqueville's *De la démocratie en Amérique* remains the canonical touchstone. What is perhaps original to Adorno is the linkage between the rise of the culture industry in America and that of Hitlerian fascism, resulting in the scandalous implication that the victory of the one over the other in World War II must be understood as "variation within a single paradigm, rather than the victory of one paradigm over another."[11] Hence the pessimistic view of popular culture in Adorno, which cannot but have been redolent of *Volk*-culture and the jargon of authenticity that had helped to underwrite fascism throughout Germany. But, as Jameson points out, "the 'Culture industry' is not a theory of culture but the theory of an *industry*, of a branch of the interlocking monopolies of late capitalism that makes money out of what used to be called culture. The topic here is the commercialization of life."[12] And, in their somewhat traditional *Ideologiekritik* of the American culture industry, Adorno and Horkheimer discover a system in which even the minutest desires of the solitary individual are caught up in a totalizing system that conditions nearly every aspect of a person's comportment toward the world and to others:

> The way in which a girl accepts and keeps an obligatory date, the inflection on the telephone or in the most intimate situation, the choice of words in a conversation, and the whole inner life as classified by the now somewhat devalued depth psychology, bear witness to man's attempt to make himself a proficient apparatus, similar (even in emotions) to the model served up by the culture industry. The most intimate reactions of human beings have been so thoroughly reified that the idea of anything specific to themselves now persists only as an utterly abstract notion: personality scarcely signifies anything more than shining white teeth and freedom from body odor and emotions.[13]

Adorno and Horkheimer's sense of the culture industry in 1947, limited as "mass culture" was to films, radio, and perhaps popular magazines, appears almost quaint in the era of satellite television, streaming internet content, and mobile phones, but their approach to the relations between discrete social acts or individual experience and a broader cultural and commercial system remains pertinent to any critical examination of the postmodern condition.

For this reason, among others, Jameson finds Adorno's only *apparently* modernist critical theory to be especially well suited to the postmodern occasion, when the total system hinted at or feared by an earlier generation of modernist thinkers (such as Max Weber, Georg Simmel, and perhaps even Karl Marx himself) has come into being in the form of "late capitalism" or globalization. "Totality," for Adorno, is a "critical category" and, he asserts that "[d]ialectical critique seeks to salvage or help to establish what does not obey totality, what opposes it or what first forms itself as the potential of a not yet existent individuation."[14] Rather than celebrating the totality, society or the economic system as a whole, Adorno's thought engages the concept, recognizing its ineluctable influence on other forms of thinking and writing. As Jameson argues, this becomes crucial to the problem of representation, where the relationship of the universal to the particular might be said to mirror "the objective tension between the social totality and its subjects." Jameson will discuss this representational crisis at greater length in *Postmodernism*, where he introduces cognitive mapping as a possible, if provisional, solution, but here he observes that Adorno's "modernist" strategy may be of value for thinking the problem of the present postmodern condition, in which "the negative, or 'critical theory,' will have definitively become a thing of the past."[15]

Indeed, Jameson finds that Adorno's infamous pessimism and gloom actually serve a salutary critical function in an era smitten with its own success. Adorno's dialectical thought, according to Jameson, may help "to restore the sense of something grim and impending within the polluted sunshine of the shopping mall—some older classical European-style sense of doom and crisis, which even the Common Market countries have cast off in their own chrysalid transmogrification, but which the USA can now better use than they can, being an older and more ramshackle society." He suggests that Adorno's bitter pessimism might have unexpectedly renewed value in the 1990s. At the triumphalist, post-Cold War moment, when facing another "end of history" (that is, Francis Fukuyama's version) in which there seem to be no viable political alternatives to liberal democracy and no meaningful opposition to multinational capitalist expansion, Jameson welcomes Adorno's sometimes unpleasant, curmudgeonly cantankerousness as a timely corrective to vapid and smug cultural contentment in advanced, postindustrial societies. In such a situation, "his bile is a joyous counter-poison and a corrosive solvent to apply to the surface of 'what is.'"[16] Looking ahead to his infamous (and sometimes misattributed) line about how it seems easier to imagine the end of the world than to envision an end to capitalism, Jameson concludes *Late Marxism* by noting that our era seems typified by a sense of "a locked social geology so massive that no visions of modification seem possible (at least to those ephemeral biological subjects that we are)." Adorno's dialectical critique befits this "new global order" in which "the relationship between the individual and the system seems ill-defined, if not fluid, or even dissolved."[17] Fortifying himself with the theoretical weapons supplied by Adorno, Jameson directs his own critical attention to the culture industry and the social totality of the postmodern condition.

Signatures of the Visible

Underscoring the shift from the social context of Adorno's mid-century critique of the culture industry to the late-century consumerist phantasmagoria of postmodernism, Jameson quips: "The question about poetry after Auschwitz has been replaced with that of whether you could bear to read Adorno and Horkheimer next to the pool."[18] By turning from a difficult figure of "high" theory and culture to the supposedly lighter entertainments of film and "mass culture," Jameson might be said to enact elements of his own theory of dialectical criticism and its role in making sense of the social totality. In *Signatures of the Visible*, also published in 1990, Jameson focuses on film and film theory in his attempt to make sense of the postmodern condition. Both *Late Marxism* and *Signatures of the Visible*, then, could be considered as prefatory to his larger project in *Postmodernism, or, the Cultural Logic of Late Capitalism*. Where the one investigates the critical theory of a supremely dialectical philosopher and cultural critic in an effort to rescue the conception of the "totality" from its then-fashionable detractors, the other explores a number of representative filmic texts from the period in order to show how their content and their form somehow reveal the determining aspects of a social totality, not to mention of history itself, rendered invisible if not unimaginable to us situated in the present, postmodern world system.

Jameson has been celebrated for the breadth of his interests; for instance, in Colin MacCabe's words, ranging "from architecture to science fiction, from the tortuous thought of the late Adorno to the *testimonio* novel of the third world," Jameson "will as readily bring the same care and attention to the deliberately complex works of high modernism as to the very different complexities of cyberpunk."[19] However, it should be clear that this ranging is based neither on mere eclecticism nor on catholicity of taste. Rather, Jameson's approach to literary and cultural criticism requires that he at least attempt to grapple with the entire cultural field in its totality, and this frequently means tackling this or that phenomenon or manifestation of the culture and society in question. This means taking the high with the low, the sophisticated with the simple, the good with the bad; of course, these categories are not symmetrical, and the dialectic as Jameson conceives it teaches that such oppositions are ultimately illusory or self-cancelling. What is more, one could argue that Jameson's own historical periodizations require that he examine works of popular culture, for as nearly all acknowledge, the late-twentieth century is no longer the age of the novel, the epic, or other supposedly lofty cultural forms, but is an era more likely to be typified by film, television, and other kinds of visual media. In fact, Jameson's interest in cinema might be considered a vestige of his high cultural or elite predilections, for in some ways the grand narrative achievement of the Hollywood films that are examined in the essays included in *Signatures of the Visible*—for example, *The Godfather*, *Jaws*, *The Shining*, *Dog Day Afternoon*, and the hypercanonical films of Hitchcock, among other lesser known titles—is analogous to that of the British or French novel in the nineteenth century. By the late-twentieth century, the names Francis Ford Coppola, Steven Spielberg, Stanley Kubrick, and Alfred Hitchcock had to be recognized as signs of a high culture, at least as much as Honoré de Balzac, Charles Dickens, Gustave Flaubert, and George Eliot would have been a hundred years before. Technologically and historically, one might say, film is itself a modern (and, perhaps, modernist) artistic form, and although that certainly does not preclude it, or the novel or the lyric poem or any other form, from being considered in the light of postmodernism, *as a form* film still hews to an older aesthetic and finds its place in a somewhat different commercial culture. Indeed, as Jameson himself muses concerning his argument in *Signatures of the Visible*, "this has very little (or nothing) to do with television, which makes me wonder whether the entire discussion is not in the nature of a post mortem on a now historical form or medium, which finds its philosophy as well as its history posthumously."[20] Nevertheless, in his meditation on film and its particular effects, Jameson adds yet another dimension to his project of dialectical criticism.

Jameson had made reference to movies throughout his career and had published a number of articles on filmmaking in general or on particular films, but *Signatures of the Visible* is his first book devoted to cinema. It contains a selection of several important essays that had been published in the 1970s and 1980s, and adds a longer, original essay, titled "The Existence of Italy," in which Jameson offers perhaps his first sustained meditation on the interrelations among realism, modernism, and postmodernism, focusing in this case on filmic texts, but nevertheless elaborating a theory suited to other cultural artifacts produced in these representational modes and historical moments. The result is a coherent attempt to bring his literary theory to bear on problems specific to visual cultures, and *Signatures of the Visible* is at once an extension of his literary critical project into another arena and an enlargement of the field of his Marxist criticism and theory.

In his introduction to the book, Jameson opens by addressing the fundamental difference between films and literary texts; while these share many overlapping characteristics, literary texts tend to lack the powerful visual sensory experience in their consumption by the reader. For, as Jameson famously opines, "The visual is *essentially* pornographic, which is to say that it has its end in rapt, mindless fascination; thinking about its attributes becomes an adjunct to that, if it is unwilling to betray its object; while the most austere films necessarily draw their energy from the attempt to repress their own excess (rather than from the more thankless effort to discipline the viewer)."[21] Jameson's sense is that postmodern society, what after all Guy Debord labeled the "society of the spectacle," is preeminently visual, such that the image—perhaps more than even the object it is an image *of* —is the dominant social form, and "all the fights about power and desire have to take place here, between the mastery of the gaze and the illimitable richness of the visual object." The underlying argument of *Signatures of the Visible* is that "the only way to think the visual [...] is to grasp its historical coming into being."[22] Thus, as in the overall project of *Postmodernism*, in this book Jameson aims to historicize something that is resolutely ahistorical. But then, the visual culture Jameson here wrestles with is itself postmodern, so this is hardly surprising.

The essays included in Part I, all previously published as journal articles, display the by now familiar critical virtuosity of Jameson's method. As was the case in his earlier conception of metacommentary and his discovery of the political unconscious, here Jameson finds in both the form and content of various movies an allegorical dimension in which a careful reader may discern a hitherto invisible or repressed social content. Although Jameson recognizes the profound differences between film and the novel, not least of which is that cinema has not really had the same function within national cultures that the novel maintained, his approach remains rather similar to that used in *The Political Unconscious*. One might also point out that *Signatures of the Visible*, quite unlike his subsequent book on cinema, *The Geopolitical Aesthetic*, contains no photographs or still images from the films under consideration, which might be said to reenact the rivalry between text and image in a way that is somewhat reminiscent of Susan Sontag's famous, intentional omission of any pictures in her groundbreaking essay "On Photography." Jameson does pay a great deal of attention to the peculiarly filmic aspects of the texts under consideration— the composition of the shot, for instance—but in general he treats these films as analogues of the novel and "reads" them accordingly.

This may be seen in the long, mostly theoretical essay "Reification and Utopia in Mass Culture," originally published in 1979 and significantly appearing as the first chapter of *Signatures of the Visible*, in which Jameson attempts to assess the ways in which works of mass culture are productive of ideological meanings beyond being merely escapist or providing distractions from the "real social conditions." As Jameson puts it (and the resonant themes of *The Political Unconscious* should be audible here as well), we can understand mass culture as "transformational work on social and political anxieties and fantasies which must then have some effective presence in the mass cultural text in order subsequently to be 'managed' or repressed."[23] He then illustrates the argument by showing how the narrative of *Jaws* discloses the social tensions attendant on the societal transformation of the economy of the United States from one of traditional labor and industry (represented by the crusty fisherman, Quint) to the late-capitalist social organization in which law-and-order (Brody) partners with wealthy science and technology (Hooper) to triumph over not only the "ill-defined menace of the shark itself," but the older New Deal-era economy of small private enterprise and traditional industries.[24] In this way, Jameson uncovers the ideological content in the form of a popular adventure story *cum* Hollywood blockbuster.

Jameson then turns to *The Godfather* films (mercifully, at that point there were only the two) in order to demonstrate a utopian aspect of this political unconscious. Whereas the idea of the Mafia itself presents an ideological argument, diverting attention from the potential "criminality" of "legitimate" business, the yearning for some collective identity in a "family" is suggestive of a more utopian impulse in the movies. In *The Godfather, Part II*, the Mafia becomes indistinguishable from business—as in the unforgettable scene in which Hyman Roth (a Meyer Lansky figure) convenes a meeting in Havana of a roomful of American business leaders, including the mobster Michael Corleone, who represents the "entertainment and gaming" industries—and the utopian content may be found in the largely unseen but powerfully transformative presence of the Cuban revolutionaries, who disrupt both American business (here embodied in Michael's plans to purchase a casino) and U.S. imperialism. A similar reversal occurs with the formerly utopian "family," which now collapses into its profoundly ideological and violent content, whether seen in the present era (in Michael's own familial dissolution) or in the past (with the murderous scenes of the young Vito Corleone in Sicily and Little Italy). Employing these unlikely examples, Jameson maintains that "all contemporary works of art [...] have as their underlying impulse—albeit in what is often distorted and repressed unconscious form—our deepest fantasies about the nature of social life, both as we live it now, and as we feel in our bones it ought rather to be lived."[25]

Jameson's essay on *Dog Day Afternoon*, "Class and Allegory in Contemporary Mass Culture," underscores and extends this dialectic of utopia and ideology by demonstrating how a film about a botched bank robbery by desperate individuals in fact discloses the possibility of a profoundly political content in the form of an allegorized class consciousness. As Jameson acknowledges in a brief afterword, this essay (originally published in 1977) attempts to trace the conceptual contours of what Jameson later calls *cognitive mapping*. It does so primarily through what he refers to, citing Freud but tacitly acknowledging Erich Auerbach, as *figuration*, which suggests the possibility of representing a seemingly unrepresentable reality through allegorical means. For Jameson, this is also thoroughly existential; it is not an abstract Marxist "science," but a vital experience of daily life in which the hierarchical class system can be discerned.[26] In the very setting of the film, a neighborhood branch of a bank, the elaborate skein of the socioeconomic power relations of a larger system may be discerned. Even the apparently white-collar workers, the bank tellers, loan officers, and manager, appear as proletarians, more akin to the *lumpen* proletariat of the sympathetic criminals (played by *Godfather* veterans Al Pacino and John Cazale), when considering the abstract, faceless system of "multinational corporations," which suggests that late capitalism itself—the mode that has rendered invisible so many of the processes of power and subjugation seen in an earlier, national form of capitalism—also makes possible a novel kind of class consciousness. Thus, perhaps, before he even knew it himself, Jameson's reading of *Dog Day Afternoon* registers the potential for a political art to approximate what had been previously understood as class consciousness, but of "a new and hitherto undreamed of kind," a practice that could also wrestle with "that new spatiality implicit in the postmodern."²⁷ Such a practice, cognitive mapping, becomes a key concept for Jameson's critical exploration of postmodernism and postmodernity, both in the *Postmodernism* book and in his more recent studies of globalization.

Although the spatiotemporal logic of Jameson's publishing history does not align itself neatly with the chronological approach to his published books that I am following, the final lines of *Signatures of the Visible* may be seen to provide an almost seamless transition from this study of film to the broader project of *Postmodernism, or, the Cultural Logic of Late Capitalism*.²⁸ Reflecting on the "return" of a modernist *art deco* in recent years, Jameson concludes by asking whether, "even within the extraordinary eclipse of historicity in the postmodern period some deeper memory of history still faintly stirs[.] Or does this persistence—nostalgia for that ultimate moment of historical time in which difference was still present—rather betoken the incompleteness of the postmodern process, the survival within it of remnants of the past, which have not yet, as in some unimaginable fully realized postmodernism, been dissolved without a trace?"²⁹ In the opening sentence of *Postmodernism*, Jameson asserts that it is "safest to grasp the concept of the postmodern as an attempt to think the present historically in an age that has forgotten to think historically in the first place. In that case, it either 'expresses' some deeper irrepressible historical impulse (in however distorted a fashion) or effectively 'represses' and diverts it, depending on the side of the ambiguity you happen to favor."³⁰ Jameson's analysis of this "attempt to think the present historically" marks perhaps the supreme achievement of his project of dialectical criticism.

Postmodernism, or, the Cultural Logic of Late Capitalism

I have suggested that *Late Marxism* and *Signatures of the Visible* might be considered as parts of, or perhaps prologues to, *Postmodernism, or, the Cultural Logic of Late Capitalism*. In fact, "The Existence of Italy," with its lengthy reflection on the historical relations among the formal modes of realism, modernism, and postmodernism, might be taken almost literally as a preface to *Postmodernism*. And given Jameson's nomination of Adorno as *the* philosopher for the postmodern epoch, *Late Marxism* may be read as an attempt to lay the theoretical foundation for Jameson's more wide-ranging and perceptive exploration of postmodernism.

Indeed, Phillip E. Wegner has suggested that Jameson's own exploration of the postmodern is, in part, made possible by his analysis of Adorno as the Marxist theorist most suited to the current cultural configuration. Borrowing the formulation of Walter Benjamin's preface to *The Origins of the German Tragic Drama*, Wegner has referred to Jameson's book on Adorno as the "epistemo-critical prologue" to *Postmodernism*.[31] Wegner convincingly argues that Jameson's approach to the problem of representing the seemingly unrepresentable postmodernity derives its force from Adorno, and perhaps more specifically from Adorno's appropriation of the Benjaminian concept of the *constellation*. Jameson provides evidence of this in his discussion of the constellation in *Late Marxism*. Citing Benjamin's assertion that "Ideas are to objects as constellations are to stars" and that, therefore, "they are neither their concepts nor their laws," Jameson concludes that "philosophical writing or *Darstellung* will consist in tracing the constellation, in somehow drawing the lines between the empirical concepts thus 'configured' together."[32] In this sense, then, Jameson's rediscovery of the model of the constellation in examining Adorno's own methodology is suggestive of the massive project Jameson himself undertakes in *Postmodernism*, according to Wegner. Where the "Idea" for Benjamin was originally "tragedy," and later "the arcades," "History," or "Paris, Capital of the Nineteenth Century," for Jameson it will become "the postmodern" itself, something that cannot be apprehended through a recitation of its key (empirical) features or even through some conceptual argument about it, but only through a process of constellating its affiliated concepts in such a way as to allow its features to become discernible in some artificial, but no less useful and meaningful configuration.

In the book itself, *Postmodernism, or, the Cultural Logic of Late Capitalism*, Jameson attaches a keyword or representative concept to each of its ten individual chapters (not counting the Introduction), which themselves have more detailed or descriptive titles. In naming such significant concepts and attaching them as labels to each chapter, Jameson suggests the "stars" that will help to form the constellation of the idea of postmodernism: Culture, Ideology, Video, Architecture, Sentences, Space, Theory, Economics, Film, and Conclusion. As Wegner argues,

Jameson's task in writing this book will be to draw the constellation that holds together an immense and at first glance seemingly unrelated variety of concepts. [...] Their significance is further born out in the fact that these concept-names, and not the particular titles, run in the header above each chapter. The chapters then develop a new and original substance for each of these concepts—not culture, ideology, sentences, or space understood in some abstract universal fashion, but rather as themselves networks taking on a specific concrete content in the current world system. These are then ultimately drawn together into a constellated—and necessarily incomplete—totality by the Idea, the name, of postmodernism.[33]

The book as a whole, then, will attempt to make visible an overall system of which various cultural texts and practices are a part.

Possibly the most striking aspect of Jameson's approach to postmodernism is his insistence that it be imagined as a system at all. For both enthusiasts and detractors of postmodern art, architecture, literature, and theory, postmodernism was understood as unsystematic and, moreover, as anti-systematic, as in Lyotard's argument that postmodern thought eschews those *grand récits* of modernity, which are themselves then conceptualized as systems. Further, by connecting the apparently disparate phenomena to a global economic system, late or multinational capitalism, Jameson grounds the concept in what the older Marxist tradition understood as the economic base, allowing this most sophisticated and complex thinker to be described as a "vulgar Marxist" (the irony of which, I'm sure, would delight him). Once postmodernism is envisioned as "the cultural logic of late capitalism," Jameson's dialectical critique of this or that postmodern characteristic or text takes on greater historical significance, for the seemingly local or isolated occurrence can be situated in a vaster structure or narrative. In summarizing the key features of Jameson's argument, it might be useful to follow Perry Anderson's lead and examine the five "moves" Jameson makes.[34] These moves are used to "outflank" the previous theories of the postmodern, while also enabling Jameson to *capture* (Anderson's word) postmodernism for Marxism.

The first such "move" has already been alluded to, and it appears in the very title of Jameson's foundational essay and book. By anchoring the elusive phenomenon in the mode of production, specifically in the most recent stage of advanced, multinational capitalism—also known as "late capitalism" in Mandel's usage, along with such affiliated conceptions as postindustrial societies, the *société de consommation* or consumer society, service economies, and, more recently, globalization—Jameson retrieves postmodernism from the more limited aesthetic or epistemological domains, and demonstrates the degree to which it must be understood as broadly historical. As we have seen, this is merely to say that Jameson's approach is Marxist, for the "sectoral validity" of these non-totalizing discourses may be granted even as the dialectical critic demonstrates that, because of their self-imposed or unconscious limitations, they are ultimately incapable of arriving at the truth they seek. In showing how postmodernism is tied to its historical situation in late capitalism, Jameson is also able to bring it into conceptual focus as a period, one that begins roughly in the late 1960s or early 1970s. This period coincides with an epoch of dramatic alterations within the global economy or, to put it more colloquially, of changing ways of doing business. The new multinational or transnational corporations are qualitatively different from businesses large and small in the industrial and monopoly stages of capitalism, when even those corporations which were heavily engaged in foreign trade tended to be discernibly national. Other features of this new economic system include "the new international division of labor, a vertiginous new dynamic in international banking and the stock exchanges (including the enormous Second and Third World debt), new forms of media interrelationship (very much including transportation systems such as containerization), computers and automation, the flight of production to advanced Third World areas, along with all the more familiar social consequences, including the crisis of traditional labor, the emergence of yuppies, and gentrification on a now-global scale."[35] Such structural transformations in the increasingly global economic system cannot but have tremendous effects upon other areas of lived experience, and the postmodern condition is thus to be understood in relation to this simultaneously overarching and underlying system.

The second "move" identified by Anderson involves the psychological effects of such social mutations, which Anderson calls the "metastases of the psyche in this new conjuncture."[36] Jameson deals with this in terms of the celebrated "death of the subject," but here specifies the material, spatial, and psychological conditions under which the prior "autonomous bourgeois monad or ego or individual" dissolves, and "the alienation of the subject is displaced by the latter's fragmentation."[37] Jameson refers to the effect of this as the "waning of affect," which does not mean that people no long feel emotion but rather alludes to a peculiarly postmodern "depthlessness." Where once the supposedly superficial or formal element could be said to reflect a core meaning in the individual self, this increasingly appears to be impossible, since for all practical purposes such a psychologically enclosed self no longer exists. At the level of culture itself, this loss of self is typified by the evanescence of a sense of historicity, most noteworthy in the perceived lack of either memory or hope. Unlike modernist art, which frequently agonized over the past or anticipated some radiant future, postmodernism in Jameson's view seems condemned to a perpetual present in which any images of the past or future become hollow simulacra—as in the fashion for "retro" clothing, for instance. Using an elegantly paradoxical phrase, Jameson refers to a "nostalgia for the present," in which even those seemingly historical productions, like period pieces, do not really attempt to represent the historical conditions as they were but rather depict our present images of what "it must have been like." Referring to E.L. Doctorow's apparently realist but actually postmodernist novel *Ragtime*, Jameson observes that "[t]his historical novel can no longer set out to represent the historical past; it can only 'represent' our ideas and stereotypes about that past (which thereby at once becomes 'pop history')."[38] This is also the basis for Jameson's famous distinction between parody and pastiche, since the essentially critical function of modernist parody is evacuated of any content, "a statue with blind eyeballs," that can still mimic but can no longer be the basis of satire.[39]

Jameson's third move, according to Anderson, is to enlarge the cultural field of postmodernism to a cultural world system itself, partially by characterizing the postmodern condition as one of dedifferentiation, in contrast to the Weberian conception of increasingly rationalized societies as divided and compartmentalized. Where some early critics of postmodernism had focused on architecture, art, literature, or philosophy, Jameson approaches postmodernism as a total system or, at least, as bearing on all of these fields and more at the same time. Hence his *Postmodernism* book deals with multiple forms—such as those listed in the "constellation" above—without attempting to reduce or limit postmodernism to a narrower field of applicability. Interdisciplinarity itself, as well as the transdisciplinary operations of Theory which came into such vogue in the 1970s and for which the name Michel Foucault may suffice as an archetypical exemplar, is not therefore merely an epistemological way of getting at the multivalenced thing called postmodernism, but is itself postmodern. The blurring of boundaries and the calling into question of previously accepted divisions is part of the postmodern condition. But lest this process appear too celebratory, it is also worth remembering that such dedifferentiation underlies the logic of globalization and the extension of a sort of American-styled, cosmopolitan, consumer capitalism throughout the world.

Similarly, in a fourth move identified by Anderson, Jameson recognized the essentially demotic nature of postmodernism, which while certainly not lacking its own hierarchies was the product of what Auerbach had referred to as an "economic and cultural leveling process."[40] Whereas modernism frequently bore the marks of an elite or an exceptional enclave (the outcast or exile, for instance), postmodernism seems resolutely immured within a mass or popular culture. The old "high/low" distinction, among others, has melted into air as the widespread blending of the commercial and the artistic in nearly all cultural domains ensures that mass culture begins to dominate all culture. The populism of postmodern works of art might be cause for celebration or for alarm, as underrepresented groups (such as women, ethnic minorities, postcolonial figures, and so forth) that may have been unwelcome in certain modernist discussions of literature or film routinely came to the fore in postmodern culture, and even "literary" fiction could find itself high on a bestseller list or turned into blockbuster movies. Of course, the dialectical flipside of the ostensibly democratic dispersion of mass cultural artefacts is the realization of the influence of what Thomas Carlyle had derided as the "cash nexus," recognizable in the well-nigh total permeation by commerce of all areas of social life.

The fifth move is one of comportment, it seems, as Anderson highlights Jameson's eccentric if not unique approach to the *valuation* of postmodernism. Above all, consistently with his position elsewhere, Jameson wished to avoid moralizing, which he saw as epistemologically unproductive and ontologically false. Many of the critics of postmodernity cast a given postmodernist work or characteristic as not only objectionable in this or that way, but morally wrong. Following Nietzsche's lead, Jameson has always maintained that behind every ethical argument lay the traces of power relationships, such that the moral or ethical often masked the truly political content of such perceptions. Moreover, the dialectic itself cautions one to be skeptical of hasty judgements, especially since the logic of the dialectical reversal dictates that what might appear "bad" at a given moment or in a discrete situation could reveal itself to be altogether "good" in another time and place. In Jameson's words, "a genuinely historical and dialectical analysis of such phenomena—particularly when it is a matter of a present of time and of history in which we ourselves exist and struggle—cannot afford the impoverished luxury of such absolute moralizing judgements: the dialectic is 'beyond good and evil' in the sense of some easy taking of sides, whence the glacial and inhuman spirit of its historical vision."[41] What is more, Jameson has conceded, as a matter of personal taste he is "an enthusiastic consumer of postmodernism," generally liking the music, architecture, food, and fashion. But he notes that "tastes, giving rise to opinions [...] have little to do with the analysis of the function of such a culture and how it got to be that way."[42] In insisting that postmodernism be understood as a cultural dominant, as the cultural logic of late capitalism (itself apprehended as the highest stage thus far of capitalist development and marked by its fundamentally multinational or global character), Jameson's argument transcends and absorbs the value-laden skirmishes of earlier discussions, such as the Habermas–Lyotard debates, and thereby transforms postmodernism from a set of epiphenomenal effects to a system in its own right. As Jameson remarks in conclusion, though he too sometimes laments his "complicity" with the word *postmodern*, he also wonders "whether any other concept can dramatize the issues in quite so effective and economical a fashion. [...] 'We have to name the system': this high point of the sixties finds an unexpected revival in the postmodernism debate."[43]

This broad-brushed survey of Jameson's "moves" within these debates as recorded in *Postmodernism, or, the Cultural Logic of Late Capitalism* has so far not touched upon what may be his most striking and memorable contribution: the concept of cognitive mapping. As Jameson himself admits at the end of *Postmodernism*, his call for a cognitive mapping on a global scale and his anticipation of a worldwide proletarianization (in his "Periodizing the 60s")[44] were really two sides of the same coin: "'Cognitive mapping' was in reality nothing but a code word for 'class consciousness'—only it proposed the need for a class consciousness of a new and hitherto undreamed of kind, while it also inflected the account in the direction of that new spatiality implicit in the postmodern."[45] I will discuss cognitive mapping further in the next chapter, but for now it is worth considering Jameson's sense of this "new spatiality" and the need for new forms of mapping.

Spatiality itself appears to have made a historic comeback in the era of postmodernity, and Jameson is joined by David Harvey (in *The Condition of Postmodernity*) and Edward Soja (in *Postmodern Geographies*) in perceiving that postmodernism ought to be characterized, at least in part, by a new, heightened sense of spatiality.[46] It is not surprising, therefore, that architecture may have been the field most actively engaged and enveloped early in the discourse of postmodernism. Jameson's famous illustration of the postmodern transmogrification of social space is found in his analysis of the Westin Bonaventure hotel in Los Angeles, a postmodern edifice in which the traditional markers of entrances or exits, indeed of inside or outside, are bewilderingly obscured. After discussing the floor plan, elevators, lobby, and other quotidian elements of the place, Jameson concludes that

> this latest mutation in space—postmodern hyperspace—has finally succeeded in transcending the capacities of the individual human body to locate itself, to organize its immediate surroundings perceptually, and cognitively to map its position in a mappable external world. It may now be suggested that this alarming disjunction point between the body and its built environment—which is to the initial bewilderment of the older modernism as the velocities of spacecraft to those of the automobile— can itself stand as symbol and analogon of that even sharper dilemma which is the incapacity of our minds, at least at present, to map the great global multinational and decentered communicational network in which we find ourselves caught as individual subjects.[47]

This is an astounding theoretical maneuver, as Jameson quickly shifts from the perceptual confusion of an individual in a scarcely legible lived space, which after all is a fairly common though no less angst-ridden experience known as "being lost," to the far vaster, abstract space of a global system, which is nevertheless the absent cause or conditioning horizon of this discrete building in Los Angeles in which the individual subject feels "out of place." A sort of existentialist crisis of representation, this cartographic anxiety requires the coordination of one's individual perspective with some sense of the larger social totality.

Jameson's proposed solution, an aesthetic of cognitive mapping, famously combines the concepts of "wayfinding" and "imageability" in the urban planner Kevin Lynch's *The Image of the City* with Althusser's theory of ideology as "the representation of the subject's *Imaginary* relationship to his or her *Real* conditions of existence."[48] In Lynch's analysis, the anxiety an individual experiences in not being able to navigate the urban environment is heightened by the lack of clear landmarks or paths, so the pedestrian seeks to form a mental image of the city for use in moving about its spaces. Lynch contrasts the geography of Boston, with its Charles

River establishing a kind of boundary and distinctive skyscrapers acting as guideposts, and Jersey City, which appears to lack those monuments that may serve as clear points of reference for one's mental cartography. Lynch argues that the inhabitants of cities without clear geographical landmarks experience a pervasive sense of alienation, as they cannot form a clear, usable, image of the place through which they move. Mappability, or imageability, therefore, becomes a crucial feature of the well-organized city, and the city dweller who can most easily form a mental picture of this space will be best able to "use" it. As Jameson summarizes it, "Disalienation in the traditional city, then, involves the practical reconquest of a sense of place and the construction or reconstruction of an articulated ensemble which can be retained in memory and which the individual subject can map and remap along the moments of mobile, alternative trajectories." But moving beyond the simpler navigation of a building's or a city's spaces, Jameson connects this cognitive mapping with Althusser's theory of ideology, in which one may form a "situational representation" of the individual subject in relation to "that vaster and properly unrepresentable totality which is the ensemble of society's structures as a whole."[49] Cognitive mapping, while still grounded in the material and spatial relations of postmodern lived experience, is thus another attempt to represent that unrepresentable totality.

In what he refers to as a "digression on cartography," Jameson illustrates the limits of the practice described by Lynch and argues for a much more broadly understood, global theoretical practice. One of the drawbacks of Lynch's model, Jameson observes, is that it is really "precartographic," describing what might be better identified as an itinerary rather than as a map. In his micro-survey of the history of mapmaking, Jameson points out that itineraries are merely "diagrams organized around the still subject-centered or existential journey of the traveler, along which various significant key features are marked." Maps, on the other hand, would need to employ artistic and technical features, perhaps also making use of such scientific instruments as the compass and the sextant, to introduce a relationship with a non-subjective totality: "cognitive mapping in the broader sense comes to require the coordination of existential data (the empirical position of the subject) with unlived, abstract conceptions of the geographic totality." With such technological developments as the globe and the Mercator projection, among other early modern innovations, the hybrid art-and-science of mapmaking begins to grapple with the more difficult question of representation itself. Cartography recognizes itself as essentially figural (or even utopian), insofar as the mapmaker here no longer attempts simply to replicate on a chart the spaces of the world or even any actual place, albeit in a scaled-down form, which is already an aesthetic or imaginative consideration, but must instead project an abstract, "unrealistic" figure that somehow stands in relation to whatever unrepresentable "real" geography lies beyond the contours of the map. That is to say, mapmaking abandons its previous "naïvely mimetic" aspirations in favor of more complicated meditations on representational form itself. "At this point it becomes clear that there can be no true maps (at the same point it also becomes clear that there can be scientific progress, or better still, a dialectical advance, in the various historical moments of mapmaking)."[50] In what might be considered another dialectical reversal, cartography becomes better able to serve its practical purpose by escaping from its adherence to such now outmoded principles of representational accuracy or fidelity to the "real" world.

As I have suggested elsewhere, the Mercator projection offers an interesting analogy for Jameson's broader sense of cognitive mapping.[51] Mercator's mathematical projection was first used to produce his influential world map in 1569. Notoriously, this process effectively distorts the geographic spaces its maps purport to represent, as objects appear larger the further they are removed from the center, that is, from the equator, thus grotesquely aggrandizing the landmasses near the North Pole, such that Greenland can appear to be larger than South America, which is actually about six times its size. That such maps served ideological purposes is well known, but Mercator's intention was neither directly ideological nor faithfully realistic; the goal was not to create an entirely accurate map, but rather a more useful one. The projection was developed in order to solve a technical, practical problem, which Jameson refers to as "the unresolvable (well-nigh Heisenbergian) dilemma of the transfer of curved space to flat charts," an essential matter for those sailing long distances across the ocean.[52] By employing charts which were drawn using the Mercator projection, navigators could set a course using straight lines, thus establishing truer courses. Obviously, such pragmatic readers would realize that the map was not "true," in the sense of a mimetically accurate depiction of the places figured on its surface, but this more fantastic representation, projecting a world that serves the purposes of sailors far better than a more realistic version might, has real effects.

"Transcoding" this history of cartography into the problematic of ideology, Jameson notes, we can substitute for this geographical space the social space in which we necessarily "cognitively map our individual social relationship to local, national, or international class realities."[53] Yet in the postmodern present, in an era of late capitalism and globalization, such mapping must itself be global. That is, "an aesthetic of cognitive mapping—a pedagogical political culture which seeks to endow the individual subject with some new heightened sense of its place in the global system—will necessarily have to respect this now enormously complex representational dialectic and invent radically new forms in order to do it justice."[54] The postmodern condition will require, not a return to the modernist practices of an earlier sociopolitical configuration, but a narrative or representational project suited to the global space of the world system.

5

Cognitive Mapping
and Globalization

Jameson concluded his widely influential 1984 essay "Postmodernism, or, the Cultural Logic of Late Capitalism" by asserting that "[t]he political form of postmodernism, if there ever is any, will have as its vocation the invention and projection of a global cognitive mapping, on a social as well as spatial scale."[1] In many of his writings in the 1980s and 1990s, Jameson endeavored to identify instances of political art that took up the call for this figuratively cartographic project and to elaborate his own theories and criticism of such work. Although one might notice that Jameson never quite wrote a full-scale study of cognitive mapping *per se*, and that he tended to refrain from using the term itself as the Nineties wore on, the concept or project remained a key aspect of his cultural criticism during this period, and it has done so, arguably, throughout his entire career. For instance, as I have mentioned in previous chapters, Jameson acknowledged that his 1977 article "Class and Allegory in Mass Culture" was an earlier attempt at making clear the processes of a cognitive mapping, *avant la lettre*, and he used the terms of the phrase in his discussion of the dialectical use of genre criticism in *The Political Unconscious*, where he noted that "realism [...] unites the experience of daily life with a properly cognitive, mapping, or well-nigh 'scientific' perspective."[2] Colin MacCabe has suggested that cognitive mapping is a crucial element of Jameson's entire critical enterprise, since it enables him to supplement the concept of the political unconscious with "an account of the mechanisms which articulate individual fantasy and social organization." Cognitive mapping provides "the missing psychology of the political unconscious, the political edge of the historical analysis of postmodernism, and the methodological justification of the Jamesonian undertaking."[3] Along with MacCabe, as well as Ian Buchanan, Phillip E. Wegner, and others, I would argue that, whatever it be named, cognitive mapping is central to Jameson's project of dialectical criticism.

Fundamental to the concept of cognitive mapping is the perceived split between the individual subject's lived experience and the structural totality that affects, undergirds, and ultimately gives meaning to that experience. Jameson's earliest considerations of Jean-Paul Sartre's existentialism or Georg Lukács's theory of the novel already speak to this basic problematic, which could also be rendered even more starkly in the older, Hegelian opposition of the subjective and the objective. Astonishingly, perhaps, for readers most familiar only with his writings on postmodernism, Jameson deploys the metaphor of the map in relation to literary practice as far back as 1968, in a brief article, "On Politics and Literature." Discussing the vocation of the political writer in the United States, a nation lacking the tradition of an oppositional political aesthetic to be found in such European artists as Louis Aragon and Bertolt Brecht, Jameson suggests that the American political writer "has to make up something like a map." As Jameson explains, the writer

> has to coordinate two different zones of experience and bring them into a coherent relationship to each other. On the one hand he has to do justice to his own lived experience, to the truth of the individual life, of the monad, to the domain if you like of psychology and of the psychological problem. But that isn't enough: then he has to situate that subjective dimension with respect to the objective, he has to bring the point in relation to the coordinates of the map, he has to give a picture of the objective structure of society as a whole and deal with matters that ordinarily have nothing to do with my own subjective experience, my own psychology, but which are rather ordinarily dealt with in political science textbooks, sociological or economic studies—all those basic questions about how the country is organized, what makes it do what it does, who runs it, and so forth—things I may *know* about intellectually but which I can't translate into the terms of my personal experience. The opposition is between subjective and objective, between mere abstract knowledge and lived experience; and the problem for the political writer—perhaps well-nigh impossible to solve—is to find some kind of real experience in which these two zones of reality intersect. But such experiences are very rare: and generally they are only abstract, or allegorical, or somehow symbolic. [...] Basically, the only way we can think our own individual lives in relationship to the collectivity is by

making a picture of the relationship. The notion of a map was such an image, or picture, or the image of an airplane from which you can look down and see masses of life, of houses and cities, disposed out below you like a map. But that's an abstract experience, and doesn't offer any genuine material for the work of art.[4]

As in Lukács's sense of a "transcendental homelessness" in a "world abandoned by God," the writer projects a map-like image of a totality that is not, or is no longer, accessible through any individual's lived experience. But Jameson's use of this spatial analogy indicates the degree to which he was already concerned with what might be considered a discernible "cartographic anxiety" of the late modern (or postmodern) existential condition.[5]

Another thing that is clear from this early commentary is that Jameson is still thinking in a national context, particularly of the apparent inability of writers in the United States to imagine a meaningful connection between individual psychology and a structural or systemic national network. But the metaphor of the abstract view or overview that is embodied in the mapping project itself is suggestive of the broader social totality that ultimately cannot be limited to a strictly domestic political economy, society, or space. As must have already been increasingly apparent in the 1960s, the national models were no longer suited to the social realities of a rapidly transforming consumer society or postindustrial capitalism, much as some Marxists and others may have resisted these expressions. In the aftermath of that tumultuous decade, and in the disappointments and retrenchments of the 1970s, it becomes clear to Jameson that the emergence of late or multinational capital is not only a new phase of the capitalist mode of production and the cultural features accompanying it, but it also presupposes a more radical break with the historical configuration of the modern world system. Following Ernest Mandel's argument in *Late Capitalism* that the present mode of multinational capital represented a third stage of capitalism—that is, one which followed the earlier stages of market and monopoly capitalism, the latter associated with what Lenin had referred to as the "age of imperialism"—Jameson adjusted his sights, recognizing that the national space could no longer appear representative of the social totality with which both individuals and groups struggled to come to terms. In his interventions into the postmodernism debates, Jameson definitively grounded these new cultural forms and phenomena in this multinational world system, which itself had become "the true ground of Being of our time."[6]

After *Postmodernism, or, the Cultural Logic of Late Capitalism*, Jameson published three books which might be viewed as elaborations on the themes laid out therein and in his other investigations into postmodernity. In a sense, then, these studies extend Jameson's previous work on postmodernism; however, his analysis of the postmodern now places a greater emphasis on globalization itself, and the world system moves from its omnipresent but less visible place in the background of cultural studies to the forefront of Jameson's inquiry. To the extent that he ever did write a book explicitly on the topic of cognitive mapping, then *The Geopolitical Aesthetic: Cinema and Space in the World System* (1992), which was based on a series of lectures presented at the British Film Institute, is that book. In it, Jameson endeavors to show how various artists working in the medium of film have, consciously or otherwise, managed to produce something like cognitive maps or "new geotopical cartographies" of the social spaces of the world system. In *The Seeds of Time* (1994), which originated as presentations in the Wellek Library Lectures in Critical Theory series at the University of California at Irvine, Jameson provides a theoretically nuanced analysis of the concept of postmodernity and its limits, while also delivering one of his most compelling arguments on utopia to date, all under the auspices of a sustained attempt to imagine the very possibility of imagining a future that is not merely the continuation of the present world system, or, in a hardly utopian alternative, the destruction of the entire world itself. Several of Jameson's significant interventions into the overall discussions about postmodernism are included in the 1998 volume, *The Cultural Turn: Selected Writings on the Postmodern, 1983–1998*, which also contains new essays specifically attuned to the dynamics of a world system in which finance capital and real estate speculation appear to be profoundly more influential on both the economic and cultural spheres than in an era when commodity production and consumption seemed to delineate the horizon of the capitalist mode. These three books, diverse as they are in the texts, media, and topics they address, signal a shift in Jameson's thinking with respect to the philosophical problem of globalization. Another book from this period, *Cultures of Globalization*, a collection of essays surveying a number of critical positions on the subject, co-edited by Jameson and Masao Miyoshi, might stand as the representative text in this transition from postmodernism to globalization in Jameson's own dialectical criticism. And yet the shift itself reveals the continuity and persistence of the problematic, for the one phenomenon (or set of phenomena) intertwines with the other, thus reciprocally giving conceptual shape to any analysis of either postmodernism or globalization or, of course, of both at the same time. Further, although Jameson's use of the explicit term *cognitive mapping* wanes in the years after *The Geopolitical Aesthetic*, the underlying concept remains crucial to his understanding of the vocation of art and literature in the age of globalization. As I suggested in Chapter 1, Jameson's lifelong project appears to be nothing less than the cultural cartography of the world system.

The Geopolitical Aesthetic

The concept of cognitive mapping, as we have seen, finds precursors in a variety of ideas and practices associated with ideology, realism, narrative form, spatiotemporal orientation, and history. But for all its similarities to or filiations with earlier forms, Jameson insists that what he means by *cognitive mapping* is particularly suited to, and situated in, a postmodern condition of multinational or global capitalism, which makes the concept or practice somewhat distinct from its predecessors. In the final section of the conclusion to *Postmodernism, or, the Cultural Logic of Late Capitalism*, significantly titled "How to Map a Totality" and drawing partially upon a 1988 essay titled "Cognitive Mapping,"[7] Jameson sketches a broadly historical production of social or cultural space that correlates with the developments of the three stages of capitalism identified by Mandel. Each requires a different existential relationship between the individual subject and the social totality of his or her life-world. And, in what itself might be thought of as a dialectical leap forward from the still subject-centered itineraries of the Kevin Lynch version of cognitive mapping discussed in the previous chapter, Jameson demonstrates how this larger and more complex notion relates simultaneously to the global space of the world system and to the narrative of history.

   Combining Henri Lefebvre's significant conception of the historical production of space with Mandel's economic analysis in *Late Capitalism*, Jameson argues that "[t]he three historical stages of capital have each generated a type of space unique to it, even though these three stages are obviously more profoundly interrelated than are the spaces of other modes of production. The three types of space I have in mind are all the result of discontinuous expansions or quantum leaps in the enlargement of capital, in the latter's penetration and colonization of hitherto uncommodified areas."[8] The overarching or unifying force throughout this historical development would thus be capital itself. In attempting to make sense of and navigate these spaces, then, a form of something like cognitive mapping would be required for each of them. However, Jameson's brief, "genealogical approach" to such spaces reveals the degree to which a literal understanding of mapping—something closer to Lynch's *imageability* or *wayfinding*—would no longer be adequate to the task of representing the social totality and the place of the individual subject within it.

The first type of space, corresponding to classical or market capitalism, conforms to the logic of the grid, "a reorganization of some older sacred and heterogeneous space into geometrical and Cartesian homogeneity." It is the space of the well-ordered city, conceived according to an Enlightenment project of disenchanting, measuring, and ordering the world, and Jameson adds that the emblematic figure for this type of space could be found in Foucault's discussion of the carceral society in *Discipline and Punish: The Birth of the Prison*; although Jameson hastens to add that, from a Marxist point of view, such an organization of space is the result of commodity production and the labor process, rather than of "the shadowy and mythical entity Foucault called 'power.'" The dominant aesthetic form correlating to this is realism, and the rise of the modern novel is associated with this historical space; Jameson duly mentions *Don Quixote*, which had served as a historico-philosophical milestone for both Lukács and Foucault, as an exemplary narrative.[9] The older modes of meaning and spatial organization evanesce, or rather, are subjugated to the abstractions and disenchantments of geometric space, but this at least makes for a relatively "mappable" social terrain. The "demystifying" realism can help to make possible a sense of place and of spatial relations in this relatively readable or decodable social context, even if it must impose the form-giving or sense-making parameters through figurative, narrative, or aesthetic means.

Later, with the emergence of monopoly capital and the age of imperialism, particularly in the late-nineteenth and early-twentieth centuries, a new sort of national space, already becoming international, emerges. The works produced in this period required another level of spatial projection, as the experience of daily life was not really adequate to understand the structures which made possible and conditioned that experience. As the problem of figuration becomes more urgent, so the techniques associated with literary modernism (such as stream-of-consciousness, montage, and spatial form) may be viewed as attempts to overcome, or at least to address, the representational crisis. As Jameson puts it,

> At this point, the phenomenological experience of the individual subject—traditionally, the supreme raw material of the work of art— becomes limited to a tiny corner of the social world, a fixed-camera view of a certain section of London or the countryside or wherever. But the truth of that experience no longer coincides with the place in which it takes place. The truth of that limited daily experience of London lies, rather, in India or Jamaica or Hong Kong; it is bound up with the whole colonial system of the British Empire that determines the very quality of the individual's subjective life. Yet the structural coordinates are no longer accessible to immediate lived experience and are often not even conceptualizable for most people.
>
> There comes into being, then, a situation in which we can say that if individual experience is authentic, then it cannot be true; and that if a scientific or cognitive model of the same content is true, then it escapes individual experience.[10]

The paradox, then, is that experience can no longer be both authentic and true, because the material grounds for a personal experience are not apprehensible directly; similarly, the models by which one ascertains the "truth" now elude individual experience. The revolutionary experiments with language and style in modernist texts reflect "an attempt to square this circle and to invent new and elaborate strategies for overcoming this dilemma." This will involve a "play of figuration," an allegorical structure by which what Jameson calls "monadic relativism" becomes a way for modernists to create, perhaps ironically, formally "closed," interior worlds of consciousness that can stand figuratively for a social totality no longer capable of being represented. As Jameson had previously revealed in his postulation of a "political unconscious," the private, self-enclosed, monadic ego in such modernist narratives becomes symptomatic of "the penetration even of middle-class lived experience by this strange new global relativity of the colonial network."[11] Although this sort of "mapping" is necessarily abstract and figurative, it nevertheless provides a method by which to bring the disparate coordinates of lived experience and the social totality into productive relation.

It is harder to detect the "quantum leap" from this form of national and colonial space to the postmodern or global space of late capitalism, but part of the answer lies in the degree to which the national space, that of the "imagined community" as Benedict Anderson so memorably defined the nation, fails to register the nearly total permeation of capital into formerly unaffected, even unheard of places. As with the often indistinct line between modernism and postmodernism, Jameson does not directly identify a moment when such a quantum leap of capitalist expansion occurs, and he even suggests that the new type of space may be partly a difference of degree: "If this is so for the age of imperialism, how much more it must hold for our moment, the moment of the multinational network, or what Mandel calls 'late capitalism,' a moment in which not only the older city, but even the nation-state itself has ceased to play a central functional and formal role in a process that has […] expanded beyond them."[12] But with the dismantling of great colonial empires, at least in their most visible forms of direct political control, a sort of withering away of the state has made room for a global or multinational space, thoroughly saturated with capital. Part of this has to do with what David Harvey has analyzed as the "suppression of distance" or "space-time compression" that postmodernity and the new technologies of late capitalism have brought with them.[13] The almost instantaneous border crossings and re-crossings, along with the development of seemingly bewildering modes of global finance and communication, make for a rather uneasy sense of place in the world system.

This postmodern spatial arrangement involves a much greater suppression of distance and saturation of space than had earlier historical stages of capital, but the sense of disorientation and anxiety related to the ever-more-complex spaces and difficulty in mapping them were already apparent at earlier stages. Jameson considers "such spatial peculiarities of postmodernism as symptoms and expressions of a new and historically original dilemma, one that involves our insertion as individual subjects into a multidimensional set of radically discontinuous realities, whose frames range from the still surviving spaces of bourgeois private life all the way to the unimaginable decentering of global capital itself."[14] Clearly, at this point, we are no longer talking about merely finding ourselves disoriented within the commercial spaces of a postmodernist building in Los Angeles; yet that visceral experience of the Westin Bonaventure Hotel is somehow emblematic of the spatial perplexity and broader, structural dilemma facing the critic or artist in the era of multinational capitalism.

Jameson's call for a "global cognitive mapping, on a social as well as a spatial scale," reflects the need for an aesthetic and political practice equipped to engage with this new spatial organization, and he recognizes that "the incapacity to map socially is as crippling to political experience as the analogous incapacity to map spatially is for urban experience."[15]

Jameson has conceded that cognitive mapping was really a sort of "modernist strategy," inasmuch as it "retains an impossible concept of totality whose representational failure seemed for the moment as useful and productive as its (inconceivable) success."[16] That is, unlike certain more postmodernist strategies that might employ a sort of Baudrillardian hyperreality or play of the simulacra in an effort to criticize the hyperreal society of the simulacrum of the present moment, Jameson's idea seemed more like the narrative figurations of a modernist epoch, attempting to give form to the fragmentary and diffuse elements of the postmodern culture. But it is also true that, in Jameson's view, the cognitive mapping he tries to envision cannot be thought of as a simple mental image of the space that one inhabits or through which one moves, even if the model supplied by Lynch is an evocative point of departure for the project of cognitive mapping. Above all, Jameson admits, the conflation of the figurative concept with literal maps both oversimplifies and effectively confuses things, since for most people "maps" are not themselves complicated and their representational accessibility is taken for granted. (But, as we have seen, even at their most practical, maps can also be extremely complex and figural representations.) Jameson states that "cognitive mapping cannot (at least in our time) involve anything so easy as a map; indeed, once you knew what 'cognitive mapping' was driving at, you were to dismiss all figures of maps and mapping from your mind and try something else." Even so, and especially knowing that it was intended as a code word for "class consciousness," Jameson insists that the spatial peculiarities of the postmodern condition or of social existence under late capitalism required a novel form specifically attuned to that "new spatiality implicit in the postmodern."[17] Hence, while cognitive mapping cannot be confused with a strictly cartographic or geographic activity, neither can one discard its "own impossible originality" by simply substituting other, less overtly spatial, code words.

In *The Geopolitical Aesthetic*, Jameson focuses attention on the ways that art and artists, in this case in the medium of film, have attempted something like cognitive mapping as a way of representing the world system in the late twentieth century, perhaps thereby clearing the ground for critique, if only implicitly. Jameson notes that cognitive mapping was intended simultaneously to describe the sort of work being done by artists or critics already and to prescribe an aesthetic and political practice suited to postmodernity. In defending his own use of cognitive mapping, Jameson asserts that "the idea has, at least on my view, the advantage of involving concrete content (imperialism, the world system, subalternity, dependency, and hegemony), while necessarily involving the program of formal analysis of a new kind (since it is centrally defined by the dilemma of representation itself)." What is more, he writes, it is an activity that individual and collective subjects almost certainly engage in, almost always and nearly everywhere, so "it is obviously encouraging to find the concept of mapping validated by conscious artistic production, and to come upon this or that new work, which [...] seems to have conceived of the vocation of art itself as that of inventing new geotopical cartographies."[18]

Jameson's argument in *The Geopolitical Aesthetic* is not only that we ought to strive for some sort of cognitive map or figural narrative of the social totality, "but that we do so all the time anyway without being aware of the process." In an era of globalization, the older forms by which individual subjects oriented themselves spatially and socially still persist, of course, but the development of a postmodern and even postnational system requires something Jameson now refers to as a *geopolitical unconscious*, "which now attempts to refashion national allegory into a conceptual instrument for grasping our new being in the world." Jameson's fundamental hypothesis, which underlies all of the other discrete theses in the chapters constituting this study, is that "all thinking today is *also*, whatever else it is, an attempt to think the world system as such."[19]

The Geopolitical Aesthetic is divided into two parts, with one longer essay focusing on Hollywood cinema comprising Part I, and a series of essays on non-American cinematic traditions (discussing films by Soviet, French, Chinese, and Filipino filmmakers). The division is only partly geographical. In separating his essay on Hollywood conspiracy films from those on Second- and Third-World cinema, Jameson suggests that the cultural circumstances of the three "worlds," an understandably problematic subdivision of the postnational world system, require different kinds of cognitive maps and national allegories. Specifically, in what might be considered a slight refinement of his controversial thesis in "Third-World Literature in an Era of Multinational Capitalism," Jameson implies that the aesthetic of cognitive mapping may take different forms and have diverse effects within the metropolitan core of Western Europe or the United States, particularly in the post-Cold War geopolitical constellation.

The long essay that constitutes Part I, "Conspiracy as Totality," provides an unexpected but clear model of a form of cognitive mapping in the era of globalization. The prevailing paranoia, resentment, and bad faith associated with the conspiracy film as a genre would seem to make it an unlikely candidate for Jameson to use as the most salient example of this theoretical practice. Yet he had earlier suggested that conspiracy could be thought of as a "poor person's cognitive mapping in the postmodern age," insofar as conspiracy is "a degraded figure of the total logic of late capital, a desperate attempt to represent the latter's system."[20] As he puts it in The Geopolitical Aesthetic, "confronted with the ambitious program of fantasizing an economic system on the scale of the globe itself, the older motif of conspiracy knows a new lease on life."[21] Notwithstanding the truth value of a given conspiracy theorist's individual claims, conspiracy provides a form of cognitive mapping that enables individual subjects to situate themselves and others meaningfully within a system that seems now understandably invisible, perilous, and unimaginably vast. By imagining or discovering a conspiracy, one suddenly gives shape to a larger social structure, inevitably tending toward the world system in its totality, thus projecting a discernible if not wholly representable, supra-individual or collective system that is apparently unknowable in our day-to-day existence, but which might be outlined somewhat allegorically through a figurative representation, such as a constellation or a map. In this way, as with Lynch's urban pedestrian, the individual subject can coordinate his or her quotidian experiences and practices with a larger spatial and social totality.

Jameson offers as a vivid example the memorable scene in Alan J. Pakula's 1976 film All the President's Men in which the two protagonist reporters are engaged in the most banal journalistic activity (that is, here, doing research at the Library of Congress), and yet the long, unexpected shot from above, places them amid the array of tables and concentric circles of the room's architecture, as the camera's point of view "literally rises from the very small (the reading room call slips) to the social totality itself." As Jameson reads this moment in the film, a utopian element reveals itself in the sudden apprehension of a totalizing spatial system, and the apparently dystopian circumstances of a vast, government conspiracy are briefly glimpsed, in a dialectical reversal, as being somehow potentially utopian after all.

For it is the impossible vision of totality—here recovered in the moment in which the possibility of conspiracy confirms the possibility of the very unity of the social order itself—that is celebrated in this well-nigh paradisal moment. This is then the link between the phenomenal and the noumenal, or the ideological and the Utopian. This mounting image, underscored by the audible emergence, for the first time in the film, of the solemn music that so remarkably confirms the investigation's and the film's *telos*, in which the map of conspiracy itself, with its streets now radiating out through Washington from this ultimate center, unexpectedly suggests the possibility of cognitive mapping as a whole and stands as its substitute and yet its allegory all at once. The mounting camera shot, which diminishes the fevered researches of the two investigators as it rises to disclose the frozen cosmology of the reading room's circular balconies, confirms the momentary coincidence between knowledge as such and the architectural order of the astronomical totality itself, and yields a brief glimpse of the providential, as what organizes history but is unrepresentable within it.[22]

This unrepresentable totality is, as Jameson makes clear, the world system itself in the era of globalization. Any form of cognitive mapping is therefore bound to emerge from a struggle to represent this unrepresentable system. "It is indeed the new world system, the third stage of capitalism, which is for us the absent totality, Spinoza's God or Nature, the ultimate (indeed, perhaps the only) referent, the true ground of Being of our own time. Only by way of its fitful contemplation can its future, and our own, be somehow disclosed."[23]

The Seeds of Time

The substantive inquiry and argument presented in *The Seeds of Time* would not appear to follow directly from Jameson's exploration of cinema and space in the world system, but this book itself represents a kind of critical cognitive mapping on Jameson's part. To borrow a line from his discussion of conspiracy, it is an attempt "to think a system so vast that it cannot be encompassed by the natural and historically developed categories of perception with which human beings normally orient themselves."[24] In truth, this study advances Jameson's argument about the relationship between what he had been calling cognitive mapping and the utopian impulse, a subject upon which he has ruminated throughout his career, but which had perhaps not been so directly addressed until now. As Buchanan has pointed out, the ostensible subject of *The Seeds of Time* is postmodernity, but it is really about utopia.[25]

The phrase "seeds of time," taken from Shakespeare's *Macbeth*, already indicates Jameson's real concern in this book. Jameson's epigraph, "... for who can look into the seeds of time / And say which grain will grow and which will not ...," alters the Shakespearean lines slightly, turning Banquo's direct address to the future-seeing witches in Act I, Scene iii into a more general sentiment in the form of a rhetorical question. Jameson begins by lamenting the then-present state of the imagination, after "the end of history," as the triumphalist rhetoric of certain post-Cold War celebrations would characterize things, in which an indistinct but pervasive anxiety concerning the future, or perhaps the lack thereof, comes to characterize the postmodern condition. As Jameson famously puts it, in a line frequently quoted (and sometimes misquoted or misattributed), "It seems to be easier for us today to imagine the thoroughgoing deterioration of the earth and of nature than the breakdown of capitalism; perhaps that is due to some weakness in our imaginations."[26] Jameson goes on to suggest that, under such circumstances, "any attempt to say what postmodernism is can scarcely be separated from the even more problematic attempt to say where it is going [...]. All postmodern theory is thus a telling of the future, with an imperfect deck."[27] In attempting to open a perspective onto a future that cannot be forecast or represented, Jameson enacts a kind of utopian theory as a means of diagnosing the present condition.

The Seeds of Time comprises three chapters, each performing a different set of operations while exploring specific areas of cultural theory and genres, including philosophy, fiction, and architecture. The first chapter, "The Antinomies of Postmodernity," is primarily critical and philosophical, as might be guessed from the Kantian title. In the second chapter, Jameson analyzes Andrei Platonov's modernist utopian novel, *Chevengur*, in which he is able to discover a distinctively Second-World culture less affected by commodity fetishism and more attuned to a visceral utopianism. Finally, in "The Constraints of Postmodernism," Jameson returns to architecture to examine the limits of this particular style or system. As he will make clear, the identification of a limit or boundary itself occasions the meditation of the new situation now modified precisely because of the awareness of this limit, which then gets incorporated into the consciousness of the situation so constituted. That is, even where one comes upon a constraint, the utopian impulse remains. Indeed, as Jameson will argue, utopia is really an attempt to think the limit.

Jameson suggests that the present age is "more propitious for the antinomy than the contradiction," for the latter implies a resolution of the initial opposition.[28] He explores four antinomies of postmodernity or, perhaps better, of contemporary thought and ideology, although he concedes that the list could be extended or even that the antinomies might, in the end, all amount to fundamentally the same thing. These antinomies may be briefly summarized. The first involves a temporal paradox, as postmodern thought simultaneously oscillates between absolute stasis and absolute change, such that the closed system of the end of history is also understood to be a perpetually swirling dynamic of creative destruction. The second invokes a spatial paradox between global homogeneity thanks to a thoroughly commodified world system and a proliferating heterogeneity related to the widespread consumerism of the system. The third antinomy relates to nature, both to the "ecological revival of a sense of Nature" and to the return of theories of "human nature," which somehow coexist with profoundly anti-foundationalist theories much in vogue among postmodern philosophers. Finally, and perhaps ultimately subsuming these others, the fourth antinomy concerns utopia itself, specifically instancing the anti-utopian celebrations of late capitalism that also unleash a sort of utopian discourse that has, if anything, become much more pronounced toward the end of the twentieth century. In staging these antinomies, in showing that they are not simply resolvable or that one side can be scientifically proven over and against its opponent, Jameson is not succumbing to a "self-defeating exercise in futility." Rather, he imagines the antinomial conflict as two quite distinct but overlapping frames of reference, "the Identity of the present confronting the immense unthinkable Difference of an impossible future, these two coexisting like eyeballs that each register a different kind of spectrum."[29]

The discussion of utopia in *The Seeds of Time* is worth lingering on for a moment, for while Jameson has continually invoked the utopian impulse throughout his career he is here explicit in his analysis of the role of utopianism in the present time. Perhaps most remarkable in this discussion is the way in which Jameson disentangles *utopia* from *dystopia*, as he forthrightly points out that the latter is hardly the opposite of the former; that would be *anti-utopia*, which is quite distinct from dystopia. Aside from having different aims and effects, Jameson observes that, formally, the dystopian narrative is driven by plot, whereas "the Utopian text does not really tell a story at all; it describes a mechanism or even a type of machine."[30] The anti-utopianism so widespread after the fall of the Berlin Wall in 1989, which was only partly reducible to anti-communism, nevertheless disclosed a utopian impulse, and Jameson maintains that "the most powerful arguments against Utopia are in reality Utopian ones, expressions of a Utopian impulse *qui s'ignore*."[31] Indeed, as Jameson goes on to show, the "the celebration of late capitalism is obliged to pass by way of the figuration of its opposite number, Utopian discourse, and to use the weapons of its arch adversary in order to glorify itself."[32] The anxieties over utopian discourse may then be understood as symptoms of a still-lingering or perhaps unconscious utopian impulse. In a manner similar to Herbert Marcuse's analysis of the "end of utopia" in the 1960s, and displaying the same kind of knack for highlighting the dialectical reversal, Jameson demonstrates that the pervasive anti-utopianism of the postmodern condition reveals the ultimate dissatisfaction with a system and, therefore, it also signals something like the desire for utopia. As he puts it elsewhere in *The Seeds of Time*, "the vocation of Utopia lies in failure; [...] its epistemological value lies in the walls it allows us to feel around our minds, the invisible limits it gives us to detect by sheerest induction, the miring of our imaginations in the mode of production itself, the mud of the present age in which the winged Utopian shoes stick, imagining that to be the force of gravity itself."[33]

And this returns Jameson to the world system once again, with the "windless closure" of late capitalism[34] and its apparently total permeation of the world's spaces. Jameson asserts that "the thinking of totality itself— the urgent feeling of the presence all around us of some overarching system that we can at least *name*—has the palpable benefit of forcing us to conceive of at least the possibility of other alternate systems, something we can now identify as our old friend Utopian thinking."[35] In this sense, "an outside and an unrepresentable exterior" to this seemingly closed or total system is made visible, or at least imaginable, precisely by critically apprehending or mapping the features of the system itself. In this way, the critique of postmodernity exhibits its own utopian imperative.

The Cultural Turn

"Exploding like so many magnesium flares in a night sky, Fredric Jameson's writings have lit up the shrouded landscape of the postmodern, suddenly transforming its shadows and obscurities into an eerie, refulgent tableau."[36] So begins Perry Anderson's foreword to *The Cultural Turn: Selected Writings on the Postmodern, 1983–1998*, a collection of essays that gathers together several of Jameson's most important previously uncollected pieces on postmodernism and that includes four newer essays which supplement and extend his theories of the postmodern. In form, *The Cultural Turn* offers a survey of Jameson's thinking on the subject, from his groundbreaking "Postmodernism and Consumer Society" (originally presented as a lecture in 1982) to "The Brick and the Balloon" (a rather contemporary essay on architecture and finance capital). Given the roughly chronological ordering of its chapters, the collection can offer some sense of the evolutionary changes to Jameson's critical approach to postmodernism and postmodernity during the period.

The four previously published essays were already well known, although their inclusion in this volume certainly makes sense as well. In addition to "Postmodernism and Consumer Society," *The Cultural Turn* includes "Theories of the Postmodern," which had appeared under different titles in *New German Critique*, as well as in Jameson's *The Ideologies of Theory* (1988) and as the second chapter in *Postmodernism, or, the Cultural Logic of Late Capitalism*. Portions of "Marxism and Postmodernism," originally published in Douglas Kellner's edited collection *Postmodernism / Jameson / Critique*, also appeared in the final section of *Postmodernism*. And "The Antinomies of Postmodernity," of course, had formed the first chapter of *The Seeds of Time*, which perhaps already represented a new phase of Jameson's thinking about postmodernity. The four new essays all respond to aspects of the postmodern phenomena that had either been given short shrift previously or that are being addressed for the first time. Jameson takes up the perversely reignited Hegelianism of Francis Fukuyama and the post-Cold War cheerleaders of globalization in "'End of Art' or 'End of History'?" In "Transformations of the Image in Postmodernity," Jameson examines more closely the distinctive dominance of the visual in postmodernism, which he had discussed in *Signatures of the Visible*, but here he surveys the permutation of "the gaze" in cultural theory from Sartre and Fanon to Foucault and, eventually, to Guy Debord, the society of the spectacle, recent cinema, and the contemporary culture industry. The final two essays, ostensibly critical reviews of recent books, are important and, I think, necessary contributions to Jameson's theory of globalization or late capitalism, for they deal with the mysteries of financial capital and speculation, which perhaps more than any other areas of economic activity have transformed the global political economy in the past 40 years.

In "Culture and Finance Capital," Jameson is able to revise and refine his argument concerning the cultural logic of late capitalism. Where the earlier postmodernism essays and Jameson's cultural theory more generally had relied on Ernest Mandel's astute division of the capitalist mode of production into three historical stages, Jameson now also enlists the theory of "internal stages" of economic cycles from Giovanni Arrighi's *The Long Twentieth Century*. Arrighi argues that financialization is itself such an internal stage, and Jameson recognizes that the contemporary explosion of global finance capital—often operating in its own mysterious sphere without ostensibly being motivated by the desire to "finance" any particular productive or consumptive activities, but existing merely for its own sake (and for its own profit, of course)—marks the present moment as an internal phase of late capitalism. Accordingly, he updates his argument on the logic of late capitalism to include a more explicit look at finance capital. As he puts it,

> Speculation, the withdrawal of profits from home industries, the increasingly feverish search, not so much for new markets (these are also saturated) as for the new kinds of profits available in financial transactions themselves and as such—these are the ways in which capitalism now reacts to and compensates for the closing of its productive moment. Capital itself becomes free-floating. It separates from the "concrete content" of its productive geography. Money becomes in a second sense and to a second degree abstract (it always was abstract in the first and basic sense): as though somehow in the national moment money still had a content—it was cotton money, or wheat money, textile money, railway money and the like. Now, like the butterfly stirring within the chrysalis, it separates itself off from that concrete breeding ground and prepares to take flight.[37]

The postmodern crisis of representation outlined in Jameson's broad, historical discussion of spaces of capital in *Postmodernism* and *The Geopolitical Aesthetic* can now be understood as part of this global system of financial exchange and circulation that seems to lack any permanent or solid landmarks at all.

In some ways, even the discussion of finance capital here, focusing on monetary policy, traditional banking, and stock markets, might appear too simple in the context of twenty-first-century global capitalism, for Arrighi and Jameson for the most part overlook the role of financial derivatives and other "exotic" instruments. As became apparent to all following the 2008 financial crises, such derivatives are the things that have made the worldwide financial system at once so opaque and so interconnected. To put it in terms of Jameson's earlier discussion of cognitive mapping, we might say that, however politically and existentially crippling the vast, unrepresentable world system might have been to the individual subject in the early twentieth century, the conditions are far more complicated today. The global economic crisis in the early twenty-first century has been caused by a thoroughly interconnected system of financial instruments that most people do not know anything about, and even those who do have little idea how systemic the risks are. As I have pointed out elsewhere,[38] a Londoner in Virginia Woolf's day may not have given much thought to the Indian tea and Jamaican sugar production that was required for that quintessentially English ritual of tea-time, but she surely would have known that they existed. Today, a few keystrokes in London or New York or Hong Kong, typed on behalf of corporate entities located, or at least registered, in Mauritius or the Cayman Islands, can affect the value of an entire national currency or determine the short-term health of a whole continent's economy, and few if any of us know which banks, hedge funds, corporations, nations, or individuals are involved. "How does one [even] know about, or demonstrate against, an unlisted, virtual, offshore corporation that operates in an unregulated electronic space using a secret proprietary trading strategy to buy and sell arcane financial instruments?"[39] The existential condition of an individual or collective subject under this phase of late capitalism is thus enveloped in a system one can scarcely even imagine, much less map. But any cognitive mapping of the present configuration must necessarily take into account this awesome network of postnational finance.

From the macro-level of the worldwide, trans- or postnational financial system, Jameson returns to the space of a single urban locale in "The Brick and the Balloon: Architecture, Idealism and Land Speculation," but this essay also attempts to map the thoroughly financialized form of capitalism in postmodernity. Partially a review of Robert Fitch's *The Assassination of New York*—a "badly organized and repetitive book" criticizing the deliberate or negligent destruction of value in New York City by urban planners and real estate speculators, among other factors—Jameson's essay is a meditation on the relationship between architecture, speculation, and urbanism. Focusing simultaneously on the developments of postmodern architecture and the mysteries of such earthy concepts as "ground rent," Jameson discerns in the notion of land speculation a sort of "fictitious capital" that effectively transforms time itself "into a kind of futures market," which in turn discloses "this new colonization of the future as a fundamental tendency in capitalism itself, and the perpetual source of the perpetual recrudescence of finance capital and land speculation."[40] Here, in what had seemed to be an article on architecture and urban decline, Jameson expands his analysis exponentially, bringing both space and time, the geographical and the historical, to bear on the most minutely quotidian and most abstruse philosophical elements of our social existence in an age of globalization. The seemingly impossible project of mapping this condition remains an imperative for dialectical criticism.

Jameson's perspective on this spatiotemporal situation may be limned from another essay written at about this same time. In "Globalization as a Philosophical Issue," originally published in *Cultures of Globalization* in 1998 and reappearing as Chapter 17 of *Valences of the Dialectic*, Jameson summarizes that moment in Hegel's *Science of Logic* when Identity and Difference are discovered to be the same thing, and when what had formerly been viewed as an antinomial opposition turns out to be in actuality a contradiction. From this "dialectical reversal," Jameson concludes:

> This is always the point we want to reach in the dialectic: we want to uncover phenomena and find the ultimate contradictions behind them. And this was Brecht's notion of the dialectic, to hold fast to the contradictions in all things, which make them change and evolve in time. But in Hegel, Contradiction then passes over into its Ground, into what I would call the situation itself; the serial view of the map of the totality in which things happen and History takes place. I like to think that it is something like this movement of the categories—producing each other, and evolving into ever new viewpoints—that Lenin saw and learned in Hegel, in his reading of him during the first weeks and months of World War I. But I would also like to think that these are lessons we can still put to use today, not least in our attempts to grasp

the still ill-defined and ever emerging effects of that phenomenon we have begun to call globalization.[41]

Here it is in the context of Hegel's grand philosophizing in the larger *Logic*, rather than an American writer's peering down from an airplane window, but Jameson's figure of "the map of the totality," now understood to be the "untotalizable totality" that is globalization, remains the key concept of his project of dialectical criticism.

6

The Thing about Modernity

In what might be considered another sort of dialectical reversal or its own ruse of history, Jameson follows up his searching analysis of postmodernism, postmodernity, and globalization by turning his critical attention toward the trenchant problems of modernism and modernity. Perhaps in a variation on Hegel's well-known comment in *The Philosophy of Right* about the Owl of Minerva taking flight at dusk, Jameson recognizes that the concept of modernity, along with its aesthetic sibling modernism, can only be truly apprehended after the fact, from the privileged vantage point afforded by postmodernity. Jameson's return to modernism, *after* postmodernism, as it were, is not entirely reflective or retrospective. As he makes clear in *A Singular Modernity: Essay on the Ontology of the Present* (2002), whose title alone suggests another aspect of the problem, the then-present, millennial moment had witnessed its own "regressions," such that the critique of postmodernity and the celebrations of the post-Cold War geopolitical order, among other things typical of the retrenchments of the 1990s, had resuscitated or given new life to the older modernist philosophies and practices. Hence, at the turn of the century, the question of modernity and modernism, for better or for worse, reemerged and took center stage.

In response to these conditions, Jameson publishes two books, which are quite different in method, scope, and effect, but which also share a fundamental conceptual space in questions of modernism, modernization, and modernity. In *Brecht and Method* (1998), Jameson examines in detail the work of the almost paradigmatically modernist German playwright, theorist, and political activist, although Jameson will also problematize the facility with which one might call Brecht a "modernist." Jameson's most thorough and painstaking critique of the concept of the "modern" is delivered in the aforementioned study, *A Singular Modernity*, which along with its "source-book," *The Modernist Papers* (2007),[1] represents the fifth of Jameson's proposed six-volume project, *The Poetics of Social Forms*. With these books, Jameson investigates what is living and what is dead in the conceptual universe of modernity, arguing for the usefulness of Brecht and the ultimate unhelpfulness of the notion of modernity for making sense of, giving shape to, and certainly attempting to change our world in the twenty-first century.

As might be expected, Jameson's primary interest in these works is not to recreate a historical situation in which the earlier modernisms could incubate and thrive, but to analyze the present situation. Ironically, perhaps, the reemergence of modernist aesthetics, philosophy, and worldviews seems itself to be a rather postmodern phenomenon. As Jameson puts it,

> What purpose can the revival of the slogan "modernity" still serve, after the thoroughgoing removal of the modern from all the shelves and shop windows, its retirement from the media, and the obedient demodernification of all but a few cantankerous and self-avowedly saurian intellectuals? It must somehow be a postmodern thing, one begins to suspect, this recrudescence of the language of an older modernity: for it is certainly not the result of any honest philological and historiographic interest in our recent past. What we have here is rather the reminting of the modern, its repackaging, its production in great quantities for renewed sales in the intellectual marketplace.[2]

The marketing of modernism, or its fundamental commodification, is entirely appropriate for a set of cultural and social phenomena that is itself so intimately related to the emergence of bourgeois social relations, industrialization, and Weberian rationalization. As a "postmodern thing," the resuscitated modernism of the late twentieth century might well be associated with what Georg Lukács had long ago analyzed as *reification*. The "thing about modernity" is, at least in part, that modernity becomes a thing, while also remaining the label attached to a process of *thing*ification in society as a whole. In his analysis of the "modern," Jameson revives the Lukácsean concept for a particularly postmodern condition, and grounds the discourse of modernity in the late-capitalist world system in the age of globalization.

Brecht and Method

In turning to Brecht, Jameson is performing a pedagogical critical act, for he sees Brecht as less a creator of an aesthetic or of a theoretical system or even of an organized political program than a useful methodological precursor. Jameson does not really make the case for Brecht's postmodernity here, as he had for Adorno in *Late Marxism*; rather, he argues strongly for Brecht's *usefulness* to us in our fitful grappling with the permutations and vicissitudes of the postmodern condition.

Brecht and Method is Jameson's fourth book devoted to a single author, and although it differs markedly in some respects from the others, it shares some of the critical themes with them, which are also, after all, lifelong concerns for Jameson's literary theory and practice. For example, just as his first book had been devoted to a study of Sartre's style, *Brecht and Method* pays a great deal of attention to Brecht's style, or, perhaps, to Brecht's diversity of styles. As Jameson astutely observes, Brecht's recognizable "style" is also problematic, since Brechtian theory and practice tends to undermine the very thing that style was to have represented. On the one hand, "there is obviously a Brechtian style, for which the expression 'turn of phrase' (the very sense of tropes, as what are *détourné*, hijacked and misdirected away from ordinary speech) is apt indeed." On the other hand, if style is to be understood as "the mark of a unique subjectivity, like a fingerprint or the sound of a familiar voice," then "Brecht's work can be observed slowly, over the years, to remove all of this, to file it down or absorb it with as few leftover traces as possible."[3] This is itself not even to mention the "Brecht" that is a label for collaborative or collective work, which Jameson views as presenting an alternative vision of style, "as though the individuality we ascribed to some period before history, with its unique qualities and obsessions, had been transcended almost at once into a collaborative subject—one which certainly seemed to have a distinctive style (the one we now call 'Brechtian') but was no longer personal in the bourgeois or individualistic sense."[4] Brecht's style, while recognizably modernist in some respects, eschews the interiority or subjectivity normally associated with modernism.

Furthermore, like *Fables of Aggression* and *Late Marxism*, *Brecht and Method* takes up an untimely writer, one who might be considered somewhat *passé* or neglected, and makes a case for the continuing relevance of his work. Unlike Wyndham Lewis, whose eccentric style and abominable politics probably won him a well-earned obscurity in twentieth-century literature, Brecht is a towering figure in modern literary studies. As Ian Buchanan suggests, however, Brecht's relative obscurity in the 1990s was likely the result of his earlier popularity or centrality in critical debates of the 1960s and 1970s. "If Brecht is dead to us today, it is because we have

Brecht fatigue—his literary star once shone so bright it seared our eyes and left us unable to see where Brecht might be able to take us in the future."[5] But as with Lewis, in Jameson's view, the formal qualities of the Brechtian work of art, particularly in their "estrangements," provided vital lessons for life in modern, capitalist societies and offer clues for making sense of our own postmodern, late capitalist world system. Similarly, the untimely Adorno, who had appeared so out of sync with the revolutionary ideas and generally liberatory vibe of the 1960s, became for Jameson the preeminent philosopher for the postmodern occasion. Although Jameson does not really make the case for Brecht's postmodernity, he emphatically argues for the usefulness of Brecht and Brechtian theory for life at the present historical conjuncture. Hence, Brecht too offers a kind of late Marxism suited to the period of multinational capitalism.

If this is so, part of the reason has to do with Brecht's commitment to "epic" theater, which breaks down the familiar dramatic or theatergoing experience into unfamiliar elements. Among the most influential concepts of Brechtian aesthetic and political theory is surely the *Verfremdungsef-fekt*, the alienation or estrangement effect.[6] Famously, Brecht wished to overturn the traditional function of theater, which from Aristotle's *Poetics* onward was to have served a socially pacifying or cathartic purpose. Estrangement tends to undermine, if not reverse, this aim. Jameson points out that the now familiar translation of the term *Verfremdungsef-fekt* as "alienation effect" is misleading, for the key concept of alienation in Marxism was rendered with a different term (that is, Marx had used the word *Entfremdung*), and "estrangement" is more in keeping with Brecht's conceptual predecessor in Russian Formalism, *ostranenia* or "making strange."[7] In practice, Brecht achieved this estrangement effect in various ways, including the use of captions or subtitles, "third-person" acting and quotations, and shocking disjunctions, such as breaking the fourth wall and addressing the audience as audience. This estrangement is both a response to and a product of the modern social condition, which Jameson refers to as autonomization but which clearly has its own ties to Marx's sense of alienation, Weber's rationalization, Niklas Luhmann's differentiation, and Lukács's reification. In other words, it relates to the fragmentations of social existence under modern capitalism.

Jameson asserts that, in literature and other cultural forms, "[m]odernist autonomization includes within itself the twin contradictory (yet dialectically identical) tendencies of the work toward minimalism on the one hand, and the mega-structure on the other." He contrasts the reduction to silence in Samuel Beckett's drama with the large and incomplete project of Robert Musil's *Man without Qualities*, arguing that both tendencies essentially enact the analytic function of literary production, that is, of breaking things down into constituent parts.[8] But this simultaneously mirrors and reacts to the reification of bourgeois society. As Jameson puts it, "Brecht's adoption of reification as a dramatic and representational 'method' [...] incorporates the spirit of the Leninist admiration for Fordism, while at the same time it seeks more immediately to restore what is truly comprehensible in human action and behavior by making that behavior incomprehensible: a realism achieved by means of Cubism might be an apt description."[9] Where Lukács had worried that such reification in the work of art merely replicated, or worse celebrated, the reification of modern societies, Brecht's position is clearly that of a politically engaged artist for whom the use of reification in art could be perceived as a form of subversion or critique. In Brecht, this becomes another form of *Ideologiekritik* in which the seemingly natural or naturalized aspects of everyday existence are revealed to be historical and social, and therefore contingent and subject to politically transformative action. As Jameson writes,

> What history has solidified into an illusion of stability and substantiality can now be dissolved again, and reconstructed, replaced, improved, "umfunktioniert." The process of aesthetic autonomization, breaking the action up into its smallest parts, thus has symbolic as well as epistemological meaning: it shows what the act "really" is, no doubt, but the very activity of breaking it up and "analyzing" it is itself a joyous process, a kind of creative play, in which the new acts are formed together out of pieces of the old, in which the whole reified surface of a period seemingly beyond history and beyond change now submits to a first ludic un-building, before arriving at a real social and revolutionary reconstruction.[10]

In effectively dramatizing or staging reification, then, Brecht produces that *Verfremdungseffekt* that shocks the viewer or reader into a kind of new wakefulness and, simultaneously, makes him or her aware of precisely what it is that had been slept through. This paradoxical reification "method" thus serves as both a critique of ideology and, one hopes, a form of political activism, as the audience may now be aware, perhaps for the first time, of previously invisible social forces affecting their lives.

This is, of course, also an aim of critical theory. As Jameson mentions at one point, Brecht might even be credited with inventing "theory" itself, at least as that becomes visible in this or that version of French structuralism or poststructuralism, which are not themselves Brechtian, obviously, but which may have been influenced by Brecht more than is usually acknowledged. In any event, Brechtian ideas were fundamental to the intellectual culture of the era, partly through the appropriation and dissemination of Brecht by Roland Barthes.[11] But this is all to say, again, that theory itself, like Brechtian thought, is not some relic of the 1960s but a vital and necessary activity for us in our present world-historical circumstances. Weighing in once more on the question of Brecht's modernity or postmodernity, Jameson concludes *Brecht and Method* by examining Brecht's notion of productivity. Distinguishing the modernist and postmodernist ideologies as analogous to the fetishism of the machine age versus that of the cybernetic or information age, Jameson argues that Brecht's estrangement effect demonstrates a capacity to invest even the disembodied postmodern or cybernetic forms of "work" with a human productivity, revealing the soul in the machine. However, Brecht's modernism, "if that is what is," is not a regression toward the earlier visions of an industrial capitalism, but an awareness of the activity inherent in the form of production, even amid the ideologies of a post-productive era, as both the free-market ideologues and "post-Marxist" critics like Jean Baudrillard have tended to celebrate.[12] In his vibrant, and perhaps proleptic, estrangements of the society of the spectacle, Brecht offers a lesson in the usefulness of criticism itself.

A Singular Modernity

Jameson's curious ambivalence with respect to modernism, or to modernity itself, is noticeable throughout his *oeuvre*. On the one hand, he clearly has some personal affection for many modernist writers, artists, musicians, architects, and filmmakers, and he has devoted a good deal of energy to the study and teaching of modernism; in such books as *Fables of Aggression* and *The Political Unconscious* and in numerous essays and lectures, Jameson has contributed much to the field of modernist studies. On the other hand, he has condemned many of the thematic or conceptual concerns associated with modernism, demonstrating that the heightened interiority or subjectivity in many modernist productions, for example, belied a repressed sense of the social or political. Furthermore, as Jameson's cultural criticism became more explicitly devoted to the problems of postmodernism and postmodernity, he found himself at times on the defensive, which in turn motivated a more polemical approach to those critics who claimed to stand for a modern or modernist sensibility over and against these postmodernist barbarians at the gate. By the end of the century, the backlash against all things associated with the postmodern, including such unrelated matters as critical theory itself, had made it possible for a certain kind of modernism or modern thought to reassert itself. Partly in response to what he considered the "regressions of the current age," Jameson's first book of the new millennium, *A Singular Modernity*, was a book-length "essay on the ontology of the present."

The "regressions" to which Jameson's project alludes during what Phillip E. Wegner has called "the long Nineties"[13] correspond to a post-Cold War political and cultural moment in the West, or in the United States at least, in which many of the concepts and forms that were thought to have been mercifully consigned to the ashbins of history had not only reemerged but were finding new and enthusiastic proponents. After critical theory had supposedly disposed of such dubious practices within modern philosophy as ethics, aesthetics, traditional political philosophy based on the autonomous individual subject, as well as economic liberalism of the quasi-religious, free-market variety, and the old "grand narratives" of history, all of these things seemed to have come back with a vengeance in the 1990s. Of course, it is only a certain kind of modernity that is valued in this new dispensation, for the neoliberal and neo-rationalist ideologues of this modernity are not interested in celebrating many of the features of what had previously been recognized as paradigmatically modern, such as actually existing socialism. In distinguishing their modernity, "the information age, and globalized free-market modernity," from the "detestable older kind," such apologists had recourse to the idea of alternate modernities, which allowed them to selectively include whatever "modern" elements are desirable, while dismissing those that are not. Jameson's title alone indicates his position on the matter.

The pun in Jameson's title (that is, the implication that modernity is "singular" in a sense of being peculiar or unique) has to do with another polemical point in his argument: namely, that there are not multiple or alternative modernities. Jameson is here responding to those who would embrace the notion of competing modernisms or modernities—for example, Latin-American, African, or Chinese modernities, which come into being autonomously and at different times than the Western modernity of Europe or the United States—thus preserving, and even celebrating, certain aspects of the "modern" while selectively dismissing undesirable features of "Western" modernity, such as the colonization and subjugation of other places and populations, along with all that attends such practices of modernization. Jameson has acknowledged that his own position on this matter was costly, since it caused many of his former friends to reject his argument and, perhaps, even to doubt his goodwill; he nevertheless remains firm in his conviction that modernity must be understood as a singular system. As he lamented in the introduction to *Jameson on Jameson: Conversations on Cultural Marxism*, "I'm sorry to say that after the publication of *A Singular Modernity*, in which the very concept of 'alternate modernities' was dismissed, my Chinese and Brazilian readers seem to have parted company with me, accusing me of being yet another Western or first world theorist preaching to the rest of the world and seeking to impose Western theories on it." However, since Jameson is resolute in affirming that modernity must be associated with capitalism itself, he maintains that "the only possible 'alternate modernity' open to us today is socialism, and that merely cultural versions of these forms of difference are not very helpful."[14] Or, as Jameson puts it in *A Singular Modernity*, "The standardization projected by capitalist globalization in this third or late stage of the system casts considerable doubt on all these pious hopes for cultural variety in a future world colonized by a universal market order."[15] To put it another way, the very processes of a singular modernity, including reification, rationalization, and the spread of capitalist markets, preclude the realization of meaningful alternatives.

Jameson's ambivalence toward modernity and modernism is on display in his preface, where he announces that, although he maintains that any understanding of modernity outside of its integral connection to capitalism will remain unsatisfactory, *A Singular Modernity* will be "a formal analysis of the uses of the word 'modernity' that explicitly rejects any presupposition that there is a correct use of the word to be discovered, conceptualized, and proposed." The same holds for modernism, "a related concept in the aesthetic sphere," and perhaps also for that notion of "late modernism" that is not to be confused any longer with postmodernism. "The project is therefore one of the ideological analysis, not so much of a concept, as of a word. What is constitutively frustrating about such analysis is that, like the pane of glass at which you try to gaze even as you are looking through it, you must simultaneously affirm the existence of the object while denying the relevance of the term that designates that existence." A tricky problem for this investigation, then, is that "the notions that cluster around the word 'modern' are as unavoidable as they are unacceptable."[16]

The first part of *A Singular Modernity* is a theoretical investigation of modernity itself, and Jameson sets out to formulate and characterize what he calls "the four maxims of modernity," which I cannot help feeling have more than a little family resemblance to the antinomies of postmodernity Jameson had explored in *The Seeds of Time*. The first maxim, which already demonstrates the unavoidability of the underlying concept, is "we cannot periodize."[17] What Jameson means by this, in part, is that "the present cannot feel itself to be a historical period in its own right without this gaze from the future, which seals it off and expels it as powerfully from time to come as it was able to do with its own immediate precedents."[18] Jameson explores this by examining "the dialectic of the break and the period," which may be seen to stand also for that of rupture and continuity or of difference and identity. Periodization, along with identifying temporal ruptures that could mark the beginnings or ends of a particular period, is an attempt to provide a meaningful historical narrative out of some Heraclitean flux of unrelated events (or, as Henry Ford called them, "one goddamned thing after another").[19] By repudiating periodization, Jameson alters the landscape of what had been a crucial, defining feature of the concept of modernity.

Jameson's second maxim, fittingly, is that "[m]odernity is not a concept, philosophical or otherwise, but a narrative category."[20] That is, modernity cannot be defined in and of itself, but only through what has been written about it. Modernity then, in a paradoxically postmodern manner of speaking, can only be characterized according to the many competing narratives in which it can be found to have been disclosed. As Jameson puts it, modernity can be considered a sort of self-referential trope, "since its appearance signals the emergence of a new kind of figure, a decisive break with previous forms of figurality, and is to that extent a sign of its own existence, a signifier that indicates itself, and whose form is its very content."[21] The *modern*, then, is largely a matter of the word's uses in historical texts, so any investigation of what had formerly been imagined as a concept must now proceed as a reading of the narratives and instances in which the trope or category can be found.

Focusing on the historical narratives in which modernity appears, Jameson comes to his third maxim: "The narrative of modernity cannot be organized around categories of subjectivity (consciousness and subjectivity are unrepresentable)."[22] This is, of course, a provocation, since modernity or modernism had likely been characterized preeminently with reference to subjectivity or consciousness, especially in literature. Jameson here acknowledges some debt to the anti-humanism associated with the theory of the 1960s, particularly that intellectual movement related to the "linguistic turn" and the poststructuralist critique of the subject in such philosophers as Heidegger, Althusser, Foucault, and Derrida (all of whom appear rather prominently in these pages, by the way). But Jameson also points out that this maxim is not to be understood as an ontological statement, but merely as a representational caveat; that is, he is not denying the existence of subjectivity, only that it can be represented. And, therefore, the specious evidence of any actual representation of consciousness ignores the fundamentally figurative nature of all such representations, which as Nietzsche long ago warned merely amount to a "mobile army of metaphors, metonyms, and anthropomorphisms."[23] Jameson then notes that the death of the subject does not mean that "we cannot tell the narrative of modernity at all," for the situation itself— as I have noted several times in this study, the Sartrean notion is never very far from Jameson's thinking—can reveal much and more of what the unreliable form of consciousness had seemed to be able to do. Thus, Jameson amends his third maxim, adding the clause, "only situations of modernity can be narrated."[24]

This, in turn, leads to Jameson's fourth and final maxim for the *bon usage* of the term *modernity*: "No 'theory' of modernity makes sense today unless it is able to come to terms with the hypothesis of a postmodern break with the modern."[25] This requirement does not also necessitate a full-blown theory of postmodernity, but it does emphasize the need for some reckoning of the situation of postmodernity. In this section, Jameson is specifically criticizing the theories of Luhmann, who ultimately reveals himself as "another ideologist of the modern as such," for Luhmann is unable to imagine, not only an alternative to the modern capitalist system itself, but also the permutations of modern capitalism in the form of globalization that render the earlier models unsatisfactory at best. Not surprisingly, Jameson maintains that the only way to adequately conceptualize or represent the modern is to do so from the vantage of our own postmodern situation.

At this point, after formulating the prolegomena to any further discussion of modernity, Jameson is ready to turn to artistic modernism. In a transitional section that bridges Parts I and II of *A Singular Modernity*,

Jameson explores some of the problems specific to aesthetic modernism, including those that reintroduce the temptations that the four maxims had been developed to thwart. In Part II, "Modernism as Ideology," Jameson takes up the earlier forms of modernism and examines their ideological functions.[26] In so doing, he allows himself a slight reprieve and periodizes the modernist trajectory from classical or high modernism to what he terms late modernism. Although Jameson does not fall into the potential traps of moralism and partisanship, he does recognize that the disruption of classical modernism by World War I left the aesthetic project of modernism incomplete, and the inevitably dystopian postwar scene helped to drain from modernism those politically progressive or utopian elements that now seemed to many either romantic or stupid. High modernism, it seems, reverted to an intensely aestheticized form, which contributed to the development of both tastes and institutions (such as a literary canon, for example) suited to that temperament. But ultimately the quest for a purely autonomous aesthetic realm founders upon the very contingencies of the artistic forms. "This is, however, a fortunate failure: for the replacement of the varied and incomprehensible Absolutes of modernism by the far more modest and comprehensible aesthetic autonomies of the late modern not only opens up the space and possibility for […] the ideology of modernism, it also enables and authorizes the production of a far more accessible literature of what can then be called a middlebrow type."[27] As Jameson concludes, the development of this late modernist aesthetic in the 1940s and 1950s creates something like a class of readers who, in drawing upon a "canon" that is presented as timeless but is itself a relic of late modernism, come to define modern culture itself. And "it is with this late modernism that postmodernism attempts radically to break, imagining that it is thereby breaking with classical modernism, or even modernity, in general and as such."[28]

The Modernist Papers

Jameson's theoretical or philosophical argument about modernity and modernism is elaborated in some detail in *A Singular Modernity*, but notably absent from that study is anything like a "reading" of a particular modernist work of art, artist, or text. *The Modernist Papers*, published six years later, rectifies this situation by supplementing the earlier book's argument with 20 essays, most of which involve interpretation and analysis of specific modernist authors or texts. A number of the essays included in *The Modernist Papers* had been previously published, but many others—some of them based on public presentations or lectures—appear in print for the first time. Taken together, the essays in *The Modernist Papers* provide a picture of Jameson's wide-ranging, but astonishingly consistent approach to modernism, as well as to narrative, form, and history. Read alongside *A Singular Modernity*, these essays demonstrate aspects of Jameson's theory while also grounding his ideas in discrete situations of reading, such that Ezra Pound, Thomas Mann, Franz Kafka, Arthur Rimbaud, James Joyce, and many others take their places in the Jamesonian critical terrain alongside such figures as Adorno, Sartre, Lukács, Barthes, and Brecht, not to mention Hegel and Marx. Jameson writes that the analyses in the essays were "meant to accompany my *A Singular Modernity* as a kind of source book."[29]

The diversity of content in *The Modernist Papers* also ensures that the readings are for the most part allowed to stand on their own, rather than to be viewed as segments of a coherent project related to the rethinking of modernity, modernism, or the modern. The essays included in *The Modernist Papers*, written over an extended period and for various occasions, all have their own individual merits, and as Jameson concedes, "This makes for a great deal of heterogeneity, both in the literary texts examined [...] and in the variety of theoretical contexts tried out over a thirty-year period."[30] Jameson's introduction provides a thoughtful reflection upon the problematic that might be said to unify these materials, apart from (but perhaps related to) the more obvious fact that all of the "primary" texts, writers, or artists under consideration would generally be labeled *modernist*. The problematic in question is the old binary opposition between form and content, a binary that Jameson grudgingly wishes to maintain even as he does his utmost to make trouble for any facile distinction between the two. In exploring the form/content interaction, Jameson also lays bare a key aspect of the modernist aesthetic and its moment.

Borrowing a crude version of Louis Hjelmslev's linguistic model, Jameson proposes to multiply the binary opposition to make four categories: the form of the form, the content of the content, the form of the content, and the content of the form. Jameson notes that, as a practical matter, "each of these combinations or perspectives will project a type of literary criticism that has its own validity as well as its own internal limitations," and that each type of criticism could thereby fall into its own prescriptive aesthetic program for writers to scrupulously follow, something Jameson wants no part of. "We cannot do without projections of the future in practical political life, but we do not have to prognosticate the future of art, something art always does for itself."[31] Jameson introduces the first three of these, partly, it seems, in order to move on to the fourth, the content of the form.[32] In his view, "the content of the form" constitutes "the only productive coordination of the opposition between form and content that does not seek to reduce one term to the other, or to posit illicit syntheses and equally illicit volatilizations of an opposition whose tensions need to be preserved at the same time that we become aware of how philosophically incompatible each of these terms is with respect to the other one."[33] For any discussion of modernism—the mode in which a supposedly pure formalism attempted to overwhelm if not eradicate content—this approach to the work of art proves especially fruitful, as we have seen in Jameson's dialectical criticism.

The overcoming of the form-versus-content argument in the context of modernism invites us to revisit what is perhaps the most notorious dispute among radical theorists over literary form and content in the twentieth century. I refer to the so-called Brecht–Lukács debate, in which the modernist experimental methods and techniques used or championed by Brecht were condemned by Lukács as retrogressive capitulations to bourgeois capitalist society. Lukács's commitment to a much earlier form of realism, such as that seen in Balzac's *La Comédie humaine*, seemed both old-fashioned and politically suspect, particularly in the 1930s when Lukács appeared to toe the Party line when it came to social realism. But the strictly formal innovations of the modernist position—which, it should be noted, was never entirely Brecht's or Lukács's view of things— also expressed a political content, which made the opposition much more complicated and interesting. Brechtian estrangement and Lukácsean representation may not, in the end, have been quite so aesthetically or politically distant from one another.

As Jameson summed it up in an essay written in the 1970s, "there is some question whether the ultimate renewal of modernism, the final dialectical subversion of the now automatized conventions of an aesthetics of perceptual revolution, might not simply be ... realism itself! For when modernism and its accompanying techniques of 'estrangement' have become the dominant style whereby the consumer is reconciled with capitalism, the habit of fragmentation itself needs to be 'estranged' and corrected by a more totalizing way of viewing phenomena."[34] Jameson finds that this new realism would derive its force from the theoretical practice of Lukács, perhaps more than from Brecht, but this would be not so much from Lukács's anti-modernist defense of realism in the 1930s as from the Lukács of *History and Class Consciousness* (1922), whose principal concerns were reification and totality. From Jameson's perspective, this renewed attention to reification would help to elevate our current thinking out of the unhelpful discourse of modernism and modernity or of the seemingly insoluble realism-versus-modernism dilemma. As Jameson elaborates,

> Unlike the more familiar concept of alienation, a process that pertains to activity and particularly to work (dissociating workers from their labor, their product, their fellow workers, and ultimately from their very "species being" itself), reification is a process that affects our cognitive relationship with the social totality. It is a disease of the mapping function whereby the individual subject projects and models his or her insertion into the collectivity. The reification of late capitalism—the transformation of human relations into an appearance of relationships between things—renders society opaque: it is the lived source of the mystifications on which ideology is based and by which domination and exploitation are legitimized. Since the fundamental structure of the social "totality" is a set of class relationships [...] reification necessarily obscures the class character of that structure, and is accompanied, not only by anomie, but also by that increasing confusion as to the nature and even the existence of social classes which can be abundantly observed in all the "advanced" capitalist countries today. If the diagnosis is correct, the intensification of class consciousness will be less a matter of a populist or ouvrierist exaltation of a single class by itself, than of the forcible reopening of access to a sense of society as a totality, and of the reinvention of the possibilities of cognition and perception that allow social phenomena once again to become transparent, as moments of the struggle *between* classes.[35]

In this vision, which clearly prefigures the concept of cognitive mapping, Jameson's call for a "new realism" would not involve any return to some simpler epoch of industrial capitalism, such as the era of Balzac or Stendhal, but would incorporate the best of what modernism had to offer—namely, for Jameson, "the violent renewal of perception in a world in

which experience has solidified into a mass of habits and automatisms"—
without sliding into the now-debased and outdated conventions of a
modernist aesthetic.[36] This relaunched Lukácsean realism, adapted for
the postmodern condition of late capitalism, would thus be an attempt to
map the spaces of the world system with a view to discovering alternative
spaces within or beyond it.

7

Other Spaces Are Possible

The conclusion to *The Political Unconscious* is titled "The Dialectic of Utopia and Ideology," and one could reasonably argue that Jameson's entire career as a literary critic and professor has been devoted to demonstrating the multifarious ways in which this dialectic plays itself out in literary and cultural texts, over and over again, and in ever more interesting permutations. The polemical edge to this demonstration can be discerned in its sometimes tacit opposition to the ultimately moralizing arguments of this or that school of criticism, which would hold that certain texts must be viewed as wholly good or bad, more with respect to a given political program than as a matter of aesthetic appeal (although the two can enfold each other, obviously). Jameson's consistently made point is that, even among fellow-travelers on the left, Walter Benjamin's famous, inextricable linkage between documents of civilization and those of barbarism must be faced with sober senses as the omnipresent challenge of any cultural criticism that hopes to have an effect on the world. As Jameson puts it in the closing lines of *The Political Unconscious*, "It is only at this price— that of the simultaneous recognition of the ideological and the Utopian functions of the artistic text—that a Marxist cultural study can hope to play its part in political praxis, which remains, of course, what Marxism is all about."[1]

Jameson's own utopianism, which of course must be understood as part and parcel of his flexible and nuanced form of ideology critique, has sometimes distinguished him from other Marxist critics, as well as from various types of theorist in the era of poststructuralism's pervasive influence on literary and cultural studies. Throughout his career, Jameson had been one of the leading proponents of, or apologists for, expressly utopian thinking, and the concept of utopia remains a more or less visible presence in all of his work. Jameson has championed a sort of utopian thought—one that draws heavily upon a Frankfurt School tradition (perhaps most closely associated, in different ways, with Ernst Bloch and Herbert Marcuse)— while constantly updating and refining his utopianism in order to reveal its relevance, even necessity, for critical theory in the current situation. Jameson has found the need to defend utopian discourse against the anti-Marxist strains of political and cultural criticism that would dismiss Marxism and the theoretical practices built upon it *as* utopian—which they take to mean idealist, unrealistic, escapist, or worse, totalitarian. But Jameson has had to work harder to retrieve the revolutionary significance of utopian discourse from an anti-utopian tradition within Marxism, that is, among Marxists who consider utopianism to be a romantic or unscientific disavowal of the practical struggles of the day—a view traceable to Marx and Engels in *The Communist Manifesto*, among other places.

However, as Jameson has put it, "Not the least unexpected thing about the 1960s was its reinvention of the question of Utopia."[2] Amid a dominant and widespread anti-utopianism, particularly in the United States in the twentieth century, Marcuse and other thinkers found in the utopian impulse a source of resistance. Referring specifically to Marcuse's social theory, Jameson has disclosed how the older Marxist antipathy for utopian discourse undergoes a dialectical reversal in an era in which class struggle has disappeared, advertising and mass culture delimit the horizon of cultural expression, and rebellion and revolt have become marketable commodities in their own right. As Jameson explained in *Marxism and Form*,

> Under these conditions, the task of the philosopher is the revival of the very idea of negation which has all but been extinguished under the universal subservience to what is; which, along with the concepts of nature and of freedom, has been repressed and driven underground by the reality principle. This task Marcuse formulates as the revival of the Utopian impulse. For where in the older society (as in Marx's classic analysis) Utopian thought represented a diversion of revolutionary energy into idle wish-fulfillments and imaginary satisfactions, in our own time the very nature of the Utopian concept has undergone a dialectical reversal. Now it is practical thinking which everywhere represents a capitulation to the system itself, and stands as a testimony to the power of that system to transform even its adversaries into its own mirror image. The Utopian idea, on the contrary, keeps alive the possibility of a world qualitatively distinct from this one and takes the form of a stubborn negation of all that is.[3]

For Marcuse, the aesthetic sphere offered the greatest opportunity for a utopian rejection of the actual and an exploration of the radical alternatives. This aspect of utopian thought, the revolutionary potential for imagining and creating alternatives to "what is," remains an energizing force in Jameson's theory of literature and culture.

Subsequent to his meditations on the discourse of modernity and the practices associated with modernism, which in the end he takes to be unpromising or failed paths for critical inquiry into the social dynamics of the present world-historical condition, Jameson turns his attention to the future and produces his most thorough and meticulous consideration of utopia to date. *Archaeologies of the Future: The Desire Called Utopia and Other Science Fictions* (2005) performs many different operations at once. It is a sequel to *A Singular Modernity* (and, perhaps, to its "source-book," *The Modernist Papers*), although it may be better to think of them as different parts of the same overall project; we now know that *Archaeologies* is the sixth and final volume in *The Poetics of Social Forms*, Jameson's still unfinished project that includes *Postmodernism, or, the Cultural Logic of Late Capitalism* (as Volume 4), *A Singular Modernity* (Volume 5), and *The Antinomies of Realism* (Volume 3), with two future works devoted to allegory and myth, respectively, yet to come. Additionally, *Archaeologies of the Future* is Jameson's critical analysis of, but also a loving tribute to, the genre or generic mode of science fiction, and the second part of the book reprints many of Jameson's most important essays on individual authors, texts, and themes in science fiction. Above all, *Archaeologies of the Future* presents Jameson's theory of utopia itself, as a literary genre, a political project, and a more diffuse impulse or desire oriented toward an unrepresentable future. At the same time, this study represents a continuation of Jameson's lifelong project and an apparently terminal landmark, albeit one that looks outward beyond the limit it demarcates, thus amounting to a summation or taking stock of the desire called utopia in the twenty-first century.

The texts published shortly after *Archaeologies of the Future* may also reflect a kind of shift in attention for Jameson, as the publication of the final volume in *The Poetics of Social Forms* marks some sort of closure, even if that project remains unfinished. Arguably, the two books that follow *Archaeologies* chronologically, *The Modernist Papers* (2007) and *The Ideologies of Theory* (2008), might be considered as a form of housekeeping; in them, Jameson reprints or publishes for the first time various essays or occasional writings produced over a span of nearly 40 years. As I discussed in Chapter 6, the former functions as a kind of "source-book" for *A Singular Modernity*, supplementing its theoretical arguments with more concrete readings of various texts, such that together *A Singular Modernity* and *The Modernist Papers* are effectively analogous to the two parts of *Archaeologies of the Future*. *The Ideologies of Theory* is an expansion of the 1988 two-volume edition, reprinting all but one of its essays but adding 13 additional essays published during the interim. And yet, the republication also serves to demonstrate the persistence of the key term, *ideology*, in this ironic, post-ideological age, while also revealing the lasting significance of dialectical criticism and theory in the larger project of making sense of the present cultural configuration. To that end, Jameson's next book, *Valences of the Dialectic* (2009), might be viewed as a crowning achievement, the copestone of the Jamesonian critical edifice, or, perhaps, a sort of *Summa Dialectica*. Like these other books, *Valences of the Dialectic* contains many essays published over the previous decades, but it also presents new material in which Jameson provides some of his most interesting and innovative thinking on the dialectic, including what turns out to be a nearly book-length study of Paul Ricoeur's *Time and Narrative*, now situated in a more properly Marxist context. Together, in their paradoxical combination of apparently conclusive summation and probing, innovative exploration, these volumes register a sort of limit or boundary, if not of Jameson's own career—thankfully, there is much more to come on that front—then of a certain perspective on the project of dialectical criticism itself, where the critic's power extends, to borrow the title of Part II of *Archaeologies of the Future*, "as far as thought can reach."

Archaeologies of the Future

In the closing lines of *A Singular Modernity*, Jameson writes that the *modern* is no longer a useful category for understanding our present, postmodern condition, and that it certainly will be of little use in helping us to change that condition. As Jameson puts it, "Radical alternatives, systematic trans-formations, cannot be theorized or even imagined within the conceptual field governed by the word 'modern.' [...] What we really need is a wholesale displacement of the thematics of modernity by the desire called Utopia. We need to combine a Poundian mission to identify Utopian tendencies with a Benjaminian geography of their sources and a gauging of their pressure at what are now multiple sea levels. Ontologies of the present demand archaeologies of the future, not forecasts of the past."⁴ In *Archaeologies of the Future*, Jameson takes up this challenge by examining the form of the utopian project and exploring the utopian impulse.

Focusing in particular on the genre or mode of science fiction, of which (following Darko Suvin) he takes utopia to be the "socio-economic subset,"⁵ Jameson connects the study of a literary form with his broader social and cultural analyses of the postmodern condition. Characteristically, close reading combines with grand philosophical explorations to provide a sweeping overview while displaying Jameson's patient attention to textual detail. As in his earlier writings, he performs a thoroughgoing formal analysis, which, by the gymnastic maneuvers of dialectical criticism turns out also to be an analysis of the political content of the literary and social text. Here Jameson carefully surveys a terrain, both imaginary and real, in which the desire called utopia is itself a sort of cognitive mapping of the alienated (and alien) social space of our time. As in so much of his work, the content and the form overlap, sometimes collapsing into one another, which can present new difficulties. Jameson acknowledges the political problems and the structural ambiguities associated with utopia. Defenders of utopia must confront a fundamental dilemma presented by the utopian text, which at first seems to provide imaginary solutions to real problems only to later become marginal to the whole system in which such problems are generated. As Jameson asks, for example, how can a text that aims to resolve all political differences be political anymore? Can the utopian text really be critical or subversive at this point? These questions are implicit in any attempt to elaborate a poetics of social forms that would mobilize the utopian impulse.

Following Marcuse, Jameson agrees that the separation of the aesthetic sphere, of art and culture, along with the spatiotemporal separation of utopia itself, from the more viscerally experienced territory of social practice in the "real world" leads to an ambiguity that can become politically crippling:

> that very distance of culture from its social context which allows it to function as a critique and indictment of the latter also dooms its interventions to ineffectuality and relegates art and culture to a frivolous, trivialized space in which such intersections are neutralized in advance. This dialectic accounts even more persuasively for the ambivalences of the Utopian text as well: for the more surely a given Utopia asserts its

radical difference from what currently is, to that very degree it becomes, not merely unrealizable but, what is worse, unimaginable.[6]

This is the inevitable danger of utopian discourse, one that is deeply embedded within its very structure. But the utopian dilemma that we face in the era of globalization is how to present radical alternatives to a system that is by its nature all-consuming, total, and global, colonizing not only the spaces of the planet but also its disparate temporalities. Radical alternatives to this system seem unquestionably "utopian" in all those negative senses in which the word had been used, to refer to projects or desires that are fantastic or unrealistic, romantic, idealistic, escapist, and the like. Still, as Jameson notes, the anti-utopians, whether consciously acting in concert with a repressive political program or, far more often, unconsciously operating in ignorance of the ideological effectiveness of such thinking, have invariably produced arguments that result in the reinforcement of the present system, effectively bolstering it against even the idea of alternatives, to the point at which the *actual* effectively becomes identical to the *possible*, and all are therefore forced to capitulate to the tyranny of "what is." In Jameson's view, such anti-utopian thinking is far more totalitarian than the utopian thought it ostensibly opposes. If the starry-eyed utopians, such as those Marx and Engels criticize in *The Communist Manifesto*, along with those who deliver such ambivalent and ambiguous texts of cognitive estrangement, are themselves not much better—a point Jameson is not at all willing to concede, by the way—then at least they are not shutting down in advance the power of the imagination itself. Jameson argues that, in the face of critics with questionable motivations and a form that is structurally unreliable, "fellow travelers of Utopia" might find a slogan of *anti-anti-Utopianism* to be the most useful working strategy.[7]

Yet, paradoxically, utopia seems to recover its sacred vocation at precisely the moment when, so the saying now goes, it seems easier to imagine the end of the world than to imagine an end of capitalism. The traditional critiques of utopian thinking or of utopian projects often centered on their inability to account for agency or their lack of a coherent picture of historical change. But these problems have only been exacerbated in our era, with both agency and historical transformation called into question by globalization in all of its totalizing force, which after the fall of "actually existing" socialism and other visible alternatives to capitalism would appear to limit in advance any utopian projections of a radically alternative future social formation. A characteristic element of the postmodern condition, it seems, is the uncertainty associated with one's position within a complex skein of social relations that has become so vast as to be nearly unimaginable. If the modern world proved difficult to map, how much more so is our own postmodern world, in which the very sources of power are now entirely disembodied, circulating around the planet via fiber-optic cables and computerized data transmissions. Even the one-dimensional society of Marcuse's era has given way to a frighteningly multi-dimensional world system that nevertheless seems as total and inescapable as any Weberian iron cage or Foucauldian panopticon. Hence, perhaps, the general disdain toward a utopianism in the pragmatist or "realistic" political theory of the day.

Although utopia, as both a literary genre and a mode of thinking, reemerged powerfully in the late nineteenth and early twentieth centuries, as witnessed in such different classics as Edward Bellamy's *Looking Backward, 2000–1887* and William Morris's *News from Nowhere*, in the years following World War I and throughout most of the twentieth century, *utopia* assumed once again an essentially pejorative meaning. Any earnest attempts to imagine a utopian society were thought to be deluded or fanciful, unrealistic at best, or else they inevitably led to nightmarish, dystopian ends. Indeed, as the utopian theorist Lyman Tower Sargent has observed, "dystopia became the dominant form of the twentieth century";[8] although, as I discussed in Chapter 5, Jameson himself argued in *The Seeds of Time* that, appearances notwithstanding, dystopia really has nothing to do with utopia, and the two are not even related by opposition, since the opposite of utopia is not dystopia, but anti-utopia. But the dystopian sentiment that appears to be so pervasive in the twentieth and now twenty-first centuries presents a challenge to any utopian form or project. In Jameson's view, this has a lot to do with "the nature of current or infrastructural organization, itself significantly modified since the onset of third-stage or neoliberal capitalism, whose content seems itself to bifurcate between faceless conspiracies on the one hand (rather than the great dictators of yesteryear) and the cyberspace of business innovation and its commodification of consumption."[9]

But it is precisely in such a world that utopian discourse is best suited to intervene. In his earlier work on postmodernism, Jameson suggested that cognitive mapping functioned as a way to understand one's position in, and as an attempt to imagine the shape of, an increasingly unrepresentable system. In the modern, and even more so in the postmodern world system, the reality of one's lived experience no longer coincides with the spatiotemporal coordinates of one's life. The existential crisis, which is also the political and aesthetic crisis, relates to the transcendental homelessness of this condition, but now emphasized in terms of a real-world problem: the individual subject's relationship to a totality of social relations now on a global scale. If, to use the urban analogy Jameson borrowed from Kevin Lynch, the individual has difficulty orienting himself or herself within a large city, how much more alienating must it be to attempt to map one's position within a national or international network of relations? *Cognitive mapping*, as Ian Buchanan has transcoded it, is another way of saying *ontology of the present*, and the utopian impulse and program therefore take their necessary positions among those archaeologies of the future that are, as must by now be clear, the dialectical counterpart to any meaningful mapping project.[10] As I have argued, utopias—by positing imaginary solutions to real problems, or by using fantasy to negate the actually existing state of affairs—project an image of a world that can be used to apprehend the totality, if only figuratively; and if such an image may not be of the "real world," or even of a plausible future world, this figural representation illustrates how the imagination conditions reality, how it makes sense of this reality and gives form to it, in ways that may be helpful at the most experiential level.[11] From that point of departure, the dimly descried or implicit alternatives to "what is" are not only imaginable in some sense, but are made to appear almost inevitable, even if we cannot quite delineate the contours of this utopian vision. As Jameson would have it, under these circumstances, it may be that all dialectical thinking, in one way or another, is somehow utopian.

Jameson concludes his long essay on "The Desire Called Utopia," Part I of *Archaeologies of the Future*, by observing that the means by which utopia is able to combine its formal and political projects are to be found in the utopian form's fundamental insistence on radical alterity. This is what Marcuse had referred to as "the scandal of qualitative difference," the imagination of a totally distinct new form of living, as opposed to the merely quantitative tinkering with this or that social problem; for example, Marcuse contrasts the mere satisfaction of well-known needs (like food, clothing, shelter) with the more properly utopian invention of new needs to be even more satisfactorily fulfilled (such as the need for beauty, peace, or solitude).[12] The blueprint depicting what such a utopian social condition would look like is itself not really possible, or perhaps even desirable, since the radical alterity of such a condition ought to require new forms of humanity to be conceived. For Jameson, the fact that the utopian form exists at all reinforces the principle of a radical break. It does so "by forcing us to think the break itself, and not by offering a more traditional picture of what things would be like after the break."[13] Utopia's formal flaw of being unable to articulate the break in terms of a practical, political transformation turns out to be a strength, allowing us "to concentrate on the break itself: a mediation on the impossible, on the unrealizable in its own right,"[14] thus preparing us for a stage yet to come. A radical alternative proposed by utopia is the utopian impulse itself, which may not only persist, but find its true home, in the age of globalization, in which so many fixed points and stable structures from an earlier *Weltanschauung* have evanesced. As in Marcuse's ironic dialectical reversal, far from occasioning an end of utopia, the postmodern condition, characterized principally by the fact of globalization and the extension of capitalism to the farthest reaches of the planetary space, may well, in Jameson's view, have engendered a renewed potential for the utopian impulse.

The dismal situation of individual and collective existence in the present political and economic situation—with the roll-back of earlier gains in unionization and the social safety net, the deregulation of industry, the disappearance or discreditation of actually or formerly existing socialisms, the environmental disasters and dire outlook with respect to climate change, the rise of ever more frightening variants of free-market and religious ideologies, the well-nigh necromantic alchemy of global finance capital, and so on—has, perhaps ironically, created a space in which the utopian impulse finds its most compelling vocation. Referring to the sense of political impasse in late capitalism, Jameson observes:

> What is crippling is not the presence of an enemy but rather the universal belief, not only that this tendency is irreversible, but that the historic alternatives to capitalism have been proven unviable and impossible, and that no other socioeconomic system is conceivable, let alone practically available. The Utopians not only offer to conceive of such alternative systems; Utopian form is itself a representational meditation on radical difference, radical otherness, and on the systemic nature of the social totality, to the point where one cannot imagine any fundamental change in our social existence which has not first thrown off Utopian visions like so many sparks from a comet.[15]

In Jameson's stubbornly resilient utopianism, the Marxist project of not only interpreting the world, but changing it, discloses itself in the form of a meticulous meditation on the impossible.

In the final essay of Part II of *Archaeologies*, Jameson concludes with his original point that "utopia as a form is not the representation of radical alternatives; it is rather the imperative to imagine them."[16] This "imperative to imagine" may go by a variety of names, of course, but one of them is surely *theory* itself. After all, theory is inherently speculative, from its etymological basis in contemplation or "looking at" (the Greek *theorein*), and the work of theory is fundamentally projective. In Jameson's dialectical theory, the projection moves always in two directions at once—into the past (history) and into the future (utopia)—and in somehow mediating between these poles consists the joyful labors of the critic. The phrase "archaeologies of the future" suggests this dual movement of the dialectic, and Jameson's excavation of the present cultural situation offers evidence of those traces of the future in our own time.

The Ideologies of Theory Redux

The publication of a new, expanded edition of *The Ideologies of Theory* in 2008 is a curious event in the historical narrative of Jameson's own career. As a practical matter, the republication of the two-volume 1988 edition in a single volume already provides a service to students and readers, and the addition of 13 more recent essays published after 1988 likely merits a new edition even for those familiar with the earlier volumes.[17] But if the original "polemic contexts" in which many of the essays were written were already becoming distant enough in the late 1980s, then the situation of many of these same critical interventions two decades later would appear to have come from another epoch entirely. Leaving aside for the moment the new additions, the reprinting of the 16 earlier essays in the post-millennial moment cannot fail to produce different effects in a new critical situation that is, as Terry Eagleton has called it, "after theory." Yet one of the more striking effects of rereading these pieces is the realization of how well so many of them continue to hold up in the present. Any collection of previously published essays will be somewhat retrospective, of course, but there is a peculiarly Janus-faced aspect to *The Ideologies of Theory* that causes one not only to look back upon the nearly 40 years' worth of critical theory represented by these articles, but also to look ahead to the situations in which such historical work speaks to a potential future criticism.

The earlier version of *The Ideologies of Theory* was published in what might be thought of as the heyday of theory in the United States, and Jameson's own contributions to theoretical discourse in literary studies, including many of the essays reprinted there, helped to establish "theory" in that place and time. Shortly thereafter, whether as a result of a strident campaign against theory (such as the generally right-wing movement that produced such momentary bestsellers as *Tenured Radicals*, *Illiberal Education*, and *Profscam*) or owing to its own success (as theory dissipated itself in a number of mainstream pedagogical or critical practices), Theory-with-a-capital-T began to wane, with respect both to its valuation within literary and cultural studies and to its reputation outside of them.[18] "Cultural studies" itself, at least as practiced and championed in the United States, became an actively anti-theoretical discourse—not to mention, as Jameson is quick to notice, an anti-Marxist one—albeit a discourse that frequently borrowed from the work of important theorists, such as Jacques Derrida, Michel Foucault, and even Jameson himself, while hollowing out the political or critical content of their writings. A number of the more recent essays included in the new edition of *The Ideologies of Theory* speak to this very situation, since Jameson is called upon to respond to anti-theoretical or "post-theory" provocations of this or that sort.

In "How Not to Historicize Theory," for example, Jameson counters an anti-theory argument concerning "The History of Theory" (that is, Ian Hunter's version of it in an article of that title) by demonstrating the persistence of a properly theoretical kind of thinking and of writing in the postmodern situation. In that essay, as in "On 'Cultural Studies'" (originally published much earlier, in 1993), Jameson recognizes that the real enemy of those anti-theoretical positions formed in reaction to the assertion of "high" theory into academic literary criticism is Marxism itself.[19] Thus, as in the earlier incarnation, but perhaps more pressing today precisely because of the purported irrelevance or absence of theory, Jameson's old Sartrean view of Marxism as the untranscendable horizon of thought exhibits its lasting power. Where Jameson began, at least as far back as 1971's "Metacommentary," by striving to show the relevance—nay, the necessity and inescapability—of Marxist theory for literary and cultural criticism, he continues more than four decades later to demonstrate the limitations of non-Marxian or anti-Marxist approaches.

Jameson's brief introduction to the new volume, focusing as it does and as the earlier introductions had not (at least, not explicitly) on the importance of ideology itself, suggests the historical shift in the discourses surrounding "theory." In 1988, Jameson's implicit polemic against those who denied the ideological character of literature or culture was cast in a discursive framework in which the terms of the debate were still more or less agreed upon. By 2008, Jameson is presumably less certain that a phrase like "ideologies of theory" will resonate with readers, and whether this is because of some imagined post-ideological or post-theoretical environment is a matter for speculation. In any case, his opening paragraph evinces a slightly apologetic or defensive, if still pedagogical, tone in explaining his continuing use of a term like *ideology* at all.

> Ideology is the mediatory concept par excellence, bridging gaps between the individual and the social, between fantasy and cognition, between economics and aesthetics, objectivity and the subject, reason and the unconscious, the private and the public. That is to say that ideology is not an achieved concept at all, but rather a problematic, itself subject to profound historical change and upheaval on both slopes of its mediatory function. It is subject also to slippage in either direction, always on the point of being absorbed by the purely subjective or dissipating out into the ideas in the air and the fashions of the zeitgeist, the values of groups and the facts-of-the-matter of their objective situations. But if ideology is grasped as either psychological or sociological, it has for all intents and purposes disappeared as a productive operation. The word, meanwhile, is inevitably tainted by history, in the form of its relationship with Marxism as a tradition and a political practice, as well as its origins in the philosophical context of a now universally criticized philosophy of the centered subject and of totality. Yet no other term or concept has been proposed to assume its multiple functions.[20]

By opening in this way, Jameson suggests that, perhaps even more so than in their situation in the late 1980s, the essays contained in this collection must somehow represent Jameson's characterization of ideology and his contention that the ideological (including the older notion of *Ideologiekritik*) maintains a vital function in literary and cultural studies today.

Ideology provides the armature upon which to hang these diverse essays, which "all seek, in their varied historical situations, to acknowledge the viral omnipresence of ideology and to identify and reformulate its all-informing and form-producing power." Although this Verso edition maintains the earlier categorical divisions of "Situations of Theory" and the "Syntax of History" for its two parts, duly assigning the newer essays to one or the other, Jameson acknowledges that the original distinction between "the ideologies inherent in various textual interpretations as such and the visions of history projected by those ideologies" has been blurred to a certain extent.[21] Perhaps the main difference is in the historical situation itself, as many of the newer essays were written after the "postmodern break," after which "the specifically literary dilemma seemed to have been enlarged to include the problem of culture as a whole." Many of the earlier essays had already begun to register this shift, but the new additions—including Jameson's forewords to Jean-François Lyotard's *The Postmodern Condition* and Jacques Attali's *Noise*, essays on architecture and film, and the article on "Benjamin's Sociological Predecessor" (that is, Georg Simmel)—indicate the degree to which Jameson's elaboration of the ideologies of theory extended beyond the traditional bailiwick of Marxist literary criticism. And yet, as I mentioned above, his twenty-first-century positions are remarkably consistent with those of his earliest essays, as he remains committed to the perspective of "Metacommentary," for instance, and his critical review of Louis Marin's *Utopiques*, "Of Islands and Trenches" (first published in 1977), remains as trenchant as ever even after his definitive study of utopia, *Archaeologies of the Future.* Indeed, Jameson revisits the dialectic of utopia and ideology by observing that to identify a dominant ideology is already to reach "the confines and limits of what our current situation allows us to think: it thereby reopens the perspective of futures unimaginable within our present time."[22]

Jameson concludes the introduction to *The Ideologies of Theory* by pointing out just how enjoyable all of this critical activity really is. Although "ideological analysis is so frequently associated with querulous and irritable negativism," Jameson stresses "the interest and delight all the topics, dilemmas and contradictions as well as jests and positions" still have for him.[23] Often forgotten amid the somber lessons of history, the incisive critiques of present situations, and the gloomy forecasts of what seems likely to come is the sheer pleasure of dialectical criticism. In Jameson's next book, which might appropriately be considered his *magnum opus* were it not for the abundance of great works in his *oeuvre*, Jameson revels in just such an enjoyment, while also making the case once more for the persistence of the dialectic and the necessity for utopian thinking in the present age.

Valences of the Dialectic

Jameson's *Valences of the Dialectic* is another monumental work that, like *Archaeologies of the Future*, seems to be at once a summation of a long career's worth of thinking on the subject and a fresh exploration of new territory for critical theory.[24] The entirety of his remarkable body of work may be connected to the project of dialectical criticism. One might say that, from the study of Sartre's style to his most recent considerations of the antinomies of realism, Jameson has never ceased to write and talk about the dialectic, dialectics, and dialectical thinking. In *Valences of the Dialectic*, he presents his most thoroughgoing defense of dialectical criticism, revisiting sites of past struggles in which dialectical thinking had been called into question or placed under siege by purportedly anti-dialectical theories, while also projecting his own critical analysis into new, perhaps unexpected areas of the contemporary world system.

In *Valences of the Dialectic*, Jameson playfully but pointedly asks, "Is the dialectic wicked, or just incomprehensible?"[25] During an epoch in which Hegelianism has been rejected by Anglo-American positivist and pragmatist philosophers, by a loosely defined poststructuralist tradition, and by social critics on both the political right and left, Jameson has sometimes appeared to be a lone voice in the wilderness of modern or postmodern critical theory in his persistence in defending and promoting dialectical criticism. Some, detecting in the concept of totality a whiff of the totalitarian, have rejected dialectical thought as wicked, perhaps, while others, particularly in the wake of postwar identitarian movements in the United States and elsewhere, as well as of the rise of poststructuralist critiques of *les grand récits* of modernity à la Jean-François Lyotard, reject the apparent negativity and the baleful teleology of the Hegelian philosophical system. Jameson's gentle taunt and broader argument are aimed at those who would prematurely consign dialectical thought to the ash bin of history.

Valences of the Dialectic surveys Jameson's own thoughts on such history over many years while also introducing new material aimed at capturing the present moment and imagining future alternatives. As with its immediate predecessors *Archaeologies of the Future*, *The Modernist Papers*, and *The Ideologies of Theory*, *Valences of the Dialectic* contains a number of previously published essays, which are worthy of renewed consideration in the present time. However, Jameson also provides for the first time a number of entirely new pieces, including a lengthy essay on "The Three Names of the Dialectic," two fascinating chapters devoted to Hegel, two interesting reflections upon commodification and cultural revolution, respectively, and what amounts to an entire book-length study of "The Valences of History." The latter is a critical and theoretical *tour de force*, which ranges from Aristotle's *Physics* and *Poetics* to Derrida's critique of Heidegger, and, along the way, performs a thorough Marxist analysis of Paul Ricoeur's monumental *Time and Narrative*, before closing with a characteristically magisterial meditation on utopia.

Valences of the Dialectic is divided into six parts, and each forms its own miniature volume, although they also work well in advancing Jameson's overall argument for dialectical thinking as a means of both understanding the world and transforming it, to recall Marx's famous eleventh thesis on Feuerbach. Jameson himself provides a helpful *précis* of the overall project in a footnote. After pointing out that the long first chapter on the "three names" of the dialectic "may serve as an introduction to the volume as a whole," Jameson lays out the plan of the rest of the book:

> The chapters on Hegel seek to establish a different case for his actuality than the one normally offered (or rejected). The second of those chapters, and the succeeding ones, examine some of the contemporary philosophical classics from a dialectical perspective [...] and also to make a case for the renewed interest in Lukács and Sartre today. A series of shorter discussions then seek to clarify various themes in the Marxian tradition, from cultural revolution to the concept of ideology; followed by a series of political discussions, which, while documenting my personal opinions on topics ranging from the collapse of the Soviet Union to globalization, nonetheless claim to demonstrate the relevance of the dialectic for practical politics. In a long final section, which confronts Ricoeur's monumental study of history and narrative, I supplement this work by supplying the dialectical and Marxian categories missing from it, without which History today can scarcely be experienced.[26]

Thus, *Valences* manages to be wide-ranging and yet coherent, combining close, careful readings of individual texts with broadly historical and philosophical discussions that draw in diverse views and traditions.

The long first chapter of *Valences* elaborates what Jameson refers to as the three "names" of the dialectic, in which various "parts of speech offer so many camera angles from which unsuspected functions and implications might be seized and inspected."[27] Thus, "the dialectic" (with the definite article) suggests something monolithic or universalizing, associated with Hegel or Marx, and tending toward singularity and totality, whereas "many dialectics" (the dialectical counterpart to the definite article being an indefinite article) allows Jameson to consider and to grapple with such supposedly anti-dialectical thinkers as Nietzsche, Bergson, and Deleuze, who will be revealed to be rather dialectical after all, as their work invariably contains dialectical moments that modify our thinking by projecting alternative universes. As he argues in chapters on Derrida and Deleuze, Jameson's view is that many such anti-dialectical thinkers wind up being dialectical without necessarily knowing it. Finally, Jameson argues that in its emphatically adjectival form—"It's Dialectical!"—the dialectic operates by somehow "rebuking your perplexity before a particularly perverse interpretation or turn of events," at which point dialectical thought can overturn "heavy-handed common sense and hidebound conventional logic" in order to "propose a startling new perspective from which to rethink the novelty in question, to defamiliarize our ordinary habits of mind and to make us suddenly conscious not only of our own non-dialectical obtuseness but also of the strangeness of reality as such."[28] In the chapter's conclusion, Jameson reiterates Henri Lefebvre's call for a spatial dialectic, "a thought mode that does not yet exist"; but he asserts that such a prospective form of the dialectic acquires increased urgency under our present conditions in an age of globalization.[29]

In the essays that follow, Jameson blends an almost ecstatic apprehension of the dialectic with a cool rehearsal of, or return to, classics of dialectic thinking. Images abound that are proper to science fiction, particularly with respect to travel in space and time, while the philosophical discourse duly maintains its allegiances to Hegel, above all, but also to Marx, Lenin, Lukács, Sartre, and other such luminous dialecticians. Because *Valences of the Dialectic* interweaves a number of startling new analyses among the older essays, the reader sometimes experiences another sort of spatiotemporal *Verfremdungseffekt*. For instance, one may be suddenly thrust into what might appear to be the moldering old debates of the 1980s, including having to relive Francis Fukuyama's post-Cold War "End of History" arguments, at one moment, and, at the next, one is invited to consider the most pressing twenty-first-century topics in terms of the dialectical reversals of Hegelian theory—as when Jameson discusses the radical transformations of global production–distribution–consumption relays made possible by Walmart, which were almost certainly unimaginable at the time some of these chapters were originally written. This diversity and apparent eclecticism can, at times, make for a bumpy ride. The chapters on Sartre, which were originally published as "Introductions" to each of the two volumes of Sartre's *The Critique of Dialectical Reason*, have a rather introductory feel. The chapter on Lukács's *History and Class Consciousness*, first published in 1988, strikes me as still quite fresh, and makes a persuasive case for the continuing relevance of that most old-fashioned of yesteryear's Hegelian Marxists; in it, Jameson demonstrates how Lukács's stolid insistence on totality can be supplemented with other categories arising from recent poststructuralist thinking to better analyze the postmodern condition. The consistency and flexibility of Jameson's positions over the years are remarkable, as his arguments for a dialectical criticism, dating back to *Marxism and Form* if not earlier, can be read in *Valences of the Dialectic* as well, but with an aspect of strange novelty that makes them seem all the more relevant in the present world-historical situation.

Throughout his career, Jameson has always managed to make use of, if not to assimilate entirely, various non-Marxist or even anti-Marxist elements to suit his purposes, which partly explains his success in engaging with postmodernism and poststructuralism when many other critics on the left eschewed them as some form of fashionable, jargon-laden nonsense. In this, Jameson might be said to have followed Marx himself, who so frequently drew upon the resources of strategic enemies like Hegel or Ricardo or Proudhon to formulate his own critique. Jameson's characteristically ecumenical and perversely counter-intuitive practice occasionally makes for some astonishing conceptual fireworks in *Valences of the Dialectic*. Perhaps the most memorable example of this expansive critical approach can be found in the chapter called "Utopia as Replication," in which Jameson makes the case for the corporate behemoth Walmart as the model for utopian thought today. The bold assertion actually follows from Jameson's earlier uses of national allegory or the conspiracy film as means of representing collectivity and totality in a bewilderingly complex world system; but here Jameson grounds his conceptual model with the technical aspects of global finance and distribution of commodities, including a brief analysis of the development, and transformative effects, of bar codes.[30] Jameson's penchant for seeing the germ of a global totality in such pedestrian minutiae of everyday life exemplifies his approach to the dialectic, and comports well with his philosophical and cultural critique of late capitalism.

The problem with such a view, some would argue, is that Jameson, in locating the seed of utopia in the expansive developments of the capitalist machinery, might appear to be unduly optimistic, or even complacent, during a period of right-wing retrenchment and the general immiseration of the working classes, who become more difficult to identify as classes in the new global reorganization of the late capitalist mode. Moreover, one might argue that Jameson's view leaves little room for a Marxist praxis, since the things against which the working class must struggle, multinational corporations and late capitalism itself, are the very things that will, by a twist of the dialectic, make possible their ultimate victory, in the form of a radically alternative social system. That is, if Walmart-styled production and distribution processes and the globalized capitalism that they both represent and engender are effectively (and ironically) forcing workers of the world to unite, and therefore helping to bring into existence the requisite conditions for a truly utopian or communistic social order to come, then what is there for Marxists to protest against or to plan for in the present conjuncture?

Jameson's response, though measured, is also highly polemical. While he has sympathy with many of the critics who quite understandably lament the injustices of the present system, and while he certainly does support tactical or strategic programs to improve conditions (such as unionization and the aim of full employment), Jameson considers the arguments of "moralizers," as he calls them, to be somewhat wrongheaded. As he puts it at one point—though the idea reappears through *Valences of the Dialectic* and elsewhere in Jameson's corpus)—"The dialectic is an injunction to think the negative and the positive together at one and the same time, in the unity of a single thought, where moralizing wants to have the luxury of condemning this evil without particularly imagining anything else in its place."[31] Jameson insists that "the dialectical union of opposites is then a social rebuke as well as a political lesson," inasmuch as the so-called "victories" or "defeats" of a given situation must be understood as moments in a larger historical ensemble whose interpretations cannot really be understood in advance.[32] This lesson ought to be valuable for both the left and the right, as what often seems a positive development from one point of view leads to a negative outcome from the other, and vice versa. As far back as *Marxism and Form*, Jameson had provided the example of the "dialectical reversals" that gave one pause in considering the nuclear age and the space race between the United States and the Soviet Union. Here, he supplies a more recent example, demonstrating how the generally leftist, Soviet-style policies of Jawaharlal Nehru in India produced the institutes of technology that made possible the spread of global capitalism, outsourcing, and so on.[33] The "logic of the situation," as Jameson has called it, which is also to say "the constant changeability of the situation, its primacy and the way in which it allows certain things to be possible and others not," is what forms the basis for his vision of dialectical criticism.[34]

Several times in *Valences of the Dialectic*, Jameson invokes the Aristotelian concept of *peripeteia*, the "reversal of fortune" or, as he prefers to think of it, the dialectical reversal. For Aristotle, the reversal makes possible some new recognition (in the Greek, *anagnorisis*).[35] Throughout *Valences of the Dialectic*—but particularly in his lengthy consideration of "Valences of History," the final section of the book—Jameson investigates the ways in which such a reversal allows one to grasp, if only tentatively and in that brief instant, the reality of the situation. Unexpectedly, but perhaps not so surprisingly given his militantly eclectic approach, Jameson discovers a model for our own time in classical literature, specifically Virgil's *Aeneid*, in which the tragic defeat of the Trojans leads to the triumphant founding of Rome. As Jameson sees it, this may be Virgil's subversively subtle warning to the great powers of Augustus's Golden Age: "you Roman victors, never forget that you are also the miserable losers and refugees of defeat and of the loss of your city and country!"[36] That something similar could be asserted in the twenty-first century concerning the U.S. empire and those triumphalist cheerleaders of globalization, whose fortunes might just as easily turn again, goes largely without saying. Such are the valences of the dialectic.

Ending on a characteristically utopian note, Jameson's study brings together disparate thinkers, texts, concepts, times and places, enfolding them in an alternative narrative that, like Hegel's *Aufhebung*, cancels, preserves, and elevates all of this material. In the already famous closing line of *Valences of the Dialectic*, he invites the reader to imagine a situation, our actual situation in fact, where "from time to time, like a diseased eyeball in which disturbing flashes of light are perceived or like those baroque sunbursts in which rays from another world suddenly break into this one, we are reminded that Utopia exists and that other systems, other spaces, are still possible."[37] In Jameson's project of dialectical criticism, the mapping of the present system is inextricably tied to the imagination of alternatives. In other words, understanding the system is not only a step in the direction of, but is itself a form of, projecting some sort of other system, if only in fitful and uncertain ways. But this projection of alternatives cannot be confused with the drafting of a blueprint of some ideal social system or with the prophetic vision of a hitherto impossible cultural organization to come. As Jameson has put it in a recent article, "Utopias do not embody the future but rather help us to grasp the limits of our images of the future, and indeed our impossibility of imagining a radically different future." He goes on to say that utopia is "the radical disturbance of our sense of history and the disruption whereby we approach a thought of the radical or absolute break with our own present and our own system. But insofar as the Utopian project comes to seem more realizable and more practical, it turns into a practical political program in our world, in the here-and-now, and ceases to be Utopian in any meaningful sense."[38] As in *Archaeologies of the Future* and in his various extrapolations of the ideologies of theory, Jameson explores the possibilities of utopian thinking as a meditation on the impossible, which becomes a particularly apt figure for theorizing the present world-historical condition in the age of globalization.

Conclusion
Reading Jameson

In my introduction I recalled a classroom scene in which Professor Jameson sketched an impromptu, rhizomatic diagram of postwar French intellectual culture through a listing of proper names and a concurrent narration of literary and theoretical concepts or practices. As a reader, I have often reflected upon that experience, since so much of Jameson's project of dialectical criticism involves the careful recitation and interpretation of the critical theory of others. This is, of course, not to suggest that Jameson's own project is somehow merely derivative, a matter of collage or montage pieced together from other theorists' writings, although I do not believe he would mind that characterization overmuch, considering that a fundamentally collective dimension is presupposed by dialectical thought. Jameson's literary theory and criticism certainly stand on their own, at least as much as those of other comparable critics. But the resolutely pedagogical spirit of the Jamesonian endeavor, combined with his disciplinary training in philology and personal commitment to literature, means that whatever else that project is, it will be dedicated to close reading, creative interpretation, and speculative thinking.[1] Jameson is himself an exemplary reader, and reading Jameson, as I suggested at the end of Chapter 1, is itself an education in the project of dialectical criticism.

The influence of other writers, critics, and theorists on Jameson's work is unmistakable, but contrary to everyday usage, such influence does not necessarily indicate a one-way street. An example of this can be found in *Late Marxism*, where Jameson discusses the readily discernible influence of Benjamin on Adorno's thought:

> But is influence to be understood simply as the transfer of some new thought from one person's head to another's? In that case, it might be preferable to talk about the awakening of new interests (not to say a whole new problematic) in the mind of the individual on the receiving end of the "influence" in question. Perhaps, however, Adorno's omnipresent theme of "mimesis" offers a new way to use this notion of

influence, which designates something that really happens just as surely as it misrepresents it. "Influence" in this new sense would then describe the ways in which a pedagogical figure, by his own praxis, shows the disciple what else you can think and how much further you can go with the thoughts you already have; or—to put it another way, which for us is the same—what else you can *write* and the possibility of forms of writing and *Darstellung* that unexpectedly free you from the taboos and constraints of forms learnt by rote and assumed to be inscribed in the nature of things. This, at any rate, is the way in which I want to grasp Benjamin's "influence" on Adorno, as just such a liberation by mimesis and as the practical demonstration of the possibility of another kind of writing—which is eventually to say: another kind of thinking.[2]

Something similar to this could likely be said for the "influence" of Adorno, not to mention Benjamin, Barthes, Brecht, Lukács, and Sartre, on Jameson's thinking. Others readily present themselves for inspection as well, such as Freud and Lacan, Althusser, Greimas, and Deleuze; or Nietzsche, Heidegger, Korsch, and Marcuse; or Kenneth Burke, Northrop Frye, Hayden White, and his old teachers Wayne Booth, Erich Auerbach, and Henri Peyre; that this list could be extended almost indefinitely is but another sign of Jameson's immense learning and catholic tastes, not to mention his philosophical commitment to the dialectic and his impossible attempt to grasp the world system in its totality. But the two figures that must be most consistently connected to Jameson's project of dialectical criticism are undoubtedly Hegel and Marx, the founder of the dialectical theory and the perfecter of it, in a manner of speaking. Although nearly everything Jameson had written throughout his career bore the traces of these two thinkers, only recently has Jameson devoted individual studies to their works. Not surprisingly, perhaps, these studies are in the form of readings.

As it happens, *The Hegel Variations: On the Phenomenology of Spirit* (2010) and *Representing Capital: A Reading of Volume One* (2011) are not only the first books that Jameson has devoted to either of these foundational thinkers, but they are the only books written by Jameson that are dedicated to the study of a single book, *The Phenomenology of Spirit* and *Capital*, respectively.[3] Although each of these books certainly stands on its own as an important interpretation of a major philosophical text, they might also be read as appendices or supplements to *Valences of the Dialectic*. In a footnote in that text, Jameson had joked that "*Valences* is something like a *Hamlet* without the prince, insofar as it lacks the central chapter on Marx and the dialectic which was to have been expected." He went on say that these "complementary volumes [...] will therefore complete the project."[4] And yet, as documents published in the form of free-standing monographs, published in consecutive years, *The Hegel Variations* and *Representing Capital* remain unique volumes within Jameson's overall body of work. Moreover, notwithstanding Jameson's own intent, these readings do not so much complete *Valences of the Dialectic* as suggest other ways of exploring the dialectic. By returning once more to these Hegelian and Marxist *ur*-texts of the dialectic, Jameson models a readerly mode of dialectical criticism that discloses not only new meanings in the works themselves, but also novel uses of them for our own time.

In these two studies, Jameson offers startling interpretations and elaborations of *The Phenomenology of Spirit* and *Capital*, at once making these very well-known books unfamiliar again, such that they now seem powerfully contemporary. In both cases, however, Jameson risks alienating some otherwise sympathetic readers, as the Hegel and Marx who emerge in Jameson's pages seem rather different from their more recognizable forms in this or that Marxist tradition. Perhaps this amounts to a Jamesonian version of Deleuze's comment about the doubling that comes with writing the history of philosophy, where "one imagines a *philosophically* bearded Hegel, a *philosophically* clean-shaven Marx."[5] In a way that is typical of Jameson's dialectical method, the familiar text becomes radically estranged in the course of his analysis. As far back as *Marxism and Form*, he had suggested that an experience of "shock" is "constitutive of the dialectic," evoking "the sickening shudder we feel in an elevator's fall or in the sudden dip of an airliner."[6] At such a moment, the mind becomes aware of itself and looks upon what had previously been taken for granted in completely new ways. Jameson's dialectical thinking, "thought to the second power,"[7] is also his model for reading, which can occasionally make for some strange interpretations. In Jameson's creative analysis of the *Phenomenology*, for example, Hegel at times comes off as a proto-poststructuralist, anticipating and parrying in advance the (only apparently) anti-dialectical thought of many poststructuralist theorists. And in *Representing Capital* one of the more astonishing assertions is that Marx in that book, and by extension, perhaps, Marxism in general, has no political theory, only an economic one, and that this is right and proper. The return to Marx's *magnum opus* marks a key moment in Jamesonian thought as well, since in this reading Jameson's own lifelong project of theorizing and analyzing narrative representation turns out to be the underlying project of *Capital* itself.

The Hegel Variations

At one level, *The Hegel Variations* presents a reading of *The Phenomenology of Spirit* in which Jameson highlights those aspects of Hegel's philosophical investigation that he finds most interesting or misunderstood. Although this is not a polemical study, Jameson nevertheless clearly wishes to rescue Hegel from the misuses or mischaracterizations of his work in a variety of social and cultural contexts, including the embrace of Hegel's conception of the "End of History" by liberalism or neoliberalism and the dismissal of his dialectical system by poststructuralism and postmodernism. In *Valences of the Dialectic*, Jameson had tried to show how many putatively anti-Hegelian theorists, such as Derrida or Deleuze, turned out to be Hegelian after all.[8] Here Jameson does something like the obverse, which in the elastic permutations of his dialectical criticism, may in fact be the same thing in the end: Jameson presents an almost postmodern Hegel, a Hegel for the era of globalization, who in his early *Phenomenology*—written in the aftermath of the French Revolution, long before his philosophy and his politics become ossified into a recognizable "Hegelianism" during his later life—produced a dynamic, open-ended system well suited to our own contemporary theoretical concerns.

The title of this book already reflects the radical departure from traditional views of Hegel's system that Jameson intends to make. Here, Hegel is not the philosopher of the rigid, iron-clad structure or of the mechanistic trajectory toward an ultimate, inevitable *telos*. Jameson invokes the musical concept of the "variation" to overcome the representational dilemma of trying "to separate the events of Hegel's text from the terms and figures in which they are presented." This will involve "the contradictory presupposition that the fundamental problem can be stated in non-representational terms."[9] The figure of theme-and-variations enables Jameson to conceptualize the project of Hegel's *Phenomenology* without recourse either to artificially static categories or to simpler versions of cyclical repetition. For, in music, a variation is not merely a modification of the previously existing, somehow stable thing called a theme. The latter is often itself "a fragile and precarious" concept. Jameson cites Adorno's *Philosophy of Modern Music*, where Adorno suggests that, in the music of Hegel's contemporary Beethoven, as in that of Adorno's own contemporary Schoenberg, "[t]he thematic material is of such a nature that to attempt to secure it is tantamount to varying it."[10] As Jameson elaborates:

> the well-nigh infinite virtuosity of the variational process itself (we often indeed begin with a variation, and only later on discover the theme as such, in its official or "original" form) at length leads to a kind of musical "critique of origins," that is to say, to the nagging doubt as to whether there ever was such a thing as the initial theme in the first place. Yet if the theme itself also comes to be considered a variation, then it turns out, in truly postmodern fashion, to have been a variation without an original, much as present-day simulacra are described as copies without originals. We therefore here arrive at a decisive moment dialectically, in which difference, by gradually extending its dominion over everything, ultimately comes to liquidate identity as such, in a well-nigh suicidal meltdown in which it must itself also disappear (inasmuch as difference is necessarily predicated on identity in the first place).[11]

In this case, the musical figure adapted from Beethoven, Schoenberg, and Adorno, becomes a model for a kind of postmodern Hegel.

Jameson's own performance in reading Hegel's *Phenomenology* is perhaps best imagined in musical terms. Each chapter plays on themes of the Hegelian text—Absolute Spirit, identity-and-difference, language, *die Sache selbst*, the master–servant dialectic, the end of history, and so on— while carefully interweaving the melodies generated by such concepts to form an almost symphonic arrangement of ideas. Jameson's characteristic attention to style, present throughout his career and harkening back to his very first book on Sartre, is also on display in *The Hegel Variations*, as he discovers in Hegel's famously convoluted sentence structure a method to that madness. For instance, "Hegel's own complex stylistic strategies show how complicated it is dialectically to show off the antithetical meanings latent in words and thoughts: for what often look like tortuous or inarticulate sentences prove to be carefully planned performances in the systematic changing of linguistic valences."[12] As usual, the content and the form cannot be long separated, and the architectonic of the *Phenomenology*, its own "ladder of forms," is for Jameson critical to the open-ended "system" of Hegelian thought.

The Hegel Variations itself enacts this open-endedness, such that Jameson's own formal organization of his study implicitly makes the case against those who view Hegel as a strictly teleological thinker or as an abstract systematizer. Jameson begins the study, in an opening chapter playfully titled "Closure," at the *end* of the *Phenomenology*, with the emergence of Absolute Spirit. Jameson actually ends *The Hegel Variations* with an ellipsis, allowing the dot-dot-dot to have the "last word," as it were, and I suggested in Chapter 1 above that this may be the most suitable way to approach Jameson's own dialectical theory conceptually, if not practically or certainly not literally. The final line of *The Hegel Variations* actually begins to restate the opening line of the book, where we "begin at the end," so in addition to the open-endedness of this study and of the Hegelian system that is its object, Jameson's book reenacts that cyclical, or as he prefers, spiral pattern that Hegel's theory of history traces. For the Hegelian philosophy of history, which becomes in a sense the foundation for all of philosophy, discloses itself, not as a teleological trajectory or a cyclical process, but as a "progression in the sense of enlargement." Here Jameson brings Marx's *Capital* to bear on the *Phenomenology*, but he insists that already in Hegel the philosophical system calls for "the subsequent enlargements of later history," such that it anticipates "the moment of imperialism (or the 'modern' in the technical sense) and now that of globalization."[13] However, as we have seen, the modern and postmodern conditions cannot be conceived, for Jameson, outside of the provenance of capitalism and late capitalism, so this Hegel who turns out to be so well suited to our own age of globalization must, it seems, pass the baton to the paradigmatic theorist of that infernal machine of capitalism, Marx himself.

Representing Capital

Just as *The Hegel Variations* is not really an introduction to the *Phenomenology*, neither is *Representing Capital* an introduction to *Capital*, although it shares with many of Jameson's other works a pedagogical tone and it undoubtedly draws upon his years of teaching Marx's texts in seminars and lectures. Jameson assumes that his readers are already familiar with both *Capital* itself and various debates within Marxism over the past century. His is less an interpretive reading of *Capital* than it is an extended and collaborative exploration of the territory as well as the map that Marx at once surveys and transforms. But all commentary is also metacommentary, and *Representing Capital* is therefore not so much an interpretation of Marx's work as a dialectical examination of *Capital*'s, and capitalism's, complex machinery.

Jameson is a literary and cultural critic, albeit one whose work has always been grounded in history, philosophy, and other disciplinary discourses, so he is perhaps correct in worrying that some readers might view this book as a "literary" reading of *Capital*. Jameson's characteristic attention to the formal qualities of the text under consideration is certainly present in *Representing Capital* as well; the discourse of literary criticism is at times brought to bear on Marx's writing, as when, for example, Jameson refers to Marx's penchant for chiasmus (for example, "the weapon of criticism cannot replace the criticism of weapons") as an example of how temporality can be introduced into what is essentially an equation.[14] However, the thrust of Jameson's argument is not literary, except insofar as he remains interested, as does recent literary theory, in the problem of representation as such. Indeed, Jameson's primary contention in his reading of the first volume of *Capital* is that the book is fundamentally concerned with representation and, more specifically, with how to represent capitalism in its totality. His astounding conclusion will be that *Capital* actually manages to do this by replicating the processes of capitalism itself, expanding by canceling out, preserving, and elevating its own puzzles until Marx's text exhausts itself by reaching its own untranscendable horizon of history.

Among the many provocations of *Representing Capital*, Jameson announces his intention to limit himself to Volume 1, afterward referring to that volume simply as *Capital* (as I henceforth shall). Jameson insists upon viewing the first volume of *Capital* as a complete work in and of itself, regardless of the subsequent volumes published by Engels or the plans laid out in the *Grundrisse* for many more parts. In fact, as Jameson acknowledges in a footnote, Marx himself delineated his plans for a six-part study in an 1858 letter to Engels, and Roman Rosdolsky in *The Making of Marx's "Capital"* identified 14 different versions between 1857 and 1868. Part of the basis for Jameson's decision to read Volume 1 as its own finished project is that is the only volume completed by Marx himself; but Jameson supplements this commonplace rationale with a bolder one: with this first volume, *Capital* is already complete, and "the layering of the posthumous volumes (falling rate of profit, ground rent, the multiple temporalities) are already laid in place here in as satisfactory a form as we are likely to need."[15] This working framework does not prevent Jameson from considering other writings, especially the *Grundrisse* and *A Contribution to the Critique of Political Economy*, but the first volume of *Capital* remains the principal text for the study.

More provocative, perhaps, is his assertion that Marx's *Capital* is not a political work. Jameson anticipates the outrage among many Marxists at such a claim, and he concludes his study with a chapter devoted to political considerations. In that section, he distinguishes political practice, strategy and tactics, from the properly economic theory of capitalism as a system. Jameson's theoretical and practical problem with those who read *Capital* as a primarily political work is that any politics will necessarily remain within the purview of the prevailing economic system. Thus, although the various political theories and practices can ideally make living or working conditions somewhat better under the capitalist mode of production, they cannot ultimately offer meaningful alternatives to that mode. This is also the crux of Jameson's opposition to the anarchists, whose opposition to the state or to state power ignores or suppresses that these are always super-structural effects, and thus epiphenomena, of the underlying economic relations which make them possible. In his "Political Conclusions," Jameson argues against the more anarchistic tradition within Marxism that focuses attention less on economic exploitation than on political domination. Jameson argues that the latter's moral or ethical emphasis "leads to punctual revolts and acts of resistance rather than to the transformation of the mode of production as such."[16] Although his adherence to the materialist categories of unemployment or exploitation allows him "to be recommitted to the invention of a new kind of transformatory politics on a global scale," he does not—and, for reasons related to his overall repre-sentational project, he probably cannot—describe such a politics. In any case, Jameson maintains that *Capital* is not a book about politics, but about unemployment, which he understands as "structurally inseparable from the dynamic of accumulation and expansion which constitutes the very nature of capitalism."[17]

In the main body of his argument, Jameson approaches his reading first by dividing Marx's book into three distinct sections to be analyzed, and then by offering more general reflections on broad ideas raised in *Capital*. Jameson views *Capital* as "a series of riddles, of mysteries or paradoxes, to which at the proper moment the solution is supplied."[18] Each solution, if it may accurately be so labeled, brings with it another problem, which the text in turn attempts to solve. In this way, *Capital* operates in a manner not dissimilar to that of capitalism, a system whose very success is predicated upon the crises that threaten it, and which must perpetually overcome the problems that threaten its self-destruction by expanding that very system, which of course inevitably makes possible even greater problems. Capitalism is "an infernal machine, a perpetuum mobile or unnatural miracle, whose strengths turn out to be what is most intolerable about it." However, in Jameson's reading, Marx's *Capital* is itself a total system, one whose function is to represent "a peculiar machine whose evolution is (dialectically) at one with its breakdown."[19] This representation is made possible, at least in part, by staging the crisis of capitalism at various levels. Ultimately, capitalism is really about overproduction and unemployment, the enforced idleness and immiseration of large numbers of the population. Hence, the mode of production reproduces itself by producing unproductive subjects. As Jameson might put it, "It's dialectical!"[20]

With Part VII of *Capital*, which Jameson takes to be the conclusion of the main body of the book, Marx introduces "The General Law of Capitalist Accumulation," which establishes that immiseration and unemployment are structurally constitutive of the capitalist system as such, rather than being mere by-products or coincidences. Noting the expansion of "pauperism" and the increase in the size of "the industrial reserve army" (that is, the unemployed), Marx literally underscores that *"This is the absolute general law of capitalist accumulation."*[21] Jameson takes this moment to be the conceptual climax of *Capital*, and it is the foundation of Jameson's contention that *Capital* is not really about labor or politics, but about unemployment.

Jameson identifies two other narrative climaxes to *Capital*, which he labels *heroic* and *comic*. The first comes in the triumphant vision of a socialism that replaces capitalism, by whatever political means (Marx does not say how) but inexorably as a matter of economics, based upon the law of the falling rates of profits, whereby "the expropriators become expropriated."[22] Jameson adds that, a decade earlier in the *Grundrisse*, Marx had noted that this transformation "would not really be on the agenda until the world market, and universal commodification, had become visible on the horizon."[23] To this heroic and revolutionary image, Marx adds a comic one, in which he describes a wealthy British capitalist who moved to Western Australia with a large fortune plus 3,000 workers in tow; these workers promptly disappeared into the bush, thus leaving the wealthy entrepreneur with no servants at all: "Unhappy Mr. Peel, who provided for everything except the export of English relations of production."[24] This comic vision of resistance and flight, according to Jameson, might be embraced by the more anarchistic strategists of the left, but offers no structural change to the capitalist mode itself.

This returns us to Jameson's point that *Capital*, and Marxism more generally, does not really offer a political theory and that, instead, its purview is properly limited to economic theory. In Jameson's view, Marx himself for the most part avoids discussing political strategies, except that he is a strongly "political animal" and his opportunism ("in the good, Machiavellian sense of the word")[25] allows him to embrace whatever seems to help at the time, be it trade unionism, legislative action, or revolutionary violence. However, much as Marx wishes to see the alleviation of suffering, Jameson argues that the political strategies can only ultimately reform the capitalist system. As with social democracy or liberal reforms, such politics can lead to the improvement of living conditions under capitalism, but it cannot result in the actual overcoming of capitalism. As Jameson put it elsewhere, "Socialism is capitalism's dream of a perfected system. Communism is that unimaginable fulfillment of a radical alternative that cannot even be dreamt."[26] This echoes Jameson's theory of utopia, in which the utopian impulse is less a matter of imagining some future ideal state and more a representation of our own imaginative limits.

Representing Capital demonstrates the degree to which representation itself must remain a crucial concern of Marxism in the age of globalization, postmodernity, or late capitalism. Jameson suggests that the simultaneously complete and unfinished book that is *Capital* does manage to represent, in a total and yet open-ended fashion, the reality of capital itself: "we can grasp the mechanism of capital as both a structure and an open-ended historical development at one and the same time." Hence, "capitalism's structure can be compared to a Rube Goldberg machine, always on the point of breaking down, and repairing itself by adding new and Ptolemaic 'axioms' […] which make it ever more unwieldy and dysfunctional." In Jameson's assiduously reflexive vision of the dialectic, a similar process occurs in our attempts to map this totality. Like Marx's *Capital*, Jameson's own *Representing Capital* becomes a machine that generates its own "boundaries and lines of flight simultaneously," conclusively leaving matters for further discussion and presenting vistas of new terrains subject to future exploration.[27]

In the end, the old tension within Marxism between voluntarism and determinism, between the activity of the class struggle and the structural form of the mode of production, or perhaps more simply between politics and history, must remain in some sort of productive tension in the labors of the Marxist critic. As I have been saying throughout this book and as Jameson's project makes clear, any attempt to formulate a radically alternative future must first and always come to terms with the scarcely representable system in which we find ourselves. Jameson summarizes the problem and its constantly evolving solution in *Valences of the Dialectic*, where he demonstrates the utopian impulse animating the critical endeavor itself:

> A Marxist politics is a Utopian project or program for transforming the world, and replacing a capitalist mode of production with a radically different one. But it is also a conception of historical dynamics in which it is posited that the whole new world is also objectively in emergence all around us, without our necessarily at once perceiving it; so that alongside our conscious praxis and our strategies for producing change, we may also take a more receptive and interpretive stance in which, with the proper instruments and registering apparatus, we may detect the allegorical stirrings of a different state of things, the imperceptible and even immemorial ripenings of the seeds of time, the subliminal and subcutaneous eruptions of whole new forms of life and social relations.[28]

The project of dialectical criticism, therefore, involves the patient, meticulous, and attentive *reading* of the situation in which we find ourselves, broadly conceived; but in this analytic and interpretive activity also lie the revolutionary forces of current and future struggles. Cultural theory cannot replace revolutionary theorizing any more than cultural practices could replace revolutionary praxis. However, to modify Marx's great dictum once again and apply it to the present age of globalization, theorists must somehow find a way to interpret the world if they have any hope of changing it. Reading Jameson, reading Jameson reading others, and reading further on our own will not amount to a satisfactorily utopian political practice in its own right; but it may well allow us as critics to gain some new understanding of the world system, to apprehend our present situation in such a way as to discern the indistinct, but nevertheless real, signs of the radically different forms emerging at the edges or the seams of its shifting spaces. We may thereby descry in Jameson's project of dialectical criticism some promising vista into the past, as well as a glimmer of a future form, embedded in the all-too-present situation in which we find ourselves. And from this altogether worldly situation, perhaps, we may project alternatives.

Notes

Introduction

1. Terry Eagleton, "Jameson and Form," *New Left Review* 59 (September–October 2009), p.123.
2. At the time of this writing, Jameson's *Antinomies of Realism* (London: Verso, 2013) had not yet appeared. I hope to consider it, along with other works, in a future project.
3. Ian Buchanan, "Reading Jameson Dogmatically," *Historical Materialism* 10.3 (2002), p.233.
4. By focusing on Jameson's books, I do not mean to overlook or somehow devalue the significance of his essays. However, many of his most influential essays have been reprinted, incorporated, or otherwise included in later books, whether in collections of essays (such as *The Ideologies of Theory* and *The Cultural Turn*), as chapters in his scholarly monographs (as when "Postmodernism, or, the Cultural Logic of Late Capitalism" became the first chapter of the book by the same title), or a hybrid of both forms (as in Part I of *Signatures of the Visible* or Part II of *Archaeologies of the Future*, which function as collections of previously published essays within books containing new material). Hence, even if one looks only at Jameson's books, one still encounters most of his well-known journal articles. (One notable exception, his controversial "Third-World Literature in the Era of Multinational Capitalism" [1986], will be discussed in Chapter 3.) In any event, for better or worse, books probably remain the privileged form of critical writing, and the trajectory of Jameson's lifelong project of dialectical criticism may be traced by looking at the books he has produced along the way.
5. See Ian Buchanan, "Live Jameson," in *Fredric Jameson: Live Theory* (London: Continuum, 2006), p.120.
6. However, this apparent lack of "productivity" is quite misleading. In addition to listing his many dozens of influential essays, lectures, and interviews produced during the 1970s and 1980s, a biographer might point out that Jameson was also at his most peripatetic during this epoch, as he moved between several academic positions, first going from the University of California, San Diego, to Yale University in 1976, then accepting a post in the University of California at Santa Cruz's innovative History of Consciousness program in 1983, before arriving at Duke University in 1985, where he established and served as chairman of the Graduate Program in Literature and where he still teaches.

7. See, for example, Alex Callinicos's trenchant critique in *Against Postmodernism: A Marxist Critique* (London: Polity Press, 1989).

8. Jameson, *Postmodernism, or, the Cultural Logic of Late Capitalism* (Durham, NC: Duke University Press, 1991), p.4.

9. Careful readers will notice the slight interruption of the chronological order, but Jameson himself notes that the essays included in *The Modernist Papers* "are meant to accompany my *A Singular Modernity*," so it seems appropriate to consider the two books in tandem. See Jameson, *The Modernist Papers* (London: Verso, 2007), p.x.

10. Jameson, *A Singular Modernity: Essay on the Ontology of the Present* (London: Verso, 2002), p.215.

11. Jameson, *Valences of the Dialectic* (London: Verso, 2009), p.612.

12. For a brief survey of many of Jameson's comments on pedagogy *per se*, see Christopher Wise, *The Marxian Hermeneutics of Fredric Jameson* (New York: Peter Lang, 1994), pp.1–24.

13. See Friedrich Nietzsche, "Schopenhauer as Educator," in *Untimely Meditations*, trans. R.J. Hollingdale, ed. Daniel Breazeale (Cambridge: Cambridge University Press, 1997), pp.125–194.

14. Jameson was at the time director of that program. I can say honestly, with only the slightest sense of irony, that I am a "certified" Marxist; the certificate, acknowledging my successful completion of the program on "Perspectives in Marxism and Society," is signed by Fredric Jameson himself (in red ink, *natürlich!*).

Chapter 1

1. I am unaware of any transcript or recording of Jameson's acceptance speech, so I rely here on my own memory of the event.

2. Jameson, *Marxism and Form: Twentieth-Century Dialectical Theories of Literature* (Princeton: Princeton University Press, 1971), p.163.

3. At the time of this writing, *The Antinomies of Realism* (London: Verso, 2013) had not yet appeared. In a 2012 interview, Jameson listed two other "forthcoming" books, one on allegory and the other on myth. These three would constitute, in reverse chronological order, the first three volumes of Jameson's long announced six-volume project, *The Poetics of Social Forms*, of which *Postmodernism, or, the Cultural Logic of Late Capitalism*, *A Singular Modernity*, and *Archaeologies of the Future* represent the last three volumes, respectively. See Maria Elisa Cevasco, "Imagining a Space that is Outside: An Interview with Fredric Jameson," *minnesota review* 78 (2012), p.89.

4. Colin MacCabe, "Preface" to Jameson, *The Geopolitical Aesthetic: Cinema and Space in the World System* (Bloomington and London: Indiana University Press and the British Film Institute, 1992), p.ix.

5. See Jameson, *Postmodernism, or, the Cultural Logic of Late Capitalism* (Durham, NC: Duke University Press, 1991), p.418.

6. Gilles Deleuze and Félix Guattari, *A Thousand Plateaus*, trans. Brian Massumi (Minneapolis, MN: University of Minnesota Press, 1987), p.12.

7. See my "Jameson's Project of Cognitive Mapping: A Critical Engagement," in Rolland G. Paulston, ed., *Social Cartography: Mapping Ways of Seeing Social and Educational Change* (New York: Garland, 1996), pp.399–416.

8. See Joseph Frank, *The Idea of Spatial Form* (New Brunswick, NJ: Rutgers University Press, 1991), pp.3–66.

9. See, for example, Slavoj Žižek, *Less Than Nothing: Hegel and the Shadow of Dialectical Materialism* (London: Verso, 2012); David Harvey, *A Companion to Marx's Capital* (London: Verso, 2010) and *A Companion to Marx's Capital, Volume 2* (London: Verso, 2013); and Terry Eagleton, *Why Marx was Right* (New Haven: Yale University Press, 2012).

10. See Jameson, *Late Marxism: Adorno, or, the Persistence of the Dialectic* (London: Verso, 1990).

11. Jameson, *The Political Unconscious: Narrative as a Socially Symbolic Act* (Ithaca, NY: Cornell University Press, 1981), pp.60–61.

12. See Georg Lukács, *The Theory of the Novel*, trans. Anna Bostock (Cambridge, MA: MIT Press, 1971).

13. Jameson, *The Modernist Papers* (London: Verso, 2007), p.ix.

14. See Alexander Nehamas, *Nietzsche: Life as Literature* (Cambridge, MA: Harvard University Press, 1985), pp.167–168.

15. See Cevasco, "Imagining a Space that is Outside."

16. Terry Eagleton, *Against the Grain: Essays, 1975–1985* (London: Verso, 1986), p.66.

17. Ibid., p.57.

18. Jameson, "Interview with Leonard Green, Jonathan Culler, and Richard Klein," in *Jameson on Jameson: Conversations on Cultural Marxism* (Durham, NC: Duke University Press, 2007), p.37.

19. Terry Eagleton, *After Theory* (New York: Basic Books, 2003), p.74.

20. Jameson, *Marxism and Form*, p.xiii.

21. Northrop Frye, *The Educated Imagination* (Bloomington: Indiana University Press, 1964), p.148.

22. See his comments in the interview "Live Jameson," in Ian Buchanan, *Fredric Jameson: Live Theory* (London: Continuum, 2006), p.124.

23. Jameson, *Sartre: The Origins of a Style* (New York: Columbia University Press, 1984), p.40.

24. Jameson, *Postmodernism*, p.16.

25. Cevasco, "Imagining a Space that is Outside," pp.93–94.

26. As Buchanan puts it in a review of several books on Jameson, "I find this trope of Jameson criticism something of a mystery—even if it were true that Jameson's style is inordinately difficult, why, as a commentator of his work,

would you admit this?"; see Buchanan, "Reading Jameson Dogmatically," *Historical Materialism* 10.3 (2002), p.238.

27. The specific enumeration of Jameson's books is made somewhat tricky by the fact that some books may "count" differently from others. I will examine 20 books, which includes some sleight of hand in treating 1988's two-volume *Ideologies of Theory* collection of essays as one book and the 2008 expanded (but single-volume) Verso edition of *Ideologies of Theory* as another. Also, I do not directly examine books where Jameson's "authorship" is of a quite different order, such as *Jameson on Jameson: Conversions on Cultural Marxism*, a collection of interviews, or *Cultures of Globalization*, an essay-collection co-edited by Jameson, although these, like many of the uncollected essays, are rightly considered important contributions to the Jamesonian corpus. Furthermore, as mentioned above, I finished drafting this study just before the appearance of Jameson's *Antinomies of Realism*, so I have not been able to give it the attention it undoubtedly deserves; I hope to examine it in detail, along with his complete *Poetics of Social Forms* project, in a future study.

28. Neil Gaiman, *The Graveyard Book* (New York: HarperCollins, 2008), p.298.

29. Kurt Vonnegut, *Breakfast of Champions* (New York: Delacorte Press, 1973), p.234.

30. Benjamin Kunkel, "Into the Big Tent," *London Review of Books* 32.8 (22 April 2010), pp.12–16.

Chapter 2

1. See the interview "Live Jameson," in Ian Buchanan, *Fredric Jameson: Live Theory* (London: Continuum, 2006), pp.122–123.

2. Jameson, "Interview with Sara Danius and Stefan Jonsson," in *Jameson on Jameson: Conversations on Cultural Marxism*, ed. Ian Buchanan (Durham, NC: Duke University Press, 2007), p.154.

3. Ibid., p.154.

4. See my "Nomadography: The 'Early' Deleuze and the History of Philosophy," *Journal of Philosophy: A Cross-Disciplinary Inquiry* 5.11 (Winter 2010), pp.15–24.

5. Walter Benjamin, "The Task of the Translator," in *Illuminations: Essays and Reflections*, ed. Hannah Arendt, trans. Harry Zohn (New York: Schocken Books, 1969), p.76.

6. See Maria Elisa Cevasco, "Imagining a Space that is Outside: An Interview with Fredric Jameson," *minnesota review* 78 (2012), p.85.

7. Adam Roberts, *Fredric Jameson* (London: Routledge, 2000), p.3.

8. Sean Homer, *Fredric Jameson: Marxism, Hermeneutics, Postmodernism* (London: Polity Press, 1998), pp.7–12. But see also Homer, "Sartrean Origins," in *Fredric Jameson: A Critical Reader*, ed. Douglas Kellner and Sean Homer (New York: Palgrave Macmillan, 2004), pp.1–21.

9. See Clint Burnham, *The Jamesonian Unconscious: The Aesthetics of Marxist Theory* (Durham, NC: Duke University Press, 1995), especially Chapter 2.

10. See Buchanan, *Fredric Jameson*, ch.2.

11. See Vincent Leitch, *American Literary Criticism from the Thirties to the Eighties* (New York: Columbia University Press, 1988), p.380.

12. Jameson, "Interview with Sara Danius and Stefan Jonsson," in *Jameson on Jameson*, p.154.

13. Jameson, "Interview with Srinivas Aravamudan and Ranjana Khanna," in *Jameson on Jameson*, p.204.

14. Jameson, *Marxism and Form: Twentieth-Century Dialectical Theories of Literature* (Princeton: Princeton University Press, 1971), pp.207, 208.

15. Jameson, *Late Marxism: Adorno, or, the Persistence of the Dialectic* (London: Verso, 1990), p.4.

16. Jameson, *Sartre: The Origins of a Style* (New York: Columbia University Press, 1984), pp.vii, xi.

17. Ibid., p.8.

18. Ibid., pp.206, 25.

19. Ibid., pp.40–63. In an astonishing example of close reading, Jameson spends over four pages analyzing Sartre's use of a single colon; see pp.54–58.

20. Jameson, *Sartre*, p.67.

21. Ibid., p.211.

22. Buchanan, *Fredric Jameson*, p.31.

23. Jameson, *Sartre*, pp.201, 202–203.

24. Ibid., p.204.

25. Ibid., p.225.

26. Jameson, "Interview with Sara Danius and Stefan Jonsson," in *Jameson on Jameson*, p.155.

27. *Burn!*, directed by Gillo Pontecorvo (1969).

28. Jameson, "Live Jameson," in Buchanan, *Fredric Jameson*, p.120.

29. But see Barbara Foley, *Radical Representations: Politics and Form in U.S. Proletarian Fiction, 1929–1941* (Durham, NC: Duke University Press, 1993); and Caren Irr, *The Suburb of Dissent: Cultural Politics in the United States and Canada during the 1930s* (Durham, NC: Duke University Press, 1998).

30. Jameson, *Marxism and Form*, p.ix.

31. Sean Homer has provided a brief history of the formation of the Marxist Literary Group by Jameson and a group of his University of California, San Diego, graduate students, including John Beverley, James Kavanagh, Gene Holland, and June Howard, in the wake of the Modern Language Association's 1968 convention in New York City. (The convention was notorious for the protests by, and arrest of, members of the newly formed Radical Caucus, and Louis Kampf, later elected president of the MLA, was himself taken into police custody.) Homer notes the perceived tension between the Marxist Literary Group and the Radical Caucus, both affiliated with the MLA, which

appears to have been rooted in a somewhat specious rivalry between theory and practice, as the former attempted to bring attention to theorizing itself, and particularly to Marxist theory, whereas the latter tended to focus on questions of the canon, pedagogy, civil rights and feminism, and equality in the profession. The principle organ of the Radical Caucus was the journal *Radical Teacher*, whereas the Marxist Literary Group focused on organizing the Summer Institute on Culture and Society and panels at the MLA convention, along with publishing its journal *Mediations*, in which Marxist theory could be explored and developed. However, as Homer notes, "a commitment to theory [...] does not preclude a concern with issues of practice," and the two groups have coexisted more-or-less collegially in the past decades. Ironically, perhaps, the successes of both organizations—in expanding canons and accessibility and in bringing Marxist theory to bear on literary and cultural studies—have probably rendered the Radical Caucus and the Marxist Literary Group less influential, though no less necessary, today. See Homer, *Fredric Jameson*, pp.28–30; see also Homer, "A Short History of the Marxist Literary Group," *Mediations* 19.2 (1995), pp.68–75. For an excellent discussion of the tumultuous events of the 1968 MLA convention, see Richard Ohmann, *English in America: A Radical View of the Profession* (Oxford: Oxford University Press, 1996), pp.27–50.

32. Jameson, *Marxism and Form*, p.xviii.
33. See Phillip E. Wegner, *Periodizing Jameson: Dialectics, the University, and the Desire for Narrative* (Evanston, IL: Northwestern University Press, 2014), ch.1.
34. Jameson, *Marxism and Form*, pp.4, 6–7.
35. Ibid., pp.30, 35.
36. Ibid., pp.43, 45.
37. Ibid., pp.60–61, 62–63, 68–72, 77.
38. Ibid., pp.82, 83.
39. Ibid., p.84–85.
40. Ibid., pp.94, 105–106.
41. Ibid., p.111; Jameson's quotation is from Herbert Marcuse, *Eros and Civilization: A Philosophical Enquiry into Freud* (Boston: Beacon Press, 1966), p.144.
42. Jameson, *Marxism and Form*, pp.120, 129. For an excellent discussion of the influence of Bloch on Jameson's thought, see Phillip E. Wegner, "Horizons, Figures, and Machines: The Dialectic of Utopia in the Work of Fredric Jameson," *Utopian Studies* 9.2 (1998), pp.58–73. For a recent reappraisal of Bloch's criticism, see Caroline Edwards, "Uncovering the 'gold-bearing rubble': Ernst Bloch's Literary Criticism," in Alice Reeve-Tucker and Nathan Waddell, eds., *Utopianism, Modernism, and Literature in the Twentieth Century* (New York: Palgrave Macmillan, 2013), pp.182–203.
43. Jameson, *Marxism and Form*, p.159.
44. Ibid., p.163.

45. See Georg Lukács, *Soul and Form*, trans. Anna Bostock (Cambridge, MA: MIT Press, 1974).

46. Jameson, *Marxism and Form*, pp.173–174, 182.

47. Ibid., pp.204–205.

48. Ibid., pp.208, 231.

49. Ibid., p.305.

50. Deleuze, *Desert Islands and Other Texts, 1953–1974*, ed. David Lapoujade, trans. Michael Taormina (New York: Semiotext(e), 2004), p.79.

51. Jameson, *Marxism and Form*, pp.306, 307.

52. Ibid., p.309.

53. Ibid., p.310.

54. See Jameson, *Valences of the Dialectic* (London: Verso, 2009), pp.41–42. More bizarre still, at least for some readers, is Jameson's argument about how Walmart's production and distribution networks form a model for utopian practice (see *Valences*, pp.411–433).

55. Nietzsche's exposition of moral frameworks based on "good and evil" versus "good and bad" can be found in *On the Genealogy of Morals*, trans. Walter Kaufmann and R.J. Hollingdale (New York: Vintage, 1969), pp.24–56.

56. Jameson, "Interview with Xudong Zhang," in *Jameson on Jameson*, p.194.

57. Jameson, *Marxism and Form*, pp.413–414.

58. Ibid., p.416.

59. The foundational text on structuralism in English is likely Richard Macksey and Eugenio Donato (eds.), *The Structuralist Controversy: The Languages of Criticism and the Sciences of Man* (1970), a collection of essays that emerged from the famous 1966 Johns Hopkins University conference, which is frequently cited as the point of arrival of structuralism, and perhaps poststructuralism, in the United States. Jonathan Culler's influential *Structuralist Poetics: Structuralism, Linguistics, and the Study of Literature* did not appear until 1975.

60. See Foucault, *The Order of Things*, trans. anon. (New York: Vintage, 1973), p.262.

61. Jameson, *The Prison-House of Language: A Critical Account of Structuralism and Russian Formalism* (Princeton: Princeton University Press, 1972), p.vii.

62. Ibid., p.v.

63. Ibid., p.5.

64. Ibid., pp.5–6.

65. Ibid., pp.22, 24.

66. Ibid., pp.43, 51, 58.

67. Ibid., pp.90–91.

68. Ibid., p.101.

69. Ibid., pp.188–189.

70. See Lukács, "Narrate or Describe," in *The Writer and the Critic*, trans. Arthur Kahn (New York: Grosset, 1970), pp.110–148.

71. Jameson, *The Prison-House of Language*, p.216.

Chapter 3

1. Jameson, "Metacommentary," *The Ideologies of Theory* (London: Verso, 2008), p.7. Except as otherwise noted, all references to *The Ideologies of Theory* will be to this expanded, one-volume edition.

2. Technically, Jameson was awarded the William Riley Parker Prize for two essays published in *PMLA* in 1971, "Metacommentary" and "*La Cousine Bette* and Allegorical Realism."

3. See Ian Buchanan, "Reading Jameson Dogmatically," *Historical Materialism* 10.3 (2002), p.226. See also Buchanan, *Fredric Jameson: Live Theory* (London: Continuum, 2006), pp.12–18.

4. Jean-Paul Sartre, *Search for a Method*, trans. Hazel E. Barnes (New York: Vintage, 1968), p.xxxiv. Barnes translates *indépassable* as "that which we cannot go beyond" and, elsewhere, as "unsurpassable."

5. Jameson, "Marxism and Historicism," in *The Ideologies of Theory*, p.452.

6. Jameson, *The Political Unconscious: Narrative as a Socially Symbolic Act* (Ithaca, NY: Cornell University Press, 1981), p.10.

7. Terry Eagleton famously referred to the Jameson of this epoch as "a shamelessly unreconstructed Hegelian Marxist, for whom after all the Derridean dust has settled and schizoid babble has subsided, [Lukács's] *History and Class Consciousness* remains the definitive text." See Eagleton, *Against the Grain* (London: Verso, 1986), p.58.

8. See, for example, the extensive bibliography for *Jameson on Jameson: Conversations on Cultural Marxism*, ed. Ian Buchanan (Durham, NC: Duke University Press, 2007), pp.241–268.

9. Jameson, *Fables of Aggression: Wyndham Lewis, the Modernist as Fascist* (Berkeley: University of California Press, 1979), p.1.

10. Wegner, "Jameson's Modernisms; or, the Desire Called Utopia," *Diacritics* 37.4 (Winter 2007), p.4. See also Wegner's *Periodizing Jameson: Dialectics, the University, and the Desire for Narrative* (Evanston, IL: Northwestern University Press, 2014). Verso republished *Fables of Aggression* in 2008.

11. Jameson, "Imaginary and Symbolic in Lacan," in *The Ideologies of Theory*, p.77.

12. Jameson, *Fables of Aggression*, pp.9–10.

13. Ibid., p.25.

14. Ibid., p.86.

15. Ibid., pp.38–39.

16. Ibid., p.94.

17. Ibid., p.103.

18. Ibid., p.184.

19. Jameson, *The Political Unconscious*, p.19.

20. Ibid., p.9.

21. Ibid., p.13.

22. Ibid., p.20.

23. Compare Terry Eagleton's conclusion in *Literary Theory* that his use of the term "political criticism" is not intended as an alternative to other types of criticism, but is meant to underscore the fact that all literary theory *is* political. See Eagleton, *Literary Theory: An Introduction* (Minneapolis: University of Minnesota Press, 1982), p.195.

24. Jameson, *The Political Unconscious*, p.75. It may be worth noting that Jameson's as yet unfinished six-volume project, *The Poetics of Social Forms*, seems to be an attempt to survey the temporal terrain outlined in this third phase of interpretation, history itself, as it will proceed from the primitive myth-making of the ancients and the romantic allegory of a pre-modern and pre-capitalist epoch in the two forthcoming volumes to the realist, modernist, and postmodernist cultural modes, themselves associated with Ernest Mandel's stages of capital (i.e., market, monopoly, and late- or multinational capitalism) and addressed in Jameson's *Antinomies of Realism*, *A Singular Modernity*, and *Postmodernism, or, the Cultural Logic of Late Capitalism*, respectively, and on to a future scarcely imaginable outside of the realm of a utopian science fiction, as Jameson has explored in the sixth and final volume, *Archaeologies of the Future*.

25. Jameson, *The Political Unconscious*, p.76.

26. Ibid., pp.99, 144.

27. Ibid., p.13.

28. Ibid., p.35.

29. Ibid., p.100.

30. Ibid., p.102.

31. Ibid., pp.289, 291.

32. Ibid., p.291.

33. Neil Larsen, in his foreword to *The Ideologies of Theory*, ably attempts to square the circle of historical survey and contemporary criticism by arguing for the representative character of these essays in Jameson's overall project. See Larsen, "Foreword: Fredric Jameson and the Fate of Dialectical Criticism," in Jameson, *The Ideologies of Theory: Essays, 1971–1986, Volume 1: Situations of Theory* (Minneapolis: University of Minnesota Press, 1988), pp.ix–xxix.

34. Jameson, "Introduction," ibid., p.xxv.

35. Ibid., pp.xxvii, xxix.

36. Ibid., p.xxvi.

37. Jameson, "Introductory Note," in *The Ideologies of Theory: Essays, 1971–1986, Volume 2: Syntax of History* (Minneapolis: University of Minnesota Press, 1988), pp.viii–ix.

38. See Jameson, "A Brief Response" [to Aijaz Ahmad], *Social Text* 17 (Autumn 1987), pp.26–28.

39. In fact, the essay does appear in *The Jameson Reader*, ed. Michael Hardt and Kathi Weeks (Oxford: Blackwell, 2000), pp.315–339.

40. Jameson, "Third-World Literature in an Era of Multinational Capitalism," *Social Text* 15 (Autumn 1986), p.69 (emphasis in the original).

41. See Aijaz Ahmad, "Jameson's Rhetoric of Otherness and the 'National Allegory'," *Social Text* 17 (Autumn 1987), pp.3–26. This essay was republished in Ahmad, *In Theory: Classes, Nations, Literatures* (London: Verso, 1992), pp.95–112.

42. Ahmad, *In Theory*, pp.96–97.

43. However, Ahmad did not necessarily agree with those who used his arguments against Jameson. Noting his own admiration for Jameson's work, Ahmad has expressed "irritation" that his critique has been used to attack Jameson's Marxism. See Ahmad, *In Theory*, p.10.

44. For a good summary of the controversy as well as a qualified defense of Jameson's position, see Neil Lazarus, *The Postcolonial Unconscious* (Cambridge: Cambridge University Press, 2011), pp.89–113.

45. Jameson, *The Political Unconscious*, p.104.

46. Ibid.

47. Jameson, "Interview with Sara Danius and Stefan Jonsson," in *Jameson on Jameson*, p.157.

Chapter 4

1. On the idea of postmodernism as a result of the perceived defeat of the Left, see Terry Eagleton, *The Illusions of Postmodernism* (London: Verso, 1996), especially pp.1–19.

2. Significantly, Habermas presented "Modernity: An Unfinished Project" as his acceptance speech upon being awarded the Theodor W. Adorno Prize in Frankfurt in 1980. A revised, English version appeared as "Modernity versus Postmodernity," trans. Seyla Ben-Habib, in *New German Critique* 22 (1981), pp.3–14; this translation was then reprinted as "Modernity—An Incomplete Project" in Hal Foster, ed., *The Anti-Aesthetic: Essays in Postmodern Culture* (Port Townsend, WA: Bay Press, 1983), pp.3–15. See also Jürgen Habermas, *The Philosophical Discourse of Modernity: Twelve Lectures*, trans. Fredrick G. Lawrence (Cambridge, MA: MIT Press, 1987).

3. For an excellent Marxist study of the poststructuralist tendency in recent French philosophy that explicitly compares it to the Frankfurt School's critical legacy, see Peter Dews, *Logics of Disintegration* (London: Verso, 1987).

4. "Postmodernism and Consumer Society," reprinted in *The Cultural Turn*, was first delivered in the form of talks presented in Germany and, more famously, at the Whitney Museum of American Art in 1982, and published in Hal Foster, *The Anti-Aesthetic: Essays in Postmodern Culture* (Port Townsend, WA: Bay Press, 1983), pp.111–125. "Postmodernism, or, the Cultural Logic of Late Capitalism," a slightly revised version of which forms Chapter 1 of Jameson's *Postmodernism*, first appeared in *New Left Review* 16 (1984), pp.52–92. Among other accolades, *Postmodernism* won the MLA's James Russell Lowell Prize, awarded to the year's outstanding book in linguistic or literary studies.

5. Douglas Kellner, "Jameson / Marxism / Postmodernism," in Kellner, ed., *Postmodernism / Jameson / Critique* (Washington, DC: Maisonneuve Press, 1989), p.2.

6. See Jameson, "Periodizing the 60s," *The Ideologies of Theory* (London: Verso, 2008), pp.512–513.

7. Jameson, *Late Marxism: Adorno, or, the Persistence of the Dialectic* (London: Verso, 1990), pp.4–5.

8. On the controversial "post-Marxist" political theory of Ernesto Laclau and Chantal Mouffe, see their *Hegemony and Socialist Strategy: Towards a Radical Democratic Politics* (London: Verso, 1985); perhaps the most famous neoliberal post-Marxist argument of the time came from Francis Fukuyama, in his infamous "End of History" essay, later expanded into his book, *The End of History and the Last Man* (New York: Free Press, 1992). On "late capitalism," see Ernest Mandel's influential study, *Late Capitalism*, trans. Joris de Brees (London: Verso, 1975).

9. Jameson, *Late Marxism*, pp.11–12.

10. Ibid., p.9.

11. Ibid., pp.139–140.

12. Ibid., pp.144.

13. Adorno and Horkheimer, *Dialectic of Enlightenment*, trans. John Cumming (New York: Continuum, 1987), p.167.

14. Quoted in Jameson, *Late Marxism*, p.232. Jameson here quotes from Adorno's "Introduction" to *The Positivist Dispute in German Sociology*, trans. G. Adey and D. Frisby (New York: Harper & Row, 1976), p.10.

15. Jameson, *Late Marxism*, pp.244–245.

16. Ibid., pp.248, 249.

17. Ibid., pp.251–252. See also Jameson, *The Seeds of Time* (New York: Columbia University Press, 1994), p.xii.

18. Jameson, *Late Marxism*, p.248.

19. Colin MacCabe, "Preface," to Jameson, *The Geopolitical Aesthetic: Cinema and Space in the World System* (Bloomington and London: Indiana University Press and the British Film Institute, 1992), p.ix.

20. Jameson, *Signatures of the Visible* (London: Routledge, 1990), p.6.

21. Ibid., p.1. Infamously, this line was selected as a "winner" of the conservative philosopher Denis Dutton's celebrated "Bad Writing Contest," presumably on the somewhat puritanical grounds that it contains the word *pornographic*. (If an unsympathetic reader were on the lookout for a more tortuous, "jargon-laden" sentence in Jameson's book, it would not be difficult to find, and I am unaware of anyone else who found this sentence confusing.)

22. Ibid., p.1.

23. Ibid., p.25. Jameson also notes that the repressive mechanisms are identical to those of modernist works, and that, from a dialectical perspective, "modernism

and mass culture are grasped as a single historical and aesthetic phenomenon" (p.21).

24. Ibid., pp.28–29.
25. Ibid., pp.31–34.
26. Ibid., pp.37–38. On the connection between Auerbach and cognitive mapping, see my *Spatiality* (London: Routledge, 2013), pp.59–62, 68–69.
27. Jameson, *Postmodernism, or, the Cultural Logic of Late Capitalism* (Durham, NC: Duke University Press, 1991), p.418.
28. Clint Burnham makes this very point in *The Jamesonian Unconscious: The Aesthetics of Marxist Theory* (Durham, NC: Duke University Press, 1995), p.217. As Burnham notes, the lines in question were likely written in chronological order, as the "Introduction" to *Postmodernism* would have been penned in 1990, after "The Existence of Italy" was completed.
29. Jameson, *Signatures of the Visible*, p.229.
30. Jameson, *Postmodernism*, p.ix.
31. See Phillip E. Wegner, *Periodizing Jameson: Dialectics, the University, and the Desire for Narrative* (Evanston, IL: Northwestern University Press, 2014), ch.3.
32. Jameson, *Late Marxism*, p.54. Jameson's quotation of Benjamin comes from *The Origins of the German Tragic Drama*, trans. John Osborne (London: Verso, 1977), p.34.
33. Wegner, *Periodizing Jameson*, ch.3.
34. See Perry Anderson, *The Origins of Postmodernity* (London: Verso, 1998), pp.54–66.
35. Jameson, *Postmodernism*, p.xix.
36. Anderson, *The Origins of Postmodernity*, p.56.
37. Jameson, *Postmodernism*, pp.14–15.
38. Ibid., p.25.
39. Ibid., p.17.
40. See Erich Auerbach, *Mimesis: The Representation of Reality in Western Literature*, trans. Willard Trask (Princeton: Princeton University Press, 1953), p.552.
41. Jameson, *Postmodernism*, p.62.
42. Ibid., pp.298–299.
43. Ibid., p.418.
44. See Jameson, "Periodizing the 60s," p.514.
45. Jameson, *Postmodernism*, pp.417–418. An earlier version of this sentence originally appeared in "Marxism and Postmodernism," Jameson's afterword to Kellner, *Postmodernism / Jameson / Critique*, p.387; hence, Jameson is reflecting in 1989 upon the stir caused by articles originally published in 1984.
46. See my *Spatiality*, especially pp.11–43.
47. Jameson, *Postmodernism*, p.44.
48. Quoted ibid. p.51, emphasis in the original. Jameson refers to Althusser, "Ideology and Ideological State Apparatuses," in *Lenin and Philosophy and Other Essays*, trans. Ben Brewster (New York: Monthly Review Press, 1971).

49. Jameson, *Postmodernism*, p.51.
50. Ibid., pp.51–52.
51. See my *Utopia in the Age of Globalization: Space, Representation, and the World System* (New York: Palgrave Macmillan, 2013), p.61.
52. See Jameson, *Postmodernism*, p.52.
53. Ibid., p.52.
54. Ibid., p.54.

Chapter 5

1. Jameson, *Postmodernism, or, the Cultural Logic of Late Capitalism* (Durham, NC: Duke University Press, 1991), p.54.
2. See Jameson, *Signatures of the Visible* (London: Routledge, 1990), p.54; Jameson *The Political Unconscious: Narrative as a Socially Symbolic Act* (Ithaca, NY: Cornell University Press, 1981), p.104.
3. Colin MacCabe, "Preface," in Jameson, *The Geopolitical Aesthetic: Cinema and Space in the World System* (Bloomington and London: Indiana University Press and the British Film Institute, 1992), pp.xii, xiv.
4. Jameson, "On Politics and Literature," *Salmagundi* 2.3 (Spring–Summer 1968), pp.22–23.
5. See Georg Lukács, *The Theory of the Novel*, trans. Anna Bostock (Cambridge, MA: MIT Press, 1971), pp.41, 88. On the notion of "cartographic anxiety" in postmodernity, see Derek Gregory, *Geographical Imaginations* (Oxford: Blackwell, 1994), especially ch.2.
6. Jameson, *The Geopolitical Aesthetic*, p.82.
7. See Jameson, "Cognitive Mapping," in Cary Nelson and Lawrence Grossberg, eds., *Marxism and the Interpretation of Culture* (Urbana, IL: University of Illinois Press, 1988), pp.347–358.
8. Jameson, *Postmodernism*, p.410.
9. Ibid., p.410. *Don Quixote* is for both Lukács (in *The Theory of the Novel*) and Foucault (in *The Order of Things*) the work that stands at the very threshold of modernity.
10. Jameson, *Postmodernism*, p.411.
11. Ibid., pp.411–412.
12. Ibid., p.412.
13. See David Harvey, *The Condition of Postmodernity: An Enquiry into the Origins of Cultural Change* (Oxford: Blackwell, 1990).
14. Jameson, *Postmodernism*, p.413.
15. Ibid., p.416.
16. Ibid., p.409.
17. Ibid., pp.417–418.
18. Jameson, *The Geopolitical Aesthetic*, pp.188–189.
19. Ibid., pp.2, 3, 4.

20. Jameson, "Cognitive Mapping," p.356; see also Jameson, *Postmodernism*, pp.37–38.
21. Jameson, *The Geopolitical Aesthetic*, 9.
22. Ibid., pp.78, 79.
23. Ibid., p.82.
24. Ibid., p.15.
25. See Buchanan, *Fredric Jameson: Live Theory* (London: Continuum, 2006), pp.113–114.
26. Jameson, *The Seeds of Time* (New York: Columbia University Press, 1994), pp.xi–xii.
27. Ibid., p.xii.
28. Ibid., p.2.
29. Ibid, pp.19, 27–28, 46, 60, and 71.
30. Ibid., p.56.
31. Ibid., p.54.
32. Ibid., p.60.
33. Ibid., p.75.
34. Jameson, "Of Islands and Trenches: Neutralization and the Production of Utopian Discourse," in *The Ideologies of Theory* (London: Verso, 2008), p.386.
35. Jameson, *The Seeds of Time*, p.70.
36. Perry Anderson, "Foreword," in Jameson, *The Cultural Turn: Selected Writings on the Postmodern, 1983–1998* (London: Verso, 1998), p.xi.
37. Jameson, *The Cultural Turn*, pp.141–143.
38. See my "Meta-Capital: Culture and Financial Derivatives," *Works & Days* 59/60 (Spring–Fall 2012), pp.231–247.
39. Edward LiPuma and Benjamin Lee, in *Financial Derivatives and the Culture of Risk* (Durham, NC: Duke University Press, 2004), p.2
40. Jameson, *The Cultural Turn*, pp.184–185.
41. Jameson, *Valences of the Dialectic* (London: Verso, 2009), p.455. Originally, "Globalization as a Philosophical Issue" appeared in Fredric Jameson and Masao Miyoshi, eds., *Cultures of Globalization* (Durham, NC: Duke University Press, 1998), pp.54–77.

Chapter 6

1. See Jameson, *The Modernist Papers* (London: Verso, 2007), p.x.
2. Jameson, *A Singular Modernity: Essay on the Ontology of the Present* (London: Verso, 2002), pp.6–7.
3. Jameson, *Brecht and Method* (London: Verso, 1998), p.19.
4. Ibid., p.10.
5. Ian Buchanan, *Fredric Jameson: Live Theory* (London: Continuum, 2006), p.39.
6. See Bertolt Brecht, "Short Description of a New Technique of Acting which Produces an Alienation Effect," in *Brecht on Theatre: The Development of*

an *Aesthetic*, trans. and ed. John Willett (New York: Hill & Wang, 1992), pp.136–147.

7. Jameson, *Brecht and Method*, pp.85–86, n.13.

8. Ibid., p.45.

9. Ibid., p.46.

10. Ibid., p.47; see also Buchanan, *Fredric Jameson*, pp.42–43.

11. Jameson, *Brecht and Method*, p.11.

12. Ibid., pp.177–178.

13. See Phillip E. Wegner, *Life between Two Deaths: U.S. Culture in the Long Nineties* (Durham, NC: Duke University Press, 2009). Demarcating the period of the "long Nineties," Wegner's book-ending events are the fall of the Berlin Wall in 1989 and the attacks on the World Trade Center and the Pentagon on September 11, 2001.

14. Jameson, "Introduction: On Not Giving Interviews," in *Jameson on Jameson: Conversations on Cultural Marxism*, ed. Ian Buchanan (Durham, NC: Duke University Press, 2007), p.7.

15. Jameson, *A Singular Modernity*, pp.12–13.

16. Ibid., p.13.

17. Ibid., p.29.

18. Ibid., p.26.

19. Ibid., pp.23, 29.

20. Ibid., p.40.

21. Ibid., p.34.

22. Ibid., p.55.

23. Ibid, pp.55–56; see Friedrich Nietzsche, "On Truth and Lie in an Extra-Moral Sense," in *The Portable Nietzsche*, ed. and trans. Walter Kaufmann (New York: Viking, 1977), pp.46–47.

24. Jameson, *A Singular Modernity*, pp.56–57.

25. Ibid., p.94.

26. No discussion of artistic modernism—particularly the view of modernism as an altogether positive and salutary development—can fail to mention the contribution of Marshall Berman, who is conspicuously absent from *A Singular Modernity*, thus perhaps sparing him from the pointed critique of Jameson's analysis. See Berman, *All That Is Solid Melts into Air: The Experience of Modernity* (New York: Penguin, 1982).

27. Jameson, *A Singular Modernity*, pp.209–210.

28. Ibid., p.210.

29. Jameson *The Modernist Papers*, p.x.

30. Ibid., p.ix.

31. Ibid., p.xiv.

32. As Jameson himself remarks, any discussion of this topic ought to acknowledge Hayden White, *The Content of the Form* (Baltimore: Johns Hopkins University Press, 1987).

33. Jameson, *The Modernist Papers*, p.xvii.

34. Jameson, "Reflections on the Brecht–Lukács Debate," in *The Ideologies of Theory*, p.447. This essay was originally published as "Reflections in Conclusion," in Theodor W. Adorno et al., *Aesthetics and Politics* (London: New Left Books, 1977), pp.196–213.

35. Jameson, "Reflections on the Brecht–Lukács Debate," in *The Ideologies of Theory*, p.447.

36. Ibid., p.447.

Chapter 7

1. Jameson, *The Political Unconscious: Narrative as a Socially Symbolic Act* (Ithaca, NY: Cornell University Press, 1981), p.299.

2. Jameson, "Of Islands and Trenches," in *The Ideologies of Theory* (London: Verso, 2008), p.386.

3. Jameson, *Marxism and Form: Twentieth-Century Dialectical Theories of Literature* (Princeton: Princeton University Press, 1971), pp.110–111.

4. Jameson, *A Singular Modernity: Essay on the Ontology of the Present.* (London: Verso, 2002), p.215.

5. See Jameson, *Archaeologies of the Future: The Desire Called Utopia and Other Science Fictions* (London: Verso, 2005), p.57; see also Darko Suvin, *Metamorphoses of Science Fiction* (New Haven: Yale University Press, 1979), p.61.

6. Jameson, *Archaeologies of the Future*, p.xv.

7. Ibid., p.xvi.

8. Lyman Tower Sargent, *Utopianism: A Very Short Introduction* (Oxford: Oxford University Press, 2010), p.29.

9. Jameson, *Archaeologies of the Future*, p.210.

10. See Ian Buchanan, *Fredric Jameson: Live Theory* (London: Continuum, 2006), p.118.

11. See my *Utopia in the Age of Globalization: Space, Representation, and the World System* (New York: Palgrave Macmillan, 2013).

12. See Herbert Marcuse, "The End of Utopia," trans. J. Shapiro and S. Weber, in *Five Lectures: Psychoanalysis, Politics, and Utopia* (Boston: Beacon Books, 1970), p.69.

13. Jameson, *Archaeologies of the Future*, p.232.

14. Ibid., p.232.

15. Ibid., p.xii.

16. Ibid., p.416.

17. *The Ideologies of Theory*, in addition to including 13 new essays, does omit one essay that had been included in the 1988 edition: "The Politics of Theory: Ideological Positions in the Postmodernism Debate." This essay formed the basis for Chapter 2 of *Postmodernism, or, the Cultural Logic of Late Capitalism*

and reappeared in *The Cultural Turn*, which likely accounts for its absence here.

18. See, for example, Paul A. Bové, *In the Wake of Theory* (Hanover, NH: Wesleyan University Press, 1992).

19. Jameson, *The Ideologies of Theory*, pp.286–301, 609–612.

20. Jameson, "Introduction," *The Ideologies of Theory* (London: Verso, 2008), p.ix.

21. Ibid., p.ix.

22. Ibid., pp.x–xi.

23. Ibid., p.xi.

24. See Wegner, "Jameson's Modernisms, or, the Desire Called Utopia," *diacritics* 37.4 (Winter 2007), pp.2–20.

25. Jameson, *Valences of the Dialectic* (London: Verso, 2009), p.102.

26. Ibid., pp.69–70, n.68.

27. Ibid., p.4.

28. Ibid., p.50.

29. Ibid., p.67.

30. Ibid., p.422.

31. Ibid., p.421.

32. Ibid., p.41. This aspect of Jamesonian thinking is discussed, with particular focus on Jameson's own style, throughout Steven Helmling's interesting study, *The Success and Failure of Fredric Jameson* (Albany: SUNY Press, 2001).

33. See Jameson, *Marxism and Form*, pp.309–310; Jameson, *Valences of the Dialectic*, pp.41–42.

34. Jameson, "Interview with Xudong Zhang," in *Jameson on Jameson: Conversations on Cultural Marxism*, ed. Ian Buchanan (Durham, NC: Duke University Press, 2007), p.194.

35. Aristotle's own example from the *Poetics* is that moment in Sophocles' *Oedipus the King* when the messenger returns to tell Oedipus the story of King Laius's unfortunate infant. Where this message was supposed to confirm that Oedipus could not have killed his father, it does just the opposite, as Oedipus now recognizes the truth of the situation, with all its horrifying implications and consequences.

36. Jameson, *Valences of the Dialectic*, p.40.

37. Ibid., p.612.

38. Jameson, "A New Reading of *Capital*," *Mediations* 25.1 (2010), p.13.

Conclusion

1. Some would dispute the image of Jameson as a philologist, but as he himself has put it, "I was really formed in what I guess you could very largely call philology, in both French and German; style studies, as it was called then, the work of people like Auerbach for example, who was my teacher at Yale";

see "Live Jameson," in Ian Buchanan, *Fredric Jameson: Live Theory* (London: Continuum, 2006), p.123.

2. Jameson, *Late Marxism: Adorno, or, the Persistence of the Dialectic* (London: Verso, 1990), p.52.

3. Of course, this assertion is problematized somewhat when one considers that the final section of *Valences of the Dialectic* itself might be taken as a book-length study of Paul Ricoeur's *Time and Narrative*, and the long chapter on Sartre in *Marxism and Form* might be considered a "reading" of *The Critique of Dialectical Reason*, not to mention the many articles and chapters, book reviews and review essays, that are devoted to a careful interpretation or analysis of an individual text.

4. Jameson, *Valences of the Dialectic* (London: Verso, 2009), p.70, n.68.

5. Gilles Deleuze, *Difference and Repetition*, trans. Paul Patton (New York: Columbia University Press, 1994), p.xx.

6. Jameson, *Marxism and Form: Twentieth-Century Dialectical Theories of Literature* (Princeton: Princeton University Press, 1971), p.306.

7. Ibid., p.305.

8. See Jameson, *Valences of the Dialectic*, especially pp.127–200.

9. Jameson, *The Hegel Variations: On the Phenomenology of Spirit* (London: Verso, 2010), pp.22–23.

10. Ibid., p.23; quoting Theodor W. Adorno, *The Philosophy of Modern Music*, trans. Anne Mitchell and Wesley Blomster (New York: Seabury Press, 1973), p.55.

11. Jameson, *The Hegel Variations*, p.24.

12. Ibid., p.43.

13. Ibid., p.115.

14. Jameson, *Representing Capital: A Reading of Volume One* (London: Verso, 2011), p.23.

15. Ibid., p.2.

16. Ibid., p.150.

17. Ibid., pp.151, 149.

18. Ibid., p.14.

19. Ibid., pp.146, 142.

20. Jameson, *Valences of the Dialectic*, pp.50–51.

21. Marx, *Capital: A Critique of the Political Economy, Volume 1*, trans. Ben Fowkes (New York: Penguin, 1976), p.798.

22. Jameson, *Representing Capital*, p.89; Jameson here quotes Marx, *Capital*, p.929.

23. Jameson, *Representing Capital*, p.89.

24. Ibid., p.90; quoting Marx, *Capital*, p.933.

25. Jameson, "A New Reading of *Capital*," *Mediations* 25.1 (2010), p.10.

26. Ibid., p.13.

27. Jameson, *Representing Capital*, pp.61–62.

28. Jameson, *Valences of the Dialectic*, p.416.

Index

Explore other books from Pluto Press

MAGICAL MARXISM
Subversive Politics and the Imagination
Andy Merrifield

'Andy Merrifield is original, erudite, politically alive and readable.'
– John Berger

Magical Marxism asks that we imagine a Marxism that moves beyond debates about class, the state and the dictatorship of the proletariat. In escaping the straitjacket of orthodox Marxist critique, Merrifield argues for a reconsideration of its potential, applying previously unexplored approaches to breathe new life into the Marxist tradition.

THE NEW URBAN QUESTION
Andy Merrifield

'Merrifield is accessible, optimistic and even fun.'
– New York Times

An exuberant and illuminating adventure through our current global urban condition, tracing the connections between radical urban theory and political activism. Merrifield identifies the new urban question that has emerged and demands urgent attention, as the city becomes a site of active plunder by capital and the setting for new forms of urban struggle, from Occupy to the Indignados.

PlutoPress
www.plutobooks.com

RED PLANETS
Marxism and Science Fiction
Edited by Mark Bould and China Miéville

'This collection shows what science fiction criticism can do when Marxist critical practice is joined by science studies and the rest of theory. The results are tremendously exciting and powerful, explaining not just a genre but our world, from the financial crash of 2008 to the utopian impulses that remain always in us.'
– *Kim Stanley Robinson*

Science fiction and socialism have always had a close relationship. This is a lively introduction for anyone studying the politics of SF, covering a rich variety of examples from Weimar cinema to mainstream Hollywood films, and novelists from H.G. Wells to Kim Stanley Robinson and Charles Stross.

PHILOSOPHIZING THE EVERYDAY
Revolutionary Praxis and the Fate of Cultural Theory
John Roberts

After modernism and postmodernism, it is argued, the everyday supposedly is where a democracy of taste is brought into being. John Roberts argues that this understanding of the everyday downgrades its revolutionary meaning and philosophical implications. Bringing radical political theory back to the centre of the discussion, he argues that the everyday should not be narrowly identified with the popular, and critiques the way in which the concept is now overly associated with consumption.

PlutoPress
www.plutobooks.com

MARXISM AND MEDIA STUDIES
Key Concepts and Contemporary Trends
Mike Wayne

A clear and concise student guide that shows how Marxist theory can illuminate media studies. Mike Wayne offers a guide to key Marxist concepts and shows how to apply them to contemporary cultural analysis. Drawing on Marx, Lukács, Gramsci, Habermas, Jameson and other writers, this book provides a comprehensive exposition of the key concepts required for a Marxist analysis of the media and current cultural trends. Re-examining such concepts as class, mode of production, culture industries, the state, base-superstructure, ideology, hegemony, knowledge and social interests, and commodity fetishism, this book ranges across film, television, the internet and print media.

BRUNO LATOUR
Reassembling the Political
Graham Harman

Bruno Latour, the French sociologist, anthropologist and long-established superstar in the social sciences is revisited in this pioneering account of his ever-evolving political philosophy. Breaking from the traditional focus on his metaphysics, the author begins with the Hobbesian underpinnings of Latour's early period encountering his shift towards Carl Schmitt then finishing with his final development into the Lippmann/ Dewey debate.

PlutoPress
www.plutobooks.com

IT'S THE POLITICAL ECONOMY, STUPID
The Global Financial Crisis in Art and Theory
Edited by Gregory Sholette and Oliver Ressler

It's the Political Economy, Stupid brings together internationally acclaimed artists and thinkers, including Slavoj Žižek, David Graeber, Judith Butler and Brian Holmes, to focus on the current economic crisis. By combining artistic responses with the analysis of leading radical theorists, the book expands the boundaries of critique beyond the usual discourse. The book argues that it is time to push back against the dictates of the capitalist logic and, by use of both theoretical and artistic means, launch a rescue of the very notion of the social.

DARK MATTER
Art and Politics in the Age of Enterprise Culture
Gregory Sholette

'With verve and urgency, Gregory Sholette explores the economics of contemporary art production in an era of neoliberalism, and outlines the promises and pitfalls of various tactics of resistance. *Dark Matter* is a salient call-to-arms.'
– *Julia Bryan-Wilson*

Art is big business, with some artists able to command huge sums of money for their works, while the vast majority are ignored or dismissed by critics. This book shows that these marginalised artists, the 'dark matter' of the art world, are essential to the survival of the mainstream and that they frequently organise in opposition to it.

PlutoPress
www.plutobooks.com

HERBERT MARCUSE
An Aesthetics of Liberation
Malcolm Miles

'Miles goes back to Marcuse's work on aesthetics to link
philosophy, art, history, political analysis and sociological
insights in a deeply humane search for the way to a better
world. This book deserves a very wide readership.'
– *Peter Marcuse, Columbia University*

When capitalism is catastrophically out of control and its
excesses cannot be sustained socially or ecologically, the ideas
of Herbert Marcuse become as relevant as they were in the
1960s. This is the first English introduction to Marcuse to be
published for decades, and deals specifically with his aesthetic
theories and their relation to a critical theory of society.

HANNAH ARENDT
A Critical Introduction
Finn Bowring

'An original and highly developed perspective on the influence of
Arendt's thinking on the social sciences.'
– *Dimitris Papadopoulos*

Hannah Arendt is one of the most famous political theorists of
the twentieth century. In this comprehensive study, Bowring
shows how Arendt's writings have influenced prominent
figures in the sociological canon, and how her ideas shed light
on some of today's most pressing social and political problems.

PlutoPress
www.plutobooks.com

MARX AND THE ALTERNATIVE TO CAPITALISM

Kieran Allen

If we are serious about finding a different way to run the post-credit crunch society, we must start by introducing alternatives to undergraduates. Kieran Allen begins the task with an accessible and comprehensive look at the ideas of Karl Marx. Dispensing with the dryness of traditional explanations of Marx, Allen shows how Marx's ideas apply to modern society. The first section briefly outlines Marx's life, the development of his work, and his key theories. The second section examines alternatives to capitalism, the concept of 'anti-capitalism' and provides concrete examples of Marx's theories in practice.

CRACK CAPITALISM

John Holloway

'Infectiously optimistic.'
– *Guardian*

Crack Capitalism argues that radical change can only come about through the creation, expansion and multiplication of 'cracks' in the capitalist system. These cracks are ordinary moments or spaces of rebellion in which we assert a different type of doing. Clearly and accessibly presented in the form of 33 theses, *Crack Capitalism* is set to reopen the debate among radical scholars and activists seeking to break capitalism now.

PlutoPress
www.plutobooks.com

Printed and bound by CPI Group (UK) Ltd, Croydon, CR0 4YY

09/06/2025

14685871-0001